MUSLIM, ACTUALLY

Previously published as *The Muslim Problem*

Tawseef Khan is a qualified solicitor specialising in immigration and asylum law, and a human rights activist with over ten years' experience working on refugee and Muslim issues. In 2016 he obtained a doctoral degree from the University of Liverpool, where his thesis explored the fairness of the British asylum system. He was a recipient of a 2017 Northern Writers Award. He is a Muslim and lives in Manchester.

MUSLIM, ACTUALLY

HOW ISLAM IS MISUNDERSTOOD
AND WHY IT MATTERS

TAWSEEF KHAN

Atlantic Books
London

Published in hardback and trade paperback as *The Muslim Problem* in Great Britain in 2021 by Atlantic Books, an imprint of Atlantic Books Ltd.

This paperback edition published in 2022.

10 9 8 7 6 5 4 3 2 1

A CIP catalogue record for this book is available from the British Library.

Paperback ISBN: 978 1 78649 953 0
E-book ISBN: 978 1 78649 954 7

Printed in Great Britain

Atlantic Books
An imprint of Atlantic Books Ltd
Ormond House
26–27 Boswell Street
London
WC1N 3JZ
www.atlantic-books.co.uk

For my brother Haseeb
And everybody out there like him

Contents

Preface to the Paperback Edition

Like many others I closely followed the news in August 2021 when the United States and its allies withdrew forces from Afghanistan and evacuated citizens from Kabul. Reading reports of human rights abuses inflicted by the Taliban in rural areas while I watched thousands of Afghans rush to Kabul airport, desperate to flee, was an incredibly bleak experience. I had grown up with the shadow of 9/11, the invasion of Afghanistan and the War on Terror always looming over me – it was why I decided to write this book. Seeing the vulnerability and pointless suffering of the Afghan people escalate once more, I felt like a young teenager again, when videos of the Taliban blowing up the Buddhas of Bamiyan, or the Americans bombing the mountains of Tora Bora left me hurt, confused and depressed.

The media began to examine the legacy of America's war in Afghanistan. On the twentieth anniversary of the Twin Towers attacks, this examination took on the legacy of 9/11. Many journalists concentrated on the psychological toll inflicted by the attacks on the American people, the lives lost on the day or in combat subsequently, and how the American view of interventionist wars had slowly changed. Few considered the legacy of 9/11 from a Muslim perspective.

This is a legacy of extraordinary rendition, kidnapping, indefinite detention, torture, targeted killings and drone attacks abroad; watchlists, surveillance, anti-terror laws and 'countering violent extremism' programmes, and racial and religious profiling at home. A legacy of families with deceased, injured or disappeared parents, siblings and children; of societies destroyed and traumatised by war and conflict; of communities stigmatised by the endless cycle of Islamophobia. A legacy in which the language and logic of the War on Terror has been reproduced far outside the West – in Burma, India, China and Sri Lanka, its leaders opportunistically casting Muslims as terrorists and national security threats and perpetual outsiders. A legacy in which Islam is always presented as a metaphor for misogyny and oppression, as we saw when restrictive abortion laws were introduced in Texas and critics invoked images of women in burqas and references to Shariah, ISIS and the Taliban.

It's a legacy in which nothing has been learnt, but what remains clearer than ever is how deliberate this ignorance is. Without such flattened, distorted representations of Muslims, the West cannot maintain the War on Terror nor the asymmetric relationships it has upheld with the Muslim communities living within its borders. It explains why, twenty years after it first used orientalist clichés to justify war in Afghanistan, the media and political establishment redeployed them to justify withdrawal. US President Biden argued that forging a functioning nation was impossible, that many had tried and failed over the centuries. He was unwilling for American forces to fight and die in a war that Afghans wouldn't fight for themselves. The media similarly blamed the Afghan people for the failure of the American mission and the Taliban's resurgence. Afghanistan was the 'graveyard of empires', whose citizens were war-hardened and corrupt; where, due to tribal and ethnic divisions and harsh geographic terrain, democracy couldn't take root. Journalists overstated the Islamic credentials of the Taliban, ignoring how the previous government of Afghanistan had also claimed to be led and inspired by Islam. They selectively wrung their hands over the safety of Afghan women and LGBT people, weaponising their identities while ignoring how Western occupation had failed to ensure their basic needs were met. They emphasised, through a reemphasis on the 'bad' brown man, that Afghan men were not deserving of safety or our compassion.

According to the Costs of War project at the Watson Institute of International and Public Affairs, the American mission in Afghanistan killed around 50,000 civilians and 70,000 military and police. Over the last two decades, it has expanded to involve counterterror operations in over 85 countries. It has caused the deaths of more than 929,000 people globally and created over 38 million refugees and displaced people. Countries like Afghanistan and Iraq (where 200,000 civilians are also estimated to have been killed during the war there) have seen so much needless destruction, so much suffering, loss and trauma. People have had their lives completely devastated. For Muslim communities living in the West, the terrain in which we forge our identities has irrevocably changed. We have had to quickly become literate in the hostility we find ourselves facing on a daily basis. We have had to find ways to adapt and succeed whilst processing that stigma. And yet, the Islamophobia train shows no sign of stopping. Despite the two decades that have passed since the beginning of the War on Terror – two decades for our leaders and commentators to improve their understanding of Islam and Muslims – we continue to be portrayed and understood in almost exactly the same way: as savages, misogynists, homophobes and outsiders. As the American scholar Sylvia Chan-Malik commented on Twitter when the Taliban returned to power in Afghanistan: '20 years later, everything has changed, yet nothing at all'.

Everything has changed, yet nothing at all. Since the last twenty years have not been enough to drive systemic change on Islamophobia I understand that the publication of this book and the year that has followed – especially a year like this – isn't either. The Coronavirus pandemic has laid bare the vulnerability of Muslim communities in Britain. According to the Office for National Statistics, between January 2020 and February 2021, Muslims had the highest death rate by faith group, with 966.9 deaths per

100,000 men and 519.1 deaths per 100,000 women. That's almost two and a half times the death rate of Christian men and twice the rate of Christian women. The government cited the existence of 'pre-existing health conditions' within communities of colour to explain away these disparities, but they were, in fact, driven by prevailing socio-economic inequalities related to housing, location and employment. We may have been living through extraordinary, anxiety-filled times, but those inequalities didn't go away.

Nor did the pervasive atmosphere of Islamophobia in Britain. In fact, Islamophobia is as tedious, repetitive and exhausting as ever. Whether our newspapers are raging about so-called 'no-go zones' in the richest, whitest areas of Manchester (Didsbury) or commentators are interrogating Muslim representatives about female imams in a religion that has no formal clergy (Emma Barnett on BBC Radio 4 Woman's Hour), we Muslims face the same old stereotypes and the same manufactured controversies. We see our leaders cashing in on Islamophobia to win voters with, for example, Keir Starmer, the leader of the Labour party, remaining silent as 1 in 4 Muslim members and supporters report direct experiences of Islamophobia within the party, or the British government rejecting the working definition of Islamophobia developed by the All-Party Parliamentary Group on British Muslims, but failing to produce its own definition more than two years on. In other parts of the West, France in particular, the discriminatory policies and laws being introduced against Muslims are incredibly frightening, serving to make the West a more difficult place for us to live and thrive. Though I fear these developments leave us more vulnerable and more politically homeless, despised by those in power and those close to us, I seek comfort and confidence in the knowledge that it's not about us, not really. Muslims are mere instruments in broader discourses – scapegoats in various Western battles around values and national identity. Indeed, if Islam is 'in crisis', as the French President Emmanuel Macron believes, it isn't alone.

What I choose to focus on where I can are the pockets of hope. At the 2020 Olympic Games, the rower Mohamed Karim Sbihi became the first Muslim to carry the flag for Great Britain at the opening ceremony. The Dutch-Ethiopian athlete Sifan Hassan became the first to medal in the 1,500 metres, 5,000 metres and 10,000 metres events at the same Games. Elsewhere, *We Are Lady Parts*, the Channel 4 comedy series about an all-female Muslim punk band, has been ground-breaking in its representation of Muslim women. Each of the five central characters are complex and different, neither victims nor terrorists. The actor Riz Ahmed recently founded the Pillars Artist Fellowship, which seeks to empower emerging Muslim directors and screenwriters towards success. While these developments aren't going to single-handedly reverse systemic Islamophobia, I hope they reflect our decision to take control and flip the narrative we hear about ourselves. I hope they also reflect an increasing desire to see and tell a different story about Muslim communities. And rather than constituting superficial, tokenistic gestures or singular achievements with no ripple effect, I hope they can be stitched together to create a movement; small, meaningful steps towards sustainable change.

I want this book to be a part of that movement. By complicating the Western narrative about Islam and about Muslim communities, I want to help create a critical mass that can capture the public's attention, challenge dominant perceptions, and demand a fairer relationship between Islam and the West. Going by my conversations this year, I am optimistic. I've received messages from readers eager to understand Islam better and grateful for the arguments I have presented, who wanted to respond meaningfully to the Islamophobia encountered in their day-to-day lives but didn't know how. I've also received messages from Muslim readers excited by the way I examine religious texts or deconstruct contemporary Islamophobia, empowered by my statements encouraging other Muslims to develop individual relationships with faith, or simply happy to be seen and represented by another

member of their tribe. I continue to believe in the power of conversations: in sharing experiences to educate and inspire others,
in meeting one another's pain and understanding it, in forging
solidarity across communities. Those are the building blocks of
real change.

Tawseef Khan, November 2021

Introduction

I was fourteen years old when, during one lunch break in high school, I burst into a classroom and announced that I'd become a pagan. My friends were sat on desks, huddled against a radiator for warmth in a room that we claimed as ours during break times; a room in the Science building that was musty with the smell of animals because it was home to two rabbits and two hamsters, a tank of terrapins and an albino rat. They shrugged in response and continued chatting. My confession came as no great surprise. We already had a pagan in the group, and a white witch too.

This was my first act of rebellion against Islam; against the dogmatic, observance-oriented Islam in which I was raised. My critique of Islam actually began much earlier, as an eight-year-old, when my mother first told me off for breaking my prayers to answer the phone. Precocious perhaps, maybe also unbelievable that I was criticizing religion at such a young age, but my mother had been teaching me about Islam since I was able to speak, and I was incredibly sensitive about being told what to do. When she chastised me in front of my cousin, I was so humiliated I began to privately question the very ritual I was participating in.

As I got older, the limits imposed on my relationship with Islam became clearer. I wasn't supposed to question doctrine; God had supposedly determined every aspect of our religious practice. To critique Islam, therefore, was to be a bad Muslim who was destined for hell. When I was old enough to pray independently, my mother began pushing me to perform my five compulsory daily prayers. She warned me about God's punishment if I didn't comply. Sometimes I would pretend to fall asleep to avoid them, but she would yank off the bedcovers and send me to wash. And in the bathroom, as I sulkily cleaned my hands, my ears, my nose, my face, my arms, my neck and then my feet, I would ask myself why God wanted this. What was the point in prayer if my heart wasn't in it? Prayer was more than a series of movements showing off my religious devotion. If God refused the prayer I had broken off in order to answer the phone, then surely God would also refuse these unhappily performed prayers I was offering as a teenager?

So my frustration had been bubbling away for several years when I adopted paganism. I knew that many Muslims would have found my behaviour disrespectful, insubordinate, insulting to Allah even, but I didn't care. I *needed* to register my complaint with Allah. I was angry with God and felt that I had every right to be. I had been deeply unhappy for such a long time. It was not the general melancholy and malaise that teenagers experience during puberty. It was rooted in my discontent with how Islam was being framed, as something based around observance, permissibility and submission.

Today I can understand my parents' decisions a little better – they were trying to shape my identity in a non-Muslim landscape as best they could. They were trying to instil me with self-worth. They wanted to save me from feeling dislocated as a British-Pakistani Muslim – from being caught between two worlds – especially as they navigated their own feelings of disorientation living in a country where they hadn't been born. But that ended up happening anyway. Using Islam in such a way led to a crisis of faith. There was nobody to talk it over with. Protesting to God seemed like the only thing I could do.

Every protest has its critics. Maybe you would have criticized mine. After all, I had no idea what paganism actually involved. Was it enough that I felt a greater 'connection' to nature than to my community? Probably not. And to all intents and purposes, I continued to live a tangibly Muslim life. It didn't occur to me to change that. Besides, I hadn't given up believing in God altogether.

I fasted (because I enjoyed it), prayed (when I couldn't get out of it) and travelled to Saudi Arabia for umrah. At the ages of fifteen and twenty-two, I performed this pilgrimage with my family. Both times, I sat inside the sacred mosque in the city of Mecca and spoke to Allah in the same way: 'I am stuck. I am angry with you. You know this. You know why.' I prayed for a solution. But as much as I sought distance from my religious identity, to get some perspective on its place in my life, the world would not allow it.

The attacks of 9/11 occurred a short time after I first registered my protest with Allah. The effect was that my personal spiritual crisis began to unfurl in the shadow of a much larger political and religious one. Before I had even developed a sense of who I was as a Muslim, I was on the back foot. I felt like I was carrying a narrative – what would become perhaps the defining narrative of our time – of a war brought to the West by terrorists inspired and guided by 'radical Islam'. In the years to come, I would be weighed down by this burden. It coloured my internal struggle and I could not escape it. I remember the jokes made by high-school acquaintances, where the punchline centred on me being a terrorist. How my friends laughed without hesitation, and I felt such impotence at having no comeback.

I went shopping with my mother in Manchester city centre the day after the London bombings of July 2005. As we walked along the high street I felt tension rising in my body. There was the distinct feeling of self-consciousness, of being monitored, of deliberation over every step in case we stoked someone's anger. The latent threat of reprisals seemed to be everywhere. Mum's hijab clearly identified her as a Muslim, and for those looking to blame the bombings on Islam, she'd be fair game. We expected it. We had already heard about the anti-Muslim attacks on the news.

Then there was a visit to Latvia in February 2007. After dinner, I walked back to my hostel in Riga with some friends. A man approached me with an invitation to attend a club he was promoting. When I declined, I watched his expression turn ugly and aggressive. 'You big Osama,' he said, as he gestured towards my facial hair. 'You very, very big Osama.'

In those years, Muslims were barely represented in public life and, when we were, media coverage was bleak and unwavering. 'We tend to write about Muslims mainly when they cause trouble,' the journalist Brian Whitaker once admitted.[1] Newspapers that had mostly ignored Muslims before 9/11 (resulting in scant knowledge about Islam amongst journalists, and even less amongst the public) were suddenly obsessed, writing almost 600 per cent more articles about us than in the years before – and that was just 2001–2002.[2] In those pieces, representation was constructed almost entirely in the context of terrorism. We went from being more or less invisible to every aspect of our existence being connected to and framed by violence and hatred. Media outlets assembled panel discussions to understand the 'trouble' with Islam. In 2005, *Jyllands-Posten*, a Danish newspaper, published caricatures of Prophet Muhammad (peace be upon him) that seemed to be a deliberate provocation to Muslims.[3] It was not just that the Prophet had been illustrated that was the problem, but that many of these representations reinforced stereotypes about Muslims in general: he was depicted with devil horns, holding a sabre and preparing for battle, and with a bomb inside his turban (which was inscribed with the shahadah – the Islamic declaration of faith). Muslims, who already existed on the margins of society, were being vilified and even further excluded. A *Daily Mail* article by Richard Littlejohn seemed to summarize feelings about Islam at the time, 'If they hate us so much, why don't they leave?'[4]

This portrayal of Muslims as illiberal and violent was regurgitated across the media. It infected everything. Even well-meaning representations upheld racist tropes; the media assumed that all Muslims were bad unless and until we could perform our 'goodness' and, when we did, these examples were celebrated as proof that some Muslims could theoretically assimilate into Western society. Young Muslims, like me at that time, saw Islam being portrayed as regressive, barbaric, bloodthirsty and incompatible with Western modernity. We tried to counteract these stereotypes and hoped that we could find a way out of this narrative. But inevitably we internalized their alienating rhetoric – how could we have avoided it? – causing us to feel split within ourselves and fight a battle with our identities.

I am a product of the construct that is the 'War on Terror'. I am one of its children. There are so many of us. I consumed its negative messaging and found myself recoiling from my religious identity. Every time a Muslim was responsible for a terror attack somewhere around the world, I lashed out at my faith and myself. My critiques of Islam became harsher. I resented my heritage and my community. I became uncomfortable openly identifying as Muslim, with Islamic practice that I had decided was shallow and performative. To greet another Muslim and give them my salaam – the most basic expression of human kinship – was something that I struggled with deeply. I had no coherent sense of self. I became extremely depressed.

And yet, despite all the years that have passed since my adolescence, I'm dismayed to see that the situation hasn't improved. If anything, it has grown worse. Young Muslims are developing their identities in a climate of unparalleled hatred, fear and stigmatization. The Right is in ascendance across the Western world, and Muslims continue to be 'othered' in new and surprising ways. This rhetoric of 'war', of the West fighting the Muslim world, and the very notion of the Muslim world as a foreign, external entity, is an ingrained and historic one. But it is more pervasive and harmful than ever before, in part because of the massive influence the media has in shaping our lives and identities, particularly the lives of young people. Human beings look to the environment around us to understand ourselves and give meaning to our existence. If the messaging coming from the media about you is negative, or one in which you don't exist at all, it causes untold damage to your self-esteem and how you move through the world.

Jawaab is a British charity that focuses on young Muslims. In 2018, they found that 61 per cent of young Muslims surveyed had either personally experienced Islamophobia or knew somebody who had; 60 per cent felt the pressure to suppress their Muslim identities, especially when travelling or operating in work environments; and 43 per cent felt conflicted in their identities, citing extremism, disenfranchisement and evolving relationships with Islam as the main reasons for this.[5] The report detailed experiences of struggling to resist negative stereotypes associated with Islam. As one young Muslim woman said: 'I've felt excluded. When you're young all you're trying to do is belong, be accepted… It's difficult being not white. Then you're not white, and you're a Muslim and female.'

I worry about how my brother is being shaped by the continuing War on Terror. When I began writing this book, he was twenty years old (I am ten years older than him) and in the middle of studying for a degree in Biology. Early on, I asked him about being a Muslim in Britain. He replied with his knowledge that no matter how busy public transport was, how crowded a university lecture happened to get, the space next to him on the bus or in the lecture hall always remained empty. He insisted that he 'didn't care' about being singled out, but I know first-hand that creating an identity in opposition to ever-present stigma isn't easy, that this identity always lacks something; it is never fully whole. My brother's knowledge of Islamophobia is still in its infancy. It will grow, and his twenties will be a critical time for him and the making of his identity. If there is a way to make that journey better – smoother – for him, I want to find it.

Across the West, the overdue conversation about race is commanding more attention than it has for years. That conversation has been forged by many different segments of our societies: the emergence of activist movements like Black Lives Matter; musicians, actors and athletes like Beyoncé, Jesse Williams and Colin Kaepernick using their celebrity to bring attention to racial injustice; social media platforms providing the space for individuals from all walks of life to learn, engage and organize; and conditions like the coronavirus pandemic in which racial inequalities become extremely difficult to ignore. Books have been integral to this conversation – through those such as *The Good Immigrant*, *Brit(ish)*, *Natives* and *Why I'm No Longer Talking to White People About Race*, British writers of colour are claiming and creating spaces where they can voice their experiences of discrimination and othering, educate and push for systemic change. But as much as I'm inspired by these conversations, the prospect of giving voice to another overdue conversation – about the West and its relationship with Muslims – is daunting. Where do I begin?

I know when the need for that conversation first dawned on me. I was born and raised in the city of Manchester. I am a proud Mancunian. The terrorist attacks that have occurred near constantly around the world over the last twenty years both horrify and depress me, even as they often barely cause a ripple in our news cycle. But as a Mancunian, I can't deny that it was the bombing of the Manchester Arena in May 2017 that had the most profound and long-lasting effect on me.

I remember lounging on the sofa as the news came in. My parents were watching a Pakistani news channel, so we heard it in Urdu first, then quickly flipped channels to watch the BBC. My body grew numb as I watched the details emerge, as I picked out various parts of my city from the coverage. I would never have imagined that Manchester could be targeted in this way.

Late into the night, my Muslim friends and I texted each other in disbelief. Our initial feelings were of heartbreak. An attack on our city felt like an attack on us. But where there was vulnerability and anger, there was also relief that we and our loved ones were safe. On any other night, I could have been there. Some of my happiest memories of Manchester involve dressing up and attending pop concerts at the Arena. So, when we texted each other that night, we also mourned the way that things sacred to us all – life and freedom, music and the innocence of youth – had been violated. Then, as the news sank in, we began to fear how this event would change things for us. What would it mean for Muslims living in Manchester, in the UK? Would we be at the forefront of the backlash?

This fear did not subside in the weeks after the attack. I watched Mancunians unite and felt heartened by the refusal to be divided, but the attack was a jolt. It was impossible to forget it and move on. Around Manchester, raids were being conducted on houses and arrests made. The bomber's links to Libya and Didsbury Mosque in South Manchester – a mosque I have visited – were under investigation. Intelligence officials continued to insist that a second attack was imminent. There was every reason to feel tense. But there was another dimension to my fear, to the fear felt by other Muslims. Amongst the calls for defiance and unity, the voices of anger and dissent felt like they were directed at me. Islamophobic hate crimes surged again.[6] Some critics demanded that Muslims condemn the attack; always there is this transferral of anger, a pressure that we bow down and atone for crimes committed by people with whom we share nothing but our faith (if we share that at all). The singer Morrissey, for example, lambasted Sadiq Khan, the Mayor of London, for his failure to condemn Islamic State, which had assumed responsibility for the bombing.[7] Other commentators restated Islam's incompatibility with the West. In this vein, the newspaper columnist Katie Hopkins chillingly tweeted the need for a 'final solution'.[8] Taken with the Westminster attack that had occurred two months before Manchester, and the London Bridge attack that took place a fortnight after, the summer of 2017 was a frightening one for us all, but especially terrifying if you were a British Muslim.

A few days after the attacks, I wrote to a number of literary agents and sent them a proposal for this book. I had been working on the idea for some time. I wanted to write something that addressed how badly Muslims were perceived in Britain and also supported young Muslims who were struggling with their identities as I once had. These motivations crystallized in the aftermath of the

Manchester terror attack. I felt a sudden urgency to communicate with the world, to speak about how Muslims were developing their identities in societies where their faith is considered poisonous. I wanted to speak about how gruelling it was to accept these successive hits to our collective self-esteem.

I was too young to fully comprehend the significance of 9/11 or even the 7/7 attacks (especially what impact they would eventually have on my life as a Muslim), but this time – with Manchester – I did. I had lived through years of Islamophobia. I was familiar with the harm it caused and could articulate that experience. For me, the Manchester attack drew a line in the sand; we could go no further down this destructive path without having a real conversation about anti-Muslim bigotry and hatred.

At the same time, the line in the sand represented to me how critical it had become to address the oppressive beliefs and practices that hold sway amongst a minority of Muslims, including those that justify violence, oppression or the marginalization of vulnerable groups (women and sexual minorities, for example). These practices are not part of the Islam I follow and recognize. Islam has ethics at its core. Like all mainstream religions, it is concerned with how we treat one another on this planet. As Prophet Muhammad once said: 'None among you is a believer until he wishes for his brothers and sisters what he wishes for himself.' So this was not simply about the beliefs that might have inspired the attack on Manchester Arena; it was about the beliefs I had been battling my entire life.

Contrary to the strategies adopted by the government, I believe that these narratives are best neutralized by Muslims themselves. I know that countless Muslims are quietly getting on with this work, but equally, many within our communities have underestimated the scale of the task before us. Their neglect has allowed our religious beliefs to be hijacked, for unjust practices to take hold; if they didn't actively encourage them, many in our communities at least watched them unfold. This narrowing of religious expression resulted in many of my early religious experiences being shaped not by autonomy, empowerment and self-direction, but by duty, authority and inflexibility. And although I am an adult now, this stagnation still registers. It still prevents us from neutralizing extremist or otherwise oppressive beliefs effectively. It still prevents some young Muslims from developing an empowered relationship with Islam.

By writing this book, I want to take the opportunity to dispel long-standing myths about Muslims that have been allowed to circulate and evolve in our societies unchecked. We are perhaps the most misunderstood – and misrepresented – minority group living in the West today. Myths exist within Muslim communities too – often along similar lines; Islam tends to be completely misunderstood by many of its own followers. By challenging the preconceptions of Muslims and non-Muslims alike, I hope to share a true picture of what it's like (and what it can look like, should you want it to) to be a Muslim living in the West today.

The fear, prejudice and hatred that are directed towards Muslim communities are more commonly described today as 'Islamophobia'. The All-Party Parliamentary Group on Muslims has defined Islamophobia as 'a type of racism that targets expressions of Muslimness or perceived Muslimness'.[9]

There's a great deal of resistance to this term being used. Some figures argue that criticizing Islam and Muslims isn't a form of racism; that describing it as such is an attempt to silence such criticisms.[10] Other objections hone in on the fact that Muslims aren't a singular race and, therefore, can't be subject to racism on grounds of their religion. Some agitators position themselves as independent and unbiased, so that their criticisms of Islam are treated as facts that they've arrived at fairly and logically.[11] But we should reflect on the reasons why a person might object to the term being used. For example, describing something as Islamophobic helps us to bring attention to bigotry. Denying the term altogether allows those propagating myths about Islam and Muslims to do so without being held accountable.

Moreover, using the term Islamophobia is appropriate in a discussion about how Muslims are treated because it's the *right* term. We use Islamophobia not because Muslims are perceived as being ethnically homogenous, but in reference to the way that Muslims are *racialized*.[12]

Let me explain what I mean by this. Race is a social construct. As a concept it was invented during the European Enlightenment to advance the superiority of one group of people over others, namely the superiority of white people over everybody else. Islamophobia, then, is a type of racism. As part of it, Muslims are constructed as a singular, homogenous group and broad arguments are used to dehumanize and assert Western moral and intellectual superiority over us. Like all forms of racism, Islamophobia is rooted in power, in particular the power held by the powerful to define the way Muslims are perceived and treated. As Muslims don't hold an equivalent amount of power and influence within British society (nor do they in other Western societies), we don't have the ability to effectively challenge the way we are portrayed. That's why it's important for us to describe anti-Muslim prejudice as Islamophobia: it isn't just bigotry, it's racism. It has that added edge. And since our constructions of race are malleable, shifting as dominant powers need, it's no defence to maintain that Muslims are not a race. For all intents and purposes, we exist as one in the minds of those who hate us.

Moreover, Islamophobia is racism because it has structural, institutional limbs. Anti-Muslim prejudice exists in all areas of public life, at every level of society, and it limits the opportunities we have access to. Examples of Islamophobia can be found within the media and the criminal justice system, in the areas of education and housing. Muslims have to engage with the reality that anti-Muslim attitudes determine their life experiences, whether in the job market, at a restaurant or even in an act as banal as obtaining car insurance.[13] In his report about the police investigation into Stephen Lawrence's murder, Lord Macpherson defined institutional racism as:

the collective failure of an organization to provide an appropriate and professional service to people because of their colour, culture, or ethnic origin. It can be seen or detected in processes, attitudes and behaviour which amount to discrimination through unwitting prejudice, ignorance, thoughtlessness and racist stereotyping which disadvantage minority ethnic people.[14]

When I say that Islamophobia is structural or institutional, I am describing how the British government has implicitly and explicitly endorsed anti-Muslim sentiment to further its own goals. There is no clearer example than Prevent, the British government's counter-radicalization programme. As part of Prevent, police officers are tasked with building relations with organizations across the UK, that are then encouraged, even forced – as teachers, doctors and other public sector workers are forced – to refer 'suspicious behaviour' to a local Prevent body.[15] This initiative has been criticized for many reasons, including its incursions on the right to free speech and its policing of 'acceptable' Muslim behaviour. (There's a cruel, hypocritical irony to the way that critics of Islam rely on free speech rights to say what they want about Muslims even as the government takes steps to curb our own rights to the same.) Prevent has criminalized countless innocent Muslims, including many young children. Teachers at one school in Luton referred a fourteen-year-old student to the Prevent authorities. His crime? He had attended school wearing a pro-Palestine badge and later tried to fundraise for Palestinian children living under Israeli bombardment.[16] Pointing out the institutional nature of Islamophobia shows not only how anti-Muslim sentiment has infiltrated all aspects and levels of British society, but also the fact that this infiltration is nearly always state-sponsored.

The state's exploitation of Islamophobia is strategic. It has been used to maintain what Reni Eddo-Lodge describes as 'systemic power'.[17] Time and time again, politicians pit Muslim communities against the rest of British society to advance their aims. Consider the 2016 election campaign for the Mayor of London. Leaflets from the Conservative candidate, Zac Goldsmith, targeted Hindu voters and claimed that Goldsmith would stand up for them, whilst Sadiq Khan, the candidate for Labour, would tax their jewellery.[18] His campaign sought to portray Khan as a terrorist sympathizer, disseminating materials that called him 'radical and divisive'. Then prime minister David Cameron pushed this line of attack at Prime Minister's Questions, accusing Khan of 'sharing a platform with extremists', including an alleged supporter of Islamic State.[19] (Cameron was later forced to apologize to the imam concerned, who was not a supporter of Islamic State at all.) Goldsmith authored an article for the *Mail on Sunday* – accompanied by a picture from the 7/7 attacks – in which he claimed that Khan 'repeatedly legitimised those with extremist views'.[20]

In August 2018, Boris Johnson used his column in the *Telegraph* to compare niqab-wearing Muslim women to letterboxes and bank robbers.[21] Pressed to apologize, he refused. Following an investigation, the Conservative Party cleared Johnson of Islamophobia, finding him to be 'respectful and tolerant'.[22] It speaks volumes about attitudes in the Conservative Party that none of their most senior politicians stepped in to criticize his comments or the outcome of the inquiry. This mealy-mouthed response, Johnson's naked (and obviously successful) calculation that such remarks would help with his goal of occupying No. 10 Downing Street, and the media's commentary have demonstrated how Islamophobia operates in our societies. Writing for the *Guardian*, Polly Toynbee accepted that Johnson's words were a clarion call to racists.[23] And yet, she went on to regurgitate familiar tropes about Muslim women lacking agency and being dehumanized by the veil.

This is what everyday Islamophobia looks like. Way back in 2011, Baroness Sayeeda Warsi warned that Islamophobia 'has passed the dinner-table test' – but it has more than passed the test. It has facilitated access to some of the highest tables in the land.[24]

There is political capital in Islamophobia; it's clearer than ever that the state and media work in tandem to extract it.

What also remains clear is that contemporary Islamophobia appears in markedly different forms to 'traditional' racism. We mistakenly restrict our understanding of racism to ugly, abusive language and behaviour. But this, paradoxically, enables racism because actual racism can be far more subtle and sophisticated. Using hints and suggestions rather than insults, it allows racist messaging to pass as harmless, as long as it doesn't contain language that is explicitly offensive.

Zac Goldsmith's campaign demonstrated the slippery insidiousness of contemporary Islamophobia. The Tories didn't explicitly call Sadiq Khan a terrorist. They simply linked his Muslim identity to the ongoing discourse around Islamic extremism. By describing him as 'radical and divisive', and by claiming that he shared platforms with extremists, the entire campaign was designed to discredit his candidacy. They used his religion to do that. With cleverly coded messages, the campaign preyed on people's fears without abusing Khan outright and, in doing so, managed to escape accountability.

But basing a campaign on Islamophobia was a colossal miscalculation, especially in a city as cosmopolitan as London. In the days after Goldsmith's article was published, his vote share plunged to 32 per cent in the polls.[25] It recovered to 35 per cent by the time of the first-round vote, but this still represented a 9 per cent drop in the Tory share on the previous election. By contrast, Khan became the most senior directly elected official in the UK, and the first Muslim mayor of a Western capital. When Khan finally called out the tone of the campaign, Goldsmith denied referencing his religious or ethnic identity and accused Khan of 'calling Islamophobia to prevent legitimate questions being asked'.[26] It's worth noting that Goldsmith has never suffered for his actions; despite losing his seat in the 2019 general election, he was awarded a life peerage and sits in the Conservative cabinet as Minister for the Environment. If anything, his racism has been and continues to be rewarded.

Our media disseminates Islamophobia with the same toxic mix of doublespeak, fearmongering and falsehood. When the child-grooming scandals blew up in Rochdale, Newcastle and Rotherham, conversations around toxic patriarchy and misogyny were employed to stigmatize Muslim communities.[27] Despite successive outcries about the treatment of vulnerable young women by the media, the victims were used as fodder to make more insidious arguments about the nature of all Muslim men. *The Times* newspaper also broke the hysteria-laden story of a white Christian child 'forced into Muslim foster care' by Tower Hamlets council.[28] The foster carers were described in terms that were a dog whistle to those who dislike Muslims; they 'didn't speak English' – one of them wore a niqab. The story alleged that they had removed a cross from the child's neck and left her 'sobbing'. The implication was that the Muslim foreignness of the carers meant they were unfit to take responsibility for this girl. In fact, Andrew Norfolk, the investigative reporter who first broke this story, is responsible for most of the Islamophobic stories published by *The Times* in recent years – almost all of which have been proven to be unfounded.[29] The effect of these stories is to amplify the anti-Muslim climate.

In just eighteen months, Miqdaad Versi from the Muslim Council of Britain won more than forty corrections from the British print media over misleading stories about Islam and Muslims.[30] The corrections have challenged reports, for example, that one in five British Muslims sympathize with jihadis, that Muslims are 'silent on terror', and that there was an 'Islamic plot' to take over a school in Birmingham, and a separate plot in Oldham. These kinds of falsified stories are directly responsible for the growth in the number of British people who see Islam as a threat to Western democracy (more than half, according to a poll conducted by YouGov).[31] And they're responsible for 31 per cent of schoolchildren believing that Muslims have taken over England.[32] Even Gary Jones, the new Editor-in-Chief of the *Daily Express*, has come to acknowledge the 'Islamophobic sentiment' within the British media.[33]

I call this barrage of negativity a destructive influence on British society because it hurts so many of us. The constant vilification and humiliation of Muslims, and the experiences of structural discrimination and state-sponsored stigma only force Muslim communities into a corner, where we are constantly defending ourselves from attack. Withstanding Islamophobia takes energy from Muslim communities – energy that could be better directed inwards. But this, as Toni Morrison argues, is its very purpose: 'The function, the very serious function of racism is distraction. It keeps you from doing your work. It keeps you explaining, over and over again, your reason for being.'[34] The endless barrage of negativity stifles the ability of Muslim communities to improve themselves, critique themselves and develop healthy self-esteems. It's also destructive because it erodes trust and relations *between* communities. It damages the way that non-Muslims perceive their Muslim neighbours, leading many to absorb unquestioningly the rhetoric that Muslims cannot live peacefully in the West. How can we live in a society where we have an irrational dislike and distrust of our neighbours?

And I call it destructive because Islamophobia puts lives at risk. The same month as the attack around London Bridge in 2017 (in which eight people were killed and forty-eight injured by three assailants), there was an incident outside Finsbury Park mosque. A white van ploughed into worshippers emerging from the mosque after tarawih prayers – the nightly prayers conducted in the evenings during Ramadan. Witnesses quote the driver as saying, 'I want to kill all Muslims' and 'this is for London Bridge' – referencing that earlier attack. Darren Osborne, the perpetrator, was sentenced to life for murder and attempted murder, with the judge identifying that his targeting of people wearing traditional Islamic dress reflected his 'ideology of hate towards Muslims'.[35] The trial revealed that Osborne had been radicalized in a matter of weeks, consuming anti-Muslim material over the Internet from Stephen Yaxley-Lennon (more commonly known by his alias, 'Tommy Robinson'), the former leader of the English Defence League (EDL), and from Britain First.

But anti-Muslim hatred is also born out of a specific historical context. What I mean by this is that the West, particularly Western Europe, has a long tradition of feeling threatened by Islam, responding by debasing Islam and racializing Muslims as 'other'. Drawing the link between this old bigotry and the anti-Muslim sentiment that exists today is vital. It helps us to appreciate the irrationality that is at the core of all anti-Muslim sentiment. Because the criticisms of Islam that circulate in our societies today aren't reasoned arguments, but myths that have been around for centuries, myths drawn from very limited interaction with actual Muslims. The belief that Muslims are violent and barbaric is, in fact, an archaic stereotype that was formulated at a time when the West had little to no experience of Islam and Muslims and even less knowledge. When reviving these arguments, Islamophobes might try to give them a sheen of reasonableness and respectability – using secular, dispassionate language, applying them to a contemporary context – but we should see through them. Throughout history, the West has used these exact stereotypes to humiliate and pigeonhole Muslims and they have the same effect today. All this supposed logic and neutrality is but mere posturing; it's to mask the cultural entitlement and hegemony that the West adopted towards Islam many centuries ago and has refused to abandon ever since.

To understand the roots of Islamophobia we must first understand Christianity. When Muslims emerged from the Arabian Peninsula in the Middle Ages, the Christians of medieval Europe were wrestling over power and doctrine. Christianity had five seats of power (Rome, Constantinople, Alexandria, Antioch and

Jerusalem) competing for influence, and it was dealing with a series of splits and schisms. For example, the East–West Schism in 1054 resulted in the separation of the Catholic and Eastern Orthodox churches. At this time, Christian Europe paid little attention to the Muslims. Islam, it assumed, was another of its deviant sects. Muslims, after all, also believe in one God and the Abrahamic prophets.[36]

But as the Muslim empires rapidly spread, Christianity couldn't afford to ignore Islam any longer. Muslims had conquered large swathes of traditionally Christian land: in Spain, North Africa and the Levant, for example, including the power bases of Alexandria, Antioch and Jerusalem. More troubling was the fact that Christians were willingly converting to Islam in substantial numbers, and this posed a huge threat to Christianity's integrity. The fear of losing followers, of being wiped out, disturbed Christian leaders and they fumbled for an explanation for this loss of face. Some leaders looked to scripture for an answer; they found it in references to the Apocalypse. Muslims were no longer viewed as belonging to the collective pantheon of wayward Christian sects. Instead, they came to be seen as the fulfilment of Biblical 'barbarians' and 'tyrants', sent by God to challenge the faithful. Once destroyed, Christianity (in its rightful form of Catholicism) would finally reign supreme.

In the absence of actual knowledge and understanding, the Christian leaders of medieval Europe concocted outrageous descriptions to explain to their followers why this particular schism, this inferior 'heresy' of Islam, was spreading across the world in place of the 'true' Christian faith. Of course, the problem was that Islam challenged not just Christianity's destiny (an un-assailable trajectory towards becoming *the* universal religion), but also the various churches' doctrines, such as the divinity of Jesus. Thus, Islam was a monster set to destroy Christianity and its followers were heretics and pagans. They reserved the worst insults for Prophet Muhammad; discrediting the Prophet delegitimized Islam itself. He was portrayed as lustful and violent, a fraud who had taken Christian theology and distorted it for his own gain. The Spanish theologians Eulogius and Paulus Alvarus associated the Prophet with the Antichrist, the former claiming that he was 'seduced by demonic illusions, devoted to sacrilegious sorcery'.[37]

Then, in November 1095, Pope Urban II delivered a sermon in which he declared Christianity in serious trouble.[38] The Holy Land was under Muslim control. '[A] people... alien to God' had tortured Christians and desecrated the Holy City, Jerusalem. They were violent, barbaric; they raped women. He called upon Europe to rise up as the 'soldiers of Christ' and take it back. The First Crusade took the Muslim regions by surprise; in recapturing the Holy Land, the Christian army massacred 30,000 Muslims and Jews in Jerusalem. Its legacy (as documented in medieval chronicles of the Crusades) was the establishment of Muslims as a 'vile and abominable race', 'fit only for extermination'.[39]

For several centuries the Crusades dragged on and, when the appetite for war petered out, a more nuanced set of personal and political relationships resumed between Muslims and Christians. But in 1492, the Spanish monarchy recaptured Spain from the Muslim Umayyads and this relationship shifted again. The monarchy expelled Muslims and Jews from the territory and those remaining were forcibly converted to Christianity. But the Spanish continued to persecute the converts, then expelled them from their territory in 1609. It's perhaps worth remembering that Europe can only be said to have a Christian identity – as critics hostile to Islam tend to argue – because Jews and Muslims were driven out.

The Spanish may have persecuted Muslims and Jews, but they still viewed them as human beings; Muslims believed in God, even if we had the 'wrong religion'.[40] And as humans, Muslims had certain rights. This soon became problematic for the colonialist endeavour. In order for Christian nations to justify their exploitation of people, their strategy had been to dehumanize them; the Spanish had done this with the indigenous Americans by identifying their godlessness (which made them subhuman in their eyes).

The Spanish thinker Sepúlveda, for example, argued that indigenous people were inhuman because they lacked souls. But when it came to exploiting the people of Africa, there was a problem: one in five was Muslim, which meant that they were not godless, and were human. The solution was to erase their religion altogether.[41]

The humanity initially offered to Muslims of Arab and Turkish heritage was curbed when the colonial powers of Europe began to encroach upon more and more of the Muslim world. The notion that Muslims belonged to a similar but different tradition was quickly eroded. It had to change. If these Muslims were still human, they couldn't be subjugated too. Accordingly, over the sixteenth and seventeenth centuries, Christian theologians returned to the debate in 1550 between the Spanish thinkers Las Casas and Sepúlveda to argue that Muslims, as a people with the 'wrong God', were also primitive and animal-like, and that subjecting them to colonial rule was necessary.

Islamophobia shifted again under the Enlightenment. Before this, Europeans had mostly used religion to justify their subjugation of Muslims and other indigenous peoples. But with the introduction of scientific theories of a racial hierarchy, the Enlightenment marked the secularization of Christian prejudice. This is crucial – Muslims went from being part of an inferior religious tradition to being an inferior group of people on the basis of logic and reason. Thus, reason is never neutral; it is also subject to bias and agenda. The Tunisian historian Hichem Djait describes Western thinkers in this period 'us[ing] first Christianity and then secular humanism as a stick to beat Islam'.[42] But secularists used Islam as a stick to beat Christianity too, or at least to encourage Christians to reflect on themselves.

Enlightenment thinkers clung to one of two stereotypes about Islam: either it was a great manipulation and deception of the masses (read: fraud), or it was a product of madness and derangement (read: fanaticism). Martin Luther believed in the imposture theory, labelling Muslims the 'arch-enemies of Christ and his Holy

Church'; 'the spirit or soul of antichrist, is the Pope, his flesh or body the Turk'.[43] The German philosopher, Immanuel Kant, opted for the latter, treating Islam as a fantasy and equating it to the many 'illnesses of the head'.[44]

Pierre Bayle, a French pioneer of the Enlightenment, was the first to take the Christian criticisms of Islam and present them in a neutral and objective style. In the *Historical and Critical Dictionary*, Bayle developed Christian characterizations of the Prophet as lustful and Muslims as lascivious (a counterpoint to Christ's chasteness and Christian morality). He argued that Prophet Muhammad's behaviour towards his wives – his purported infidelity and violence towards them – was unfair to women, and this proved that he was not a genuine prophet. Moreover, he agreed with Christians who discredited the rapid spread of Islam by claiming that Christianity had, at least, spread peacefully, whereas Islam was spread by force. Muslims were mostly peaceful in practice, Bayle agreed, but the Quran 'requires them to persecute the infidels'.[45]

These secular criticisms of Islam often served a higher purpose. They were a call for Christians to recognize their flaws and accept the transition towards a secular political system. Though the overriding issue was the role of religion in post-Enlightenment European society, when Christians fought back against calls for a separation between religion and the state, Islam suffered again, with hateful stereotypes permeating deep into Western thought. The Anglican theologian, Humphrey Prideaux, took it upon himself to prove that Islam, not Christianity, was the real fraud. In 1697, he published a biography of Prophet Muhammad, *The True Nature of Imposture Fully Displayed in the Life of Mahomet*. This book portrayed the Prophet as tyrannical, fanatic and fraud-ulent, and ended up wielding a great deal of influence over the eighteenth century, taking these old ideas about Islam and making them commonplace across British society. In 1746, his book was published in the United States and was so popular there that it had to be published two more times at the end of the century.[46]

Over time, Enlightenment thinkers and then the Orientalists used their beliefs in science, empiricism and reasoning to explain their domination and dehumanization of Muslim people. This became an exercise in proving that the West had intellectual, cultural and moral supremacy over Muslims. The French philosopher Volney travelled across Egypt and, upon his return, described Islam as crude and anti-scientific, reflecting the 'barbarism' that it had emerged from.[47] Ernest Renan, the French historian of religion, argued that 'different peoples have different abilities to move along this path... There is a hierarchy of peoples, languages and cultures... The Semitic spirit and Islam have conquered the world, but it can produce nothing else.'[48] In Renan's view, Islam was incompatible with science; a Muslim scientist couldn't exist and had never truly existed in history.[49]

The sociologist Karl Marx asserted that Islam was inherently xenophobic and used this assessment to legitimize European colonization of the Muslim world.[50] It's not hard to draw a line between his claim and the arguments made by Islamophobes today. The same distrust of the Quran, of Muslims and our intentions is alive in Western societies.

The Orientalists' obsession with comparing Europe to the Muslim world had the effect of constructing a wall of separation between them. Europe was civilized and superior; Muslims were inferior because Islamic ideology was inferior. Later, as Muslim countries began to obtain their independence from European colonization, these assumptions continued to dictate how the West understood Islam. As the American professor Khaldoun Samman contends, Western thinkers saw Muslim nations struggle with modernity and concluded that it was because of 'cultural deficiencies'.[51] Muslim societies were underdeveloped because they still looked to Islam for guidance and this doctrine was intrinsically defective and ill-equipped to assist them.

Scholars like the Puerto Rican sociologist Ramón Grosfoguel have charted the evolution of Western racism from biological racism to cultural racism.[52] Today the word 'race' is rarely mentioned, but that doesn't matter. Parts of Western society are still fixated on establishing the inferiority of specific groups, and within this religion plays a prominent role. It is religion that is now denounced as barbaric, savage, primitive, underdeveloped and so on, not the people themselves. This was devised precisely as a way of evading accusations of racism, even as the arguments and underlying stereotypes remain unchanged.

This is the tradition in which British-American historian Bernard Lewis speaks when arguing that Muslim stagnation is a product of the 'classical Islamic view'.[53] Islam had enjoyed 'its moment', he felt, albeit during a simpler time. But in the modern era, Muslims couldn't rise again. To progress, we would have to let go of Islam entirely. This belief that Islam was incompatible with the modern era led Samuel Huntington to posit the 'clash of civilizations' theory in 1993. He argued that the West – politically, culturally, economically and technologically advanced – needed to prepare itself for constant conflict with a civilization that was its exact opposite.[54] This kind of argument ignores the factors to blame for stagnation in Muslim societies, such as the violence of colonization, Western interventions into domestic politics, corrupt leadership, fragile borders and economic failures. Thinkers like Lewis and Huntington felt that the flaws were to be found within Islam, and this is precisely where Islamophobic rhetoric situates itself today.

Clearly, there is a through line between contemporary anti-Muslim bigotry and the history I have described above. For much of the latter half of the twentieth century, the West was relatively quiet on the Muslim front. It was preoccupied with the Cold War enemy of the Soviet Union ('Islamists' were useful then, nurtured and funded to help destabilize the Soviet Union) and, in its anti-Arab and anti-Palestinian depictions, Islam tended to be curiously absent. But after the Iranian Revolution in 1979, the Rushdie Affair in 1989 and then, most critically, the collapse of the Soviet Union in the early 1990s, the West needed a new common enemy to rally its societies around. The West dipped into its considerable well of historic anti-Muslim bigotry, and contemporary Islamophobia emerged in line with the theses advanced by Huntington and Lewis.[55]

Of course, the language of Islamophobia has evolved over time. It comes to us in a secular, dispassionate context and, because it comes primarily from the 'enlightened' West, we are to believe that it is a product of reason. But at its heart, contemporary Islamophobia is the same as it has been throughout history. It's motivated by fear and insecurity. It's focused on proving the inferiority of Islam. It redeploys the exact same arguments. And it is based on scant understanding of Islam and how the faith is actually practised. Anti-Muslim attitudes are full of contradictions. Islamophobes are terrified of Islam and Muslims (i.e. they're quick to claim that Muslims want to impose Shariah law across the West), and yet they are intent on establishing our inferiority. Equally, it's strange to realize that Islamophobes and some conservative Muslims are frequently united in their belief that there is a single Islam. But if we are to be successful in demolishing anti-Muslim stereotypes and correcting the mistaken assumptions that some Muslims hold about their own faith, we need to see through these myths and appreciate their historical contexts.

The history of Islamophobia, and all the many misconceptions and prejudices that have accumulated over time, are thus long overdue the kind of interrogation that will ultimately lead to their abolition. This is what this book does, examining the most significant issues in the debate surrounding Islam today to interrogate what we understand of Islam and Muslims and hold those understandings to account.

1

'Muslims Don't Integrate'

One Christmas, my aunt invited our extended family to her house for dinner. We split the menu: one family made canapés; one roasted a leg of lamb; one prepared the trimmings. The day before, I went out with my mum to buy two turkeys, which we brined in a bath of salt and spices. The following morning, we marinated them and put them in the oven; every hour we took them out and basted them with their juices. In the afternoon on Christmas Day, thirty of us gathered together. We laid out the food on the dining table and, after several photographs, we settled down to eat.

This scene plays out in countless Muslim households, not just in the West, but across the world. I remember a visit to Pakistan many years ago. On Christmas Eve, my cousin took me to the livestock market. We purchased a live turkey and gave it to the nearby butcher. He handed us a carcass, plucked and skinned, and I carried it home in a plastic bag. The next day, we cooked it in a tandoor oven, covered in yoghurt and spices, and ate it with mashed potato and roasted vegetables. My Pakistani family, who are mostly unfamiliar with Western Christmas traditions, relished the experience.

When I was six years old, my schoolteacher knitted miniature stockings for every student in her class. We hung them on a Christmas tree that stood in the middle of our classroom and,

at the end of term, we took them home. I remember it vividly –
the novelty and excitement. Once I emptied the stocking of its
sweets, I carried it everywhere. That year, it accompanied me to
Pakistan and I recall clutching the stocking carefully when I rode
on a horse-drawn carriage for the very first time. As a child, my
parents took me to visit Father Christmas every year. His grotto
sat in the middle of the Arndale Centre in Manchester, a line of
families coiled permanently around it. Each time, my parents
waited for over an hour so that I could do what other children did
– meet Father Christmas and get a Christmas present from him.

Sometimes I wonder why my parents were so laidback, why
they didn't worry about these things conflicting with our faith. At
high school, I was part of the choir. Every Christmas and Easter, we
performed a series of concerts in the city's churches. At home, my
parents listened to me practising the hymns and carols about Jesus;
sometimes they asked me to perform them in front of the family.
I asked my mother about this once and she replied with typical
nonchalance: 'Well, Jesus is our prophet too, you know. We just
don't see him as the Son of God.' Then she dismissed my question
altogether. 'There's nothing wrong with any of this, with singing
carols, with Christmas dinners. There's no harm to it at all.'

The Christmas break marks a rare moment in the year when
my family isn't working, when we're able to relax and spend quality
time together, when we can nourish ourselves with food and television. I might be a Muslim, but it has been easy to make space in
my life for Christmas. Knowing that, across the country, people
are coming together like my family does, I feel connected to something bigger and more profound than the limits of my existence.
I am a Muslim, but Christmas does this for me. I see no problem
with that. So it hurts to witness the conflicts that are created by
something as innocent as Muslims celebrating Christmas.

In recent years, *The Great British Bake Off* has become Britain's
most successful cultural export. The show has been sold to

196 territories and the series format licensed to at least twenty. Wholesomeness plays a large part in its success. There's little of the melodrama that reality television is renowned for. *Bake Off* is a simple baking competition and, trophy aside, the victor is promised very little in the way of reward. But it has also exposed the progressively tribal (and Islamophobic) nature of Western society.

The finale to the sixth series was the most-watched show of 2015, viewed by over 15 million people in Britain. The winner was Nadiya Hussain, a thirty-year-old woman from Luton. Nadiya's success was potent. A friend of mine, who shares Nadiya's Bengali heritage, recalled the night of the finale. Her entire family had huddled around the television to watch it. And when Nadiya won, every single one of them – even the stoic-looking uncles – cried with happiness. I can only imagine what Nadiya's success meant to those men, who had come to Britain in the 1960s and 1970s, who had never seen a British Bengali like them achieve such public success, who never thought it was possible.

Nadiya was extremely popular with the public and this popularity appeared to break boundaries. Here was a Muslim woman who wore the hijab; she obsessed over cake and talked openly about her struggle with anxiety. It was far removed from the stereotypes that portray Muslim women as fragile and oppressed. But her presence on the show didn't only humanize Muslim women, it seemed to help alter perceptions of Muslims as a whole. Professor Ted Cantle at the Institute of Community Cohesion claimed Nadiya had done more 'for British-Muslim relations than 10 years of government policy'.[1]

Nadiya's popularity has allowed her to transition into a media career. She now fronts cookery shows on television and publishes novels and recipe books; Nadiya is one of the most famous Muslim figures in Britain. But the price of her success is an endless torrent of abuse.

In October 2017, Nadiya published a column for BBC *Good Food* magazine, sharing her Christmas recipes and tips. A summary of the article was published in the *Mail Online*. Soon, the comments section beneath was inundated with messages from furious readers: 'Telling us how to celebrating Christmas? Are you ******* serious. The media is out of control with its pc agenda [sic]'; 'Christmas advice from a Muslim! How dare a Muslim woman offer her thoughts on celebrating Christmas'; 'Why do I want tips about how to celebrate Christmas from this woman? Would she like mine on how to celebrate Eid?'[2]

On Twitter, Nadiya wrote that she had read the messages before going to sleep. They had given her nightmares. Later, she said:

> I get abuse for merely existing. Too brown to be English. Too Muslim to be British. Too Bengali to eat fish fingers! There is no end! I exist, we all do! Some days I hate myself for simply breathing the same air that I am so often told I am not entitled to.[3]

This is the harm of Islamophobia – the pain of never being enough for some. It's no coincidence that Nadiya has linked her struggle with anxiety to racism she experienced as a child.[4] We end up directing the rejection and abuse inwards, at great personal cost. What's unfair about this isn't just the hate; it's that Islamophobes can't decide what they want from us. First they claim that Muslims won't integrate. The Danish People's Party, for example, demands that Muslims celebrate Christmas to prove their 'Danishness'.[5] But when we do, Islamophobes complain that we're diluting and undoing the Western way of life.

Nadiya's experience made me reflect on this contradiction. In the West, minorities are expected to shoulder the burden of integration; we keep peddling the stereotype that Muslims refuse to integrate into our societies. But here was a Muslim who had won the most popular competition on television, being the best at that quintessentially British pastime – baking. What more did the haters want from her? Which other measure of integration did they prefer? I soon realized that if Nadiya's baking excellence, her honesty and approachability, and her participation in a key Western holiday weren't enough to insulate her from Islamophobia, the criticisms actually had nothing to do with her conduct. And I understood that if Nadiya couldn't be insulated from the abuse (not that I'm saying she should be, simply because she's successful or visible, a 'good immigrant'), the rest of us had no chance. The problem wasn't her integration. The problem was her existence; the audacity that somebody could feel they belonged, to such an extent that they took up space in our media.

At the same time, Christmas is a flashpoint for puritanical Muslims fearful that our communities are abandoning Islam whilst living in the West. Last Christmas Day, when my turkeys were roasting in the oven, I decamped to the living room and logged on to Twitter. I scrolled down my timeline, past food photographs and Christmas anecdotes, past articles about television specials and affirmations for the lonely. It was all so heart-warming. 'Merry Christmas' was trending.

There's a long-running conversation about whether Muslims can celebrate Christmas and I saw this reflected on Twitter too. The vast majority of tweets were jovial, making fun of those arguing that saying the words 'Merry Christmas' was sinful, or 'haram'. But there were a few posts – backed by videos from religious preachers – that insisted Christmas was wrong.

I clicked on the videos. The preachers had two main objections: that imitating non-believers was a sin and that celebrating a non-Muslim festival was bid'ah – a betrayal of Islamic doctrine or heresy. After watching a video with Assim Al-Hakeem, a conservative Saudi scholar, I searched out videos featuring Zakir Naik and Mufti Menk. Both Naik and Menk hold considerable influence in some Muslim communities. Naik is an Indian preacher and Menk the Grand Mufti of Zimbabwe; both argued that getting involved in Christmas was the same as endorsing the belief that Jesus was the Son of God and that, they claimed, was blasphemous.

I laughed at these arguments, remembering how Prophet Muhammad fasted on the day of Yom Kippur in solidarity with the Jewish tribes of Medina. The scholars of Al-Azhar University, the most prestigious religious institution in Sunni Islam, had also clarified this issue. In 2009, they said, 'There is no harm in congratulating non-Muslims with whom you have a family relationship, or that are neighbours of yours.'[6] I particularly enjoyed a comment written in Urdu on Twitter, addressed to the joyless Muslim preachers that interfered in our lives with their inane remarks. It went along the lines of: 'My commitment to Islam isn't so fragile that wishing somebody a "Merry Christmas" could weaken my faith. Develop your own faith in God so that Christmas wishing seems ordinary and doesn't hurt your religious views.'

But there's no doubt that as easily as I dismiss this panic amongst Muslims, there are those who are deeply conflicted by it. When I started thinking about Muslim stereotypes around integration, I returned to these videos, wondering why some Muslims, especially those of us living in the West, are so compelled by a narrative that renders *any* involvement in Christmas a sin. The videos reminded me of the arbitrary conflict drawn between Islam and the most important celebration in the Western calendar. That conflict, triggered here by the mere words 'Merry Christmas', represented a whole canvas of barriers sewn together by leaders in our communities, intent on making life more difficult for us than it needs to be.

I asked the British poet and activist Suhaiymah Manzoor-Khan about how she understood the conversation about integration to operate within and outside Muslim communities. She pointed out that both of these conversations were completely separate, although they superficially appeared to be parallel:

What I mean by that is, the first conversation [the Islamophobes claiming that Muslims don't integrate] is about race and nation. The second conversation [conservative Muslims arguing that we mustn't integrate] stems from a very legitimate question about what it means to have faith in a secular society. What does it mean to try to live a life of submission to divine will in a society that doesn't cater to that?

It's worth thinking this point through. Certain Muslims do have reservations about celebrating Christmas simply because it is an expression of the Christian faith. Some go on to believe that participating in another religion's festivals and beliefs may contradict their commitment to Islam. But Manzoor-Khan's argument concerns Muslims for whom Christmas raises bigger questions about identity and their place in Western society. Many Muslims oppose parts of Western culture only because they are afraid of losing their own norms, so rejecting Christmas is a symptom of that. She added: 'A lot of this [hostility] is the voice of traumatized generations of migrants who are trying to hold on to cultural norms that are threatened by living in a society where they're completely minoritized and excluded.' From personal experience, I know this to be true: though my parents were relaxed about Christmas when I was a child, they had certain limits (for example, we weren't allowed to have a Christmas tree). But these boundaries disappeared in my adulthood; they went on to embrace every Christmas tradition that I brought into our home, and that is, I believe, because they felt the task of ensuring I grew up with a strong grasp of my religious and cultural identities was complete.

Although the conversations around integration that take place both within and outside of Muslim communities are only casually connected, I still believe it's worth having them simultaneously. Very often, Muslims end up rejecting the West using the exact same logic and rhetoric that Islamophobes level at us – as the controversies around Christmas make clear.

What are we referring to when we talk about integration? For decades, Britain never bothered with a coherent integration policy. It still doesn't have one. But in March 2018, the government published an 'Integrated Communities Strategy Green Paper' which at least defined what it meant by integration. Integrated communities, it said, are ones 'where people – whatever their background – live, work, learn and socialize together, based on shared rights, responsibilities and opportunities'.[7] This is helpful, but only to an extent. Social cohesion is ultimately about all communities enjoying the same right to fully participate in society. Integration is actually then, I believe, the work of eliminating discrimination and generating this equality of opportunity.

Other countries have been thinking about integration far longer than Britain and have more to offer on what it involves.[8] The Australian policy on multiculturalism ends up describing it as a kind of social contract. We all receive the same rights and responsibilities; upholding those responsibilities benefits everyone and forges a proper society. The National Integration Plan of Germany sets out what those responsibilities would look like. For newcomers to German society, it's the responsibility to get involved, to accept its legal system and to show belonging by learning the language. For the government, it's the responsibility to offer courses and opportunities that facilitate integration. For broader German society, it's the responsibility to show acceptance, tolerance and a willingness to welcome people.

Here in the UK we never talk about integration like this in the mainstream. It sounds unrealistic and utopian; it doesn't offer scapegoats and shallow answers, but this is the reality: integration needs us all to play our role in society for it to work. In Britain, integration is often used as shorthand for talking credibly and authoritatively about the failures of immigration, but the two things are not the same. Nor does integration have anything specifically to do with race. Integration involves us all. The very act of living in a community is to understand that we have responsibilities to each other, and that we receive benefits in exchange for carrying out those duties.

But the competing narrative of integration insists on portraying it as the process of society accepting an outsider. Think about this idea for a minute – that integration is about being accepted; the contours of power quickly reveal themselves. When integration is about acceptance, receiving societies have all the power: they get to decide what integration looks like whilst accepting no responsibility for making that process easier. And when that power between parties is so imbalanced, integration quickly becomes a demand for minorities to assimilate into society whilst constantly proving their loyalty and gratitude (as the threat of rejection and retraction looms constantly over them).

By assimilate, I'm referring to the idea that minorities should conform to the majority point of view; that we should resemble, in our public and private selves, mainstream society. But that's not integration. Real integration is motivated by a desire to bring communities together. Assimilation is motivated by cultural insecurity. It's concerned with approving the behaviour of minority groups; with controlling their identities and narcissistically reminding them of how benevolent the society that once received them (or their ancestors) happens to be.

This is exactly how Muslims experience the integration conversation. Our communities are stereotyped as being unwilling to integrate. We are criticized for failing to learn the languages of the countries we live in, of eking out separate existences for ourselves in ghettoes far from the (white) mainstream. We're accused of weakening national cultures and values by dressing differently, eating different food and belonging to a different belief system. This stereotype has been built over many years, but the War on Terror gave it a new dimension. Integration (or lack thereof) became the reason why Muslims born and raised in the West carried out terrorist attacks. Experts argued that religious extremism was attractive to them only because these individuals had failed to integrate, and political figures followed tack. Western societies had been careless, they argued, failing to notice that some Muslims hadn't sufficiently integrated. But this wouldn't be tolerated any longer.

In December 2006, then British prime minister Tony Blair made his infamous speech on multiculturalism. Blair reflected on the 7 July bombings in London, which had been carried out by four home-grown (Muslim) attackers. Their actions, Blair said, had 'thrown into sharp relief the nature of what we have called, with approval, "multicultural Britain"'.[9] The bombers may have been integrated in terms of lifestyle and education, but they hadn't accepted British values. And this specific failure had shed light on how the blind encouragement of diversity in Britain had led to 'separation and alienation' from the values that defined the nation. Britain's accepting nature had been abused, he claimed, and this had led to growing 'unease' in society about how well integrated minorities truly were.

Blair's speech was aimed squarely at Muslims. He made it clear that poor integration wasn't a problem in other communities, but within 'a minority' of the Muslim community. And that minority needed to be reminded of its duty to integrate and respect British values. 'Our tolerance is what makes Britain, Britain. So conform to it; or don't come here.' He went on to rail against forced marriages, disrespect for women amongst Muslim men and Shariah law.

The speech was also a transparent attempt to appeal to the voters of Middle England, who had been encouraged by endless media coverage to view Muslims as bogeymen. It signalled the increasingly bullish tones that Western political leaders would come to adopt on the topic of integration. Criticizing poor Muslim integration was no longer forbidden territory. In fact, it became the sort of rhetoric even mainstream politicians were expected to deliver. So in 2010, when the German politician Thilo Sarrazin published his book *Germany Abolishes Itself*, in which he lambasted Muslims for failing to integrate and bringing no benefit to Germany, the book's controversy and subsequent popularity forced concessions from Angela Merkel, the German Chancellor: 'Of course, the approach to build a multicultural society and to live side-by-side and to enjoy each other has failed, utterly failed.'[10]

Merkel went back on this in her 'Wir Schaffen Das' ('We Can Do This') speech of 2015, which preceded an open-door policy that let 800,000 refugees into the country. But Merkel is, above all, a pragmatist, adjusting her political positions to reflect the public mood, so her immigration policies have shifted rightwards again in response to rising anti-immigration sentiment and the growing popularity of far-right movements.[11]

Back in 2010, leaders across Europe scrambled to follow Merkel's willingness to criticize integration. In February 2011, Prime Minister David Cameron argued that the previous government's 'doctrine of state multiculturalism' had encouraged 'different cultures to live separate lives'. He said, 'We've even tolerated these segregated communities behaving in ways that run completely counter to our values.' A few days later, the French president, Nicolas Sarkozy, asserted, 'The truth is that in all our democracies we have been too preoccupied with the identity of those who arrived and not enough with the identity of the country that welcomed them.'[12] The Spanish and Australian leaders made similar pronouncements.

This is a lesson in how bigotry moves from the margins to the centre. Like this, Western leaders have mainstreamed (and legitimized) the far-right contention that Muslim integration was always doomed to fail. Such a dynamic was plain to witness in the Netherlands. The Dutch far-right politician Geert Wilders maintains that Islam is incompatible with European society and as such threatens its values: 'Dutch values are based on Christianity, on Judaism, on humanism. Islam and freedom are not compatible.'[13] In the run-up to the 2017 elections, the Dutch prime minister, Mark Rutte, made a show of rejecting Wilders, ruling out a coalition with his Freedom Party (PVV). But Rutte then borrowed Wilders' rhetoric. In January 2017, he published an open letter calling for migrants to accept Dutch cultural standards. People who 'refuse to adapt, and criticize our values' should 'behave normally, or go away', he wrote.[14] Dutch people were tired of those who harassed LGBT people, whistled at women in short skirts or branded 'ordinary Dutch people racists'. This is how it always works; mainstream politicians launder Islamophobic discourse, making it palatable for the masses, believing it will aid their chances of seizing or sustaining power.

But the example of Geert Wilders makes clear that beneath talk of Muslim unwillingness to integrate is the stereotype that we simply *can't* integrate because our beliefs and values contradict those in the West.

When the Democratic Party decided to nominate Barack Obama as its candidate for the 2008 presidential election, the reaction of the American Right reflected this belief that Western and Islamic values are fundamentally contradictory.[15] Obama's familial connections to Islam fed conspiracies that he was a secret Muslim, which was why he couldn't be trusted to lead the United States or respect its constitutional values. The right-wing blogger, Pamela Geller, for example, described him as 'the jihad candidate'. During Obama's presidency, she accused him of 'using all branches of the government to enforce the Shariah. [His is the] first Muslim presidency, just eight years after 9/11.'[16]

The Somali-American congresswoman Ilhan Omar has faced racism of a similar slant. In one such incident in February 2019, Omar found herself tagged on Twitter by the representative for New York, Lee Zeldin. He uploaded an antisemitic voicemail that he'd received – one that had nothing to do with Omar – and asked her: 'Would love to know what part of this hate filled, anti-Semitic rant you disagree with? I disagree with all of it. Do you?' But Omar isn't the only one; time and time again, Muslims who aren't even in the public eye are expected to prove their allegiance to Western values. These are purity tests designed for Muslims to fail. No matter what, Muslims will never be able to show that we are integrated, that we share the West's values. We will never be believed and so there will always be something lacking in our evidence.[17]

And these narratives on Muslim integration are deeply embedded within Western society. According to a YouGov poll in February 2019, substantial numbers in the West believed that Islam clashed with their country's values: 53 per cent in Germany, 49 per cent in France, 37 per cent in the US and 32 per cent in the UK.[18] An image always existed in the Western imagination of Muslims as a wildly intolerant, invasive group of people. But this virulent image has resurfaced and persuaded Westerners so successfully that many are even prepared to physically defend themselves from cultural attack. In 2019, Hope Not Hate found that 32 per cent of Britons believed in 'no-go areas' existing across the country due to the dominance of 'Shariah law'; 30 per cent said that they would support a campaign to stop mosque building in their area – 21 per cent would maintain this support even if the matter became violent.[19] Impulses of this kind are ascendant everywhere in the West.

So how do we begin to unpick the stereotype that Muslims won't integrate? Let's start with the fact that Muslims *do* integrate. This was the conclusion of a study by the Bertelsmann Foundation in 2017.[20] The study looked at the Muslim populations of five European nations – Austria, France, Germany, Switzerland and the United Kingdom – surveying 10,000 people, and it focused on five components of successful integration: language, education, employment, social connections and emotional connections to the country concerned. From generation to generation, the study found, Muslim integration increased in these countries. For example, an average of 76 per cent of second-generation Muslims learned the national language as their first language; 67 per cent stayed in school until their seventeenth birthday; and 75 per cent of Muslims spent their free time with non-Muslims. These statistics offer a strong rebuttal to the arguments that Muslims don't learn the national language, that we drop out of school and meaningful employment due to sheer laziness, and that we refuse to socialize outside of our religious communities.

The research also provides insight into the specific successes and failures of Muslim integration in each country. In Germany, for example, Muslims are successfully integrated into the job market. Unemployment amongst German Muslims was no different to the national average. But Germany has a strong economy, high demand for labour and the German government actively promotes economic integration through job placement initiatives and language courses. By contrast, it failed on education: only 36 per cent of Muslim children completed school until the age of seventeen. This is because the German school system disadvantages children from lower socio-economic and migrant backgrounds.[21] From the age of eleven, children are separated according to ability, but that ability is mostly determined by German language proficiency. So a school system that already fails to provide enough support to those who speak German as a second language then goes on to treat poor German skills as proof that a child is less capable or even has a learning disability. As a result, children from disadvantaged backgrounds tend to enter the lower tier for secondary education, fail to complete it and then enter the labour market without even a school degree. There, they might find a job, but it will likely be a low-skilled, low-paid position, making it almost impossible for them to escape the cycle of social disadvantage.

In comparison, 90 per cent of French Muslim children stayed in school until the age of seventeen. But this didn't translate to success in the job market either. Unemployment of Muslims stood at 14 per cent, compared to a national average of 8 per cent. In a tight job market, where Muslims and non-Muslims are educated to the same level, the disparity indicates that employers are discriminating against Muslims.

Indeed, this is proven through the research. Between 2008 and 2009, 22,000 people were surveyed in France with the aim of comparing the prospects of French citizens with immigrant backgrounds to those without such backgrounds. The subsequent report, *Trajectories and Origins*, was published in 2015.[22] People with non-French heritage were *socially* integrated, it concluded, despite stereotypes to the contrary. They had diverse social connections, good academic qualifications and French language skills. But because they spent longer being unemployed, they faced significant barriers to achieving *economic* integration.

The French economist Marie-Anne Valfort has illustrated this barrier fantastically. She carried out a social experiment on the experiences of French Muslims in the job market. Over 2013–2014, she prepared 6000 fictitious CVs, some with 'Muslim-sounding names', and used them to make job applications.[23] Recording the outcomes, Valfort discovered that her Muslim applicants were far less likely to receive a callback from an employer than their Catholic and Jewish counterparts (10 per cent compared with 21 per cent and 16 per cent). French Muslim men, she found, were also less likely to be contacted than Muslim women. At best, a Christian man submitted five applications before an employer contacted him, but a Muslim man would have to submit twenty.

Valfort's research unambiguously proves that prejudice has a huge role to play in high unemployment amongst French Muslims. Unsurprisingly, it has been difficult to pin this kind of conclusion down because France considers itself a 'colour-blind' nation and is resistant to data collection on race. But research constantly sheds light on the institutional discrimination that Muslims face in the West. In Britain, for instance, discrimination in the job market hits Muslim women hardest, particularly amongst those of Pakistani and Bangladeshi heritage.[24] This is despite the fact that Muslim women achieve more university degrees than Muslim men.[25]

According to the Office for National Statistics, in 2015 35 per cent of British Muslim women were in employment, compared to 69 per cent of non-Muslim women. There are complex reasons for this, some of which include the decision some Muslim women make to not work. But there is also plenty of anecdotal evidence illuminating the vulnerability of Muslim women to discrimination, for example, because of their clothing choices – a decision effectively legitimized by the European Court of Justice in 2017, when it ruled that a ban of political or religious signs in the workplace, including headscarves, wasn't necessarily discriminatory.[26]

We also need to recognize the impact of Islamophobia on mobility and integration. Imagine that you and your community are constantly accused of refusing to integrate. It doesn't encourage or inspire cohesion; conversely, it breeds resentment and a desire to separate. Our governments need to be especially aware of this – forcing integration doesn't work. For example, in 2018 the Danish government decided to implement twenty-five hours per week of compulsory day care for children from ethnic minority 'ghettoes', where they would be taught about 'Danish values'.[27] But this will have a bitter legacy in those communities because they have been portrayed as poor, uneducated and full of crime, and because these policies assume that Muslim parents aren't fit to raise their own children. Since the Danish government also proposed to dock the welfare benefits of any family who refused to send their child to the day care and even demolish immigrant neighbourhoods, Danish Muslims are essentially being punished for being different.

I spoke to the Danish curator and film-maker Saadat Munir who confirmed that this was the case:

> Almost all Danish political parties see immigrants, especially Muslims, as a problem. I live in one of these ghettoes and we are going to be homeless in 2024. But actually, I disagree with the term, 'ghetto'. It's a way of covering up Islamophobia and migrant-phobia in Danish society. These areas weren't ghettoes when the homes were built to house Turkish guestworkers in the 1980s. And the areas that the government offers to relocate us to either are too expensive for our families to afford, or they become new ghettoes, only further away from the centre. My personal take is that all of this is only going to create bigger divisions within our society, between ethnic Danes and ethnic minorities most of all.

Sometimes I wonder if this is the precise intention, a fulfilment of what the British author Douglas Murray said in his speech to the Dutch parliament in 2005: 'Conditions for Muslims in Europe must be made harder across the board: Europe must look like a less attractive proposition.'[28] It certainly feels that way.

So why does the stereotype about Muslims refusing to integrate persist when it's both damaging and untrue? It's because this conversation isn't and hasn't ever been about Muslim integration. It's a dishonest conversation, constructed on deliberately misleading terms, because many people benefit from the deceit.

A narrative of Muslim culpability helps Western governments and politicians to evade personal responsibility. In 2017, David Cameron appointed Dame Louise Casey to conduct a review of integration in Britain. Casey's subsequent report, published in 2016, blamed low employment rates amongst Muslim women on patriarchy within Muslim communities rather than acknowledging bias in the job market.[29] The report also criticized poor English language skills within Pakistani and Bangladeshi communities without recognizing the connection between language skills amongst recent migrants and the availability of courses. The Conservative government has been cutting the funding for ESOL (English for Speakers of Other Languages) courses since 2010, whilst insisting that anyone settling in Britain 'should learn the language of the country' (so said in May 2014 by then Culture Secretary, Sajid Javid).[30]

Muslims provide our political class with a scapegoat for rising inequality, diverting public attention from austerity politics and neoliberal policies. Those situated near the bottom of the ladder, like the white working class, are encouraged to blame Muslims and immigration (and both together) for their circumstances. But Muslims aren't to blame, not when governments haven't invested enough in public services to ensure that the needs of our growing societies are met. Moreover, pitting minorities against one another stops us from talking about how inequality cuts across racial lines. Somebody who is Black, Pakistani or Bangladeshi is three times more likely to be unemployed than somebody who is White British. Fifty-nine per cent of Bangladeshi children, 54 per cent of Pakistani children and 47 per cent of Black children in Britain live in poverty.[31] Reporting on the barriers to social mobility faced by young Muslims in 2017, the Social Mobility Commission found that 46 per cent of British Muslims live in ten of the most deprived local authority districts.[32] The working class in our countries isn't just white; a significant proportion is Muslim too.

Finally, blaming Muslims is easier than reflecting on our own culpability – the reality of our personal racism. The responses to Nadiya Hussain's Christmas column were an illustration of this; objections to 'free speech' and 'political correctness' are a disguise for racist intolerance and always have been.

Of course, there are Muslims who don't want to integrate, who are content to live quiet lives disengaged from mainstream society. And of course there are also Muslims who refuse to integrate because they believe integration compromises their religious beliefs. But they remain a minority. The vast majority of Muslims *are* well integrated into Western societies. We integrate in spite of these societies rather than because of them. We integrate under a climate of hate and hostility, and we do so whilst experiencing immense structural inequality. I grew up in a predominantly Muslim area and witnessed talk, even amongst my extended family, of how hard opportunities are to come by, how difficult social mobility is to achieve when you have limited access.

Moreover, it's vital to stress that our faith and cultures are not barriers to this process. The so-called conflict of values is a misnomer, enmeshed in the stories that the West tells about itself. The Enlightenment is valorized as a solely Western achievement and so are the values it is said to have produced. In the eighteenth century, the German philosopher Hegel argued that the Muslim world's defining achievement had been 'to hand on Greco-Roman civilization to modern Europe', after which, nothing but 'sensual enjoyment and oriental repose' remained in those societies.[33] But the truth is that the Enlightenment owes a significant debt to the rest of the world. As Richard Baldwin notes, '[M]uch of the European revival was based on the ideas, institutions and technologies borrowed from the advanced civilizations in the Middle and Far East.'[34]

However, the Western debt to the Muslim world is particularly weighty, since the Enlightenment wouldn't have been possible without the magnificent convergence of innovation and achievement that took place during the Islamic Golden Age, in so many areas at the same time: law, jurisprudence, theology, philosophy, mathematics, physics, chemistry, biology, engineering, astronomy, geology, geography, medicine and medical surgery, and so much more.

Al-Khwarizmi, the father of modern algebra, developed the rules required to solve linear and quadratic equations, using not just geometry as the Greeks had done, but also decimal fractions, irrational numbers and geometric measurements. He made similar advancements in arithmetic (introducing Arabic numerals to Muslim society), trigonometry and astronomy. Ibn Sina's *The Canon of Medicine* (and the work of other Muslim physicians) forms the basis of all modern medicine. Ibn Rushd took the Greek philosophical tradition and developed it in a monotheistic context. Even after the Golden Age, without the work of Ibn Khaldun, there would be no science of culture, known today as sociology. And Copernicus could not have made his many achievements in the field of mathematical astronomy without directly lifting from the work of Muslim astronomers such as Urdi, Tusi and Ibn al-Shatir. We take many parts of the modern world for granted without realizing the instrumental role that Muslims played in their invention. Some of those things include medical surgery, hospitals, aeroplanes, universities, cameras, toothbrushes, musical scales and even coffee.

Detractors often argue that Muslim scientific innovation occurred in spite of Islam rather than because of it. The Orientalist scholar Ernest Renan insisted that Islamic philosophy had evolved outside of the religious tradition: 'science had indeed existed and been tolerated inside Islamic society, but the scientists and philosophers were not really Muslims'.[35] Even contemporary authors like Christopher de Bellaigue and Justin Marozzi, who've written *The Islamic Enlightenment: The Modern Struggle Between Faith and Reason* and *Islamic Empires: Fifteen Cities that Define a Civilization*, present Islam as the enemy of progress. But many of these intellectuals identified strongly with Islam and were inspired by a rationalist school of Islamic theology that actively promoted knowledge production.

Rather than weaponizing its values, the West should reflect on how their development was only possible because of its successful transition to modernity, and how this transition would not have been possible without the labour and subjugation of colonized peoples, including Muslims. In *How the West Came to Rule: The Geopolitical Origins of Capitalism*, Anievas and Nişancioğlu explain that, without the combination of 'American land, African slave labour and English capital', Britain wouldn't look remotely the way it does today. In *The Dutch Atlantic*, Nimako and Willemsen show how freedom for European citizens was only secured through denying others the same freedoms.[36] Even today, our liberal and democratic values are only possible because of our economic prosperity, which is built and maintained through the dominance and exploitation of Third-World societies. So how great (and how Western) are our so-called values really?

Furthermore, what the West considers unique about itself – its commitment to democratic values – does not belong to it exclusively. The Abbasid Empire observed the rule of law; its judiciary was completely independent of the government. And its judicial system employed oral evidence and juries almost four hundred years before the English instituted juries in their own court system. Most traditional Muslim empires were secular, observing a separation between religion and politics. Even today, what the West considers special about itself is a set of values desired and respected by people across the world. The wish to live in a democratic society, where freedom and human rights are guaranteed, is a universal one, not the sole preserve of Westerners. This may appear to be an overstatement, but as the Indian economist Amartya Sen has pointed out, though democracy might not be universally practised or uniformly accepted, across the world, democracy is viewed as a human right.[37]

During the Arab Spring protests that began in 2010, for example, Muslims rebelled because they were tired of living under corrupt, undemocratic and authoritarian leaders; they took to the streets to call for more equal and representative societies. The same was true for the Gezi Park protests of 2013 in Turkey, which were motivated by the Turkish government's growing tyranny, or the 2019 protests in Algeria and Sudan. Even where Muslims are living under autocratic regimes or fragile democracies, the desire for freedom and representation is strong. In 2012, Pew found that 81 per cent of people in Lebanon desired democracy, 71 per cent in Turkey and 67 per cent in Egypt.[38] And these societies didn't just want democracy; they specified wanting to live in societies that valued competitive elections and free speech.

In Tunisia – the Arab Spring's only success – we have a budding example of how Islam can come together with democratic values as a political reality. The ousting of autocrat Zine El Abidine Ben Ali was followed by the first ever free and fair elections in 2011 and then 2014. In the first election, the Islamic party, Ennahdha, was victorious, and though the party stepped down after the political crisis of 2013–2014, it has continued to support the country's process of embedding democratic values throughout Tunisian society. Thus, in the municipal elections of 2018, there were legally mandated diversity quotas for women, the disabled and the young.

It is tempting to believe that these changes illustrate the West's success in exporting its values to these areas, but as I explained above, democratic values are not foreign to Islam. I suggest that we invoke a remembrance of our heritage to make this clear: Muslims don't require a reformation similar to that which occurred within Christianity and produced Protestantism. We simply need to return to our inclusive, diverse and innovative roots.

To give an example of such remembrance, the Magna Carta tends to be lauded as the oldest constitution in the world, the first to set out a contract of rights and responsibilities between the state and citizen in 1215. But Islam has an example of a written constitution that is 600 years older. In 622, Prophet Muhammad established a multireligious polity in the city of Medina. His Constitution of Medina set out the rights of the different groups living under it.

It's also worth thinking over the selectivity of Western logic. It reifies the Magna Carta as part of the founding myth of Western liberalism, but overlooks the fact that the document was forgotten for several hundred years until it became important again in the seventeenth century, and that the document privileges the aristocracy whilst limiting the rights of women and Jews. It's worth remembering that the West didn't champion democracy domestically until very late on. For example, in the UK, universal male suffrage didn't exist until 1918 and that was only to get conscripts to fight in the First World War.

At the same time, the West likes to take credit for exporting democracy to the Muslim world, whilst arguing that Muslims are 'not ready for free and fair elections' and doing all it can to promote undemocratic leaders and regimes.[39] But when have Muslim states been able to trial democracy without intervention? In truth, the Western promotion of democracy, as the deposition of Saddam Hussein in Iraq proved, has less to do with values and more to do with its own goals and interests.[40]

Taking credit for the buds of democracy in the Muslim world allows the West to perpetuate the myth of its own supremacy whilst justifying continued interventions into these countries. But it's worth reflecting on how fragile Western democracies themselves are. The USA Patriot Act 2001 resulted in the dilution of many civil liberties, and essentially authorized the rendition of foreign nationals to undemocratic regimes where they could be tortured. More recently, in the light of spending irregularities during the Brexit campaign by Vote Leave and accusations of Russian interference in the 2016 US elections, to attacks by the British Parliament on its judiciary, democracy may be a value championed by the West, but it is a vulnerable one that requires constant vigilance and protection. There's an argument to be made that Western democracy, particularly in neoliberal economies like the United States, is a sham, where moneyed elites ensure the winning candidate is one who will defend their interests.[41] At times it feels that the West is so focused on seeing itself as the custodian of democracy abroad, it cannot see how democracy is decaying beneath our noses.[42]

At the same time, I want to challenge Muslims who fear or believe that living in the West poses fundamental questions for our faith. There is nothing in Islam that should make this difficult. Hossein Askari, economist and professor at George Washington University, has tried to find the world's nations that best reflect Islamic values. Islamic values, he argues, cover four main areas: free markets and sound regulations (to deliver economic prosperity); good governance (which commits to eradicating poverty and corruption, and to the rule of law); respect for human rights and equality of opportunity; and a contribution to global politics (focused on creating a more peaceful world).[43]

Thus, Askari looked at the economic policies, legal systems, human rights records and foreign policies of 208 countries and territories. His first report, published in 2014, saw Western countries coming out on top: Ireland first, followed by Denmark, Luxembourg, Sweden, the UK, New Zealand, Singapore, Finland, Norway and Belgium. Malaysia was the highest-placed Muslim country at 33, followed by Kuwait at 48 and the United Arab Emirates at 64. Overall, Muslim governments performed incredibly poorly, failing to incorporate basic Islamic teachings into their governance, and they haven't fared much better in successive reports. Askari commented: 'We must emphasize that many countries that profess Islam and are called Islamic are unjust, corrupt, and underdeveloped and are in fact not "Islamic" by any stretch of the imagination.' The research confirms what I always believed: far from creating conflict with our faith, living in the West could help us to align our lives closer to the ideals of Islam.

What about the Muslims who believe that we can't (or shouldn't) integrate? I remember one afternoon when I was still in high school. I was sat alone in the cafeteria devouring my lunch before choir practice. Three boys from my year group approached my table and bombarded me with questions. 'Why do you sing in the choir? Don't you know that Islam forbids music?' I was much too young for theological answers back then, but I immediately recalled the musicality of the Quran and the call to prayer; and I thought about the ubiquity of devotional music, such as qawwali, in our home. 'That's not my interpretation,' I replied, and carried on eating. Years later, the accusation persisted, bothering me enough to look into it.

I bring up the issue of music in Islam here because, by addressing the supposed condemnation of music in Islam, I hope to show Muslims and Islamophobes that faith is not a barrier to integration. Moreover, I want to illustrate how conflicts constructed between the West and Islam can be resolved. Those insisting that music is haram often use the Quran as their source, though the text makes no reference to music. Conservative preachers cite verse 31:6, which refers to 'distracting tales' intended 'to lead others from God's way'. But this verse isn't concerned with music; it's about those who use wordplay to make fun of the Quran. Similarly, the negative reference to '[enticing] whichever you can with your voice' in 17:64 refers to the devil, which the Quran makes clear from the next line: 'But Satan does not promise them except delusion.'

We are 1400 years from when the Quran was written, so when reading it, we need to use our common sense and understanding of Islamic ethics and values if we want it to guide us. Would it make sense, for example, for Islam to ban music? What purpose would that serve? Who would it serve? Certainly not God, who wouldn't have created songbirds if music was so despicable.

Though we both fear and revere it, Shariah also has a role to play in this. Under the guidance of the Shariah, an Islamic ruling must meet one of four objectives: it must uphold justice, prevent harm, remove hardship or protect. If a law doesn't meet these criteria, it cannot be Islamic. These are complicated questions, but they can also guide our internal dilemmas, particularly around integration. So what would this mean for music? It can't be right to ban music; doing so wouldn't meet any of these objectives. There's no valid reason to justify it.

We should think of the Quranic ethos when the text is silent on a modern dilemma or use the Shariah framework when religious guidance contradicts itself. To evaluate Hadith – the written record of the Prophet's words and behaviours – we can also use the system of evaluation that was created by Muslim scholars centuries ago and has been used ever since. If, for example, two Hadiths contradicted one another, I would start by trying to evaluate the authenticity of the Hadiths through these scholarly commentaries and, failing that, I'd rely on my internal voice. What do I – guided by the scholarship out there – believe is God's true expression? This might sound alarming, but it's no different to how scholars generally deal with problematic Hadith. As the South African theologian Farid Esack explained: 'People are trying to reassess Hadith not in terms of the chain of narrators but in terms of the content… how valid the idea in it is.'[44] My suggestion is an extension of that practice. But this doesn't mean that people can use their internal voice to interpret negatively; not all interpretations are valid, as Esack clarifies:

> I basically use the argument that the Qur'an is a living text that it can only be understood in context but that this does not mean that all contextual readings are equally valid. And I never spoke about an authentic meaning; I always spoke about greater authenticity and the whole notion that greater authenticity lies with the marginalized that is still very much at the heart of my theological approaches.

When I was younger, I realized that the Quran couldn't always provide me with black-and-white answers to my questions. That's when I started to develop my own framework, applying logic to my dilemmas, asking myself, 'Am I doing something wrong? Does this hurt somebody?' This is how it was in the past. The great philosopher Al-Kindi, for example, argued that music had healing qualities, creating joy and calm out of grief and depression. Common sense is important; the Quran talks of Islam as the 'middle' or 'moderate' path [2:143], the path of least resistance. Every rule must have a logical reason behind it and mustn't be harsh. Because of this, there's no reason to think that life in the West could pose problems for our faith and vice versa.

The constant talk of values and conflicts reflects a crisis that has little to do with integration. These conflicts are always about nation and identity and who is permitted to belong.

The myths that we tell ourselves in the West to create coherent national identities have always been exclusionary; hinged on the creation of an oppositional 'other'. Those who don't fit in with or subscribe to these stories of exceptionalism are the people we consider incapable and undeserving of belonging. This is not new. In 1978, the scholar Edward Said wrote in his seminal text, *Orientalism*, that the concept of Europe has always existed in opposition to Islam; from the outset, the West built an identity that was based on its superiority to the Muslim world.[45]

But what does it mean to be British today? In 1993, then prime minister John Major described Britain as the country of 'long shadows on county grounds, warm beer, invincible green suburbs, dog lovers and pools fillers and – as George Orwell said – "old maids bicycling to holy communion through the morning mist"'.[46] He suggested that Britain would remain so in fifty years' time, despite the fact that this description seemed comically outdated, even in 1993. I'd argue that 'Britishness' is historically forged from whiteness, composed of four possible people: the English, Welsh, Scottish and Northern Irish. A 'unique' national character was created, consisting of resilience and self-reliance, shaped by the way that Britain, a small island, historically punched above its weight. That is reflected in the way we treat the British Empire and victory in the Second World War as our greatest achievements.[47]

The same is true for France. Politicians and media commentators maintain that the country is the product of a unique culture. Laïcité, the founding principle of the French Republic, is a form of secularism that unites citizens under shared values rather than affiliations based on gender, ethnicity or religion, for example. As a result, it bans all form of religious expression from being a part of the public space.[48]

But these nationalist myths are ultimately hollow; they're selective retellings of the truth. They leave out a long history of ethnic diversity in Britain; they erase the brutality of British colonialism; and they lead us to believe that triumph in the Second World War was because of Britain alone, not Allied cooperation and manpower from the Commonwealth. Similarly, French secularism operates selectively. The state still subsidizes 36,000 churches (paying the salaries of much of the clergy) and school holidays revolve around Catholic festivals. This country remains inexorably shaped by Catholic tradition.

There's good reason for this – we need stories to unify us. After all, John Stuart Mill defined a nation as one where citizens are 'united among themselves by common sympathies which do not exist between themselves and others'.[49] But we also need those stories to evolve and reflect our societies as they change.

This need is perhaps most obvious when looking at the place of Muslims in Western societies. Muslims haven't been granted unconditional acceptance and national identity has remained an excusatory fantasy. In Germany during the 1960s, for example, when the post-war economy was booming, the German government invited workers from Turkey to fill labour shortages, expecting them to return once these needs were met. So when the Turkish 'guestworkers' decided to remain in Germany, it was a problem; because they weren't white, they unsettled the idea of what it meant to be German. The same happened in Britain in the 1950s, with workers invited from the Commonwealth to rebuild a country decimated by war. It led to Enoch Powell's infamous 'Rivers of Blood' speech in 1968, in which he warned about the loss of white identity (and supremacy) in Britain.

This tension between identity and belonging continues today. In 2018, the German football player, Mesut Özil wrote an open letter hitting out at the Islamophobic abuse he'd experienced in Germany. When Germany won the World Cup in 2014, he was hailed a national hero. But when the team performed poorly four years later, Özil said that he was singled out for criticism. After a game against Sweden, for example, a German fan came up to him and told him to 'piss off you Turkish pig'. The politician Bernd Holzhauer called him a 'goat-fucker'. Özil said: 'I am German when we win, but I am an immigrant when we lose. This is because despite paying taxes in Germany, donating facilities to German schools and winning the World Cup with Germany in 2014, I am still not accepted into society, I am treated as being "different".'[50]

Mesut Özil's letter is a clear-sighted deconstruction of belonging to the West whilst Muslim. His belonging to Germany was conditional, hinged on success. And though the German football team's performance in the 2018 World Cup was a collective failure, the fact that he was Muslim meant that he alone was isolated and attacked, and made to feel like he didn't belong. But Özil is still a rich football player, and his affluence enables him to call this dynamic out with a degree of protection and to protest his mistreatment by retiring from international football. It's worth considering how little power young Muslims have in their lives to hit back when their belonging is undermined too.

Belonging has never been granted to Muslims because it is assumed that we can never be loyal to the West. The British philosopher Roger Scruton expressed this sentiment in 2006, accusing British politicians of believing 'the proposition that pious Muslims from the hinterlands of Asia would produce children loyal to a secular European state'.[51] Consider the experience of Mo Farah, the long-distance runner who moved to Britain as a child. Moments after winning gold in the 10,000m race at the London 2012 Olympics, a journalist asked him whether he would have preferred to run for Somalia. Farah replied: 'Look mate, this is my country. This is where I grew up. This is where I started life. This is my country and when I put on my Great Britain vest I'm proud, very proud.'[52]

Hybrid identities of this kind are not new to the West, but they're only threatening when held by racialized minorities. A white person with immigrant heritage doesn't have his or her loyalty constantly questioned. Mesut Özil pointed this out in his letter. The German media constantly foregrounds his Turkish heritage, emphasizing his foreignness, but the Polish heritage of footballers Lukas Podolski and Miroslav Klose is almost never mentioned. The difference in treatment is even clearer when you consider that Özil was slated for posing for a picture with the Turkish President Erdoğan, but when his teammate Lothar Matthäus met Vladimir Putin, the German media was silent.

Yet, Muslims have proven their connection to the West. Research commissioned by Channel 4 (and conducted by ICM

Unlimited) showed that British Muslims identified with Britain as their home; 86 per cent of Muslims polled felt a strong sense of belonging to Britain, 88 per cent considered Britain a good place to live and 78 per cent were keen to integrate.[53] In 2016, 87 per cent of Germans of Turkish origin felt closely connected to the country.[54] Sam Harris has argued that European Muslims exploit the values of their host nation, whilst showing 'little inclination' to acquire them, but I disagree.[55] It is because Muslims recognize the stability and safety of these societies – in contrast to the struggles of Muslim nations – that they find belonging in the West (and continue to, despite rejection).

There's a significant degree to which the obsession with loyalty reflects Western sensitivity about who is allowed to criticize. Muslims, like other minorities, are expected to be grateful that Western societies were magnanimous enough to accept us. So when we criticize the West, it's viewed as a mark of disloyalty and ingratitude. When Özil published his open letter, rather than support him, his teammates questioned his patriotism and loyalty. The future of the German football team, said Manuel Neuer, was 'about having players again who are indeed proud to play for the national team'.[56] In a country where being accepted as Black and Brown and German remains even less possible than being accepted as Black and Brown and British, Özil's criticisms about belonging and identity were razor-sharp. But overdue as they might have been, they failed to ignite a national conversation because the comments stung too much, and stung only because they came from a German-Turkish Muslim. It's worth comparing this reaction to the footballer Gary Neville. 'We have a racism problem in the Premier League and in England,' he said in January 2020.[57] Sky Sports host David Jones remarked that this was part of 'an important discussion'.

What if the West recognized the place of Muslims in society? Imagine how that would change the dialogue on education in general and faith schools in particular.

Many European politicians have declared their opposition to Islam playing a role in our schools. In Denmark, the prime minister and leader of the Social Democrat party, Mette Frederiksen, called for Muslim schools to be banned, describing Islam as a barrier to integration.[58] In France, right-wing politicians have opposed the teaching of Arabic in public schools, treating it as a gateway towards religious extremism. In Britain, the panic around the Islamification of our schools showed up in the 'Trojan horse' scandal of 2014. Fake documents alleged that teachers and governors were plotting an 'Islamic' takeover of several (secular) state schools in Birmingham. Despite the salacious and misleading media coverage (former teachers accused the schools of using prefects as 'morality squads', installing expensive speaker systems to broadcast the call to prayer and playing extremist propaganda videos in classrooms), the accusations themselves were thoroughly debunked.[59]

Faith schools have been a part of Western society for centuries. Historically, the Church monopolized education, fomenting a connection between teaching and religion that exists to this day. As of 2016, there were over 6800 faith schools in the British state system, of which only 28 were Muslim.[60] The rest belong to other religions: 4700 Church of England, 2100 Catholic, 33 Jewish and 28 Methodist. In France, where there are no state-funded faith schools, instead there are 8500 Catholic schools, 300 Jewish schools and fewer than 100 Muslim schools in the private sector. Judging from the number of column inches devoted to the issue, it's clear that many people are concerned about Muslim faith schools and remain unconvinced that they have a place within Western society. I would argue that they do have a place in our societies and, moreover, that they add to an existing tradition. All parents are entitled to send their children to a school of their choice, so Muslim parents should be no different in this respect. The real question should be one of defining their place in our education system.

But faith schools, as a litmus test of how welcoming Western societies are to communities belonging to faiths other than Christianity, are controversial. Critics of faith schools argue that they're divisive, fuelling segregation along religious and ethnic lines. Faith schools are condemned for allowing religious parents to carve out separate lives for their children, away from the mainstream. These arguments overlook Muslim diversity. Muslim communities in the West are extremely heterogeneous, belonging to different cultures, races and languages, making cultural or racial segregation unlikely.

Moreover, there are several benefits to having Muslim faith schools. They offer Muslim students help with their self-worth – a place to forge new identities that fuse together different traditions, rather than forcing loyalty to one religious or cultural tradition over another. In 2009, the head of Islamia School in London, Abdullah Trevathan, said: 'This school is about creating a British-Muslim culture, instead of, as I've often said in the press, conserving or saving a particular culture.'[61]

Muslim schools have untapped religious potential. Critics want us to believe that faith schools are hotbeds of radicalization and intolerant teaching, but they provide an opportunity to do the exact opposite; to teach children about the inclusivity of Islam. The Islamia School is a good example of this, which introduces its pupils to Islam via jurisprudence, not rules and regulations. By also teaching them classical Arabic, it provides Muslim students with the interpretive tools to create an empowering relationship with faith. Learning of this kind could really help Muslim communities. It would allow our communities to develop a body of Muslim scholars and leaders who are trained at home. And because they are trained at home and come from those specific communities, they would be better positioned to support them than imams imported from abroad. It's no coincidence that the Islamia School's academic performance is particularly strong (in June 2018, they had a 99 per cent GCSE pass rate at grade C or higher); they've created an exceptional learning environment.[62]

But religion is not the only reason why Muslim parents choose faith schools for their children. We have to stop analysing the decisions taken by Muslims through the prism of religion. Low academic attainment is often a much bigger factor. In Britain, for example, boys from poorer Pakistani and Bangladeshi families perform especially badly at school. Research has documented how young Muslims often feel a sense of alienation and disaffection at school for reasons including 'religious discrimination; Islamophobia; the lack of Muslim role models in schools; low expectations on the part of teachers; time spent in [extracurricular] mosque schools; the lack of recognition of the British Muslim identity of the student'.[63] Thus, Muslim parents believe faith schools can address these issues, hoping a different religious and cultural environment will allow their children to overcome structural disadvantage.

And that makes sense. Many faith schools have strong academic reputations. In France, Averroès High School in Lille is one of the highest-ranking schools in the country.[64] In 2016, the Danish think tank Kraka found that independent Muslim schools produced better students than the national average.[65] The environment was credited; the schools fostered a culture of discipline and mutual respect between teachers and students. Even the British Department for Education has acknowledged that, 'Many faith schools are high-performing and are more likely to be rated Good or Outstanding by Ofsted than non-faith schools.' Muslim state schools are three times as likely to be rated as such than their secular equivalents, in fact.[66]

Certainly, some tensions and issues still exist between religion and education. In the private sector, some British Muslim schools have poor academic standards or fail to stick to national curricula. But the solution is to ensure the registration and regulation of these schools, not to shut them down altogether.

The need for all sides to compromise on this issue was laid clear by one specific incident. In January 2019, Muslim parents began to protest outside the gates of Parkfield Community School in Birmingham. The focus of their objection was the school's 'No Outsiders' programme, which provides LGBT-inclusive relationship education. The lessons weren't 'age appropriate', argued the parents, and they needlessly sexualized children as young as five. But the families also appeared to have reservations on religious grounds, as one parent said to the media: 'Children are being told it's OK to be gay, yet 98 per cent of children at this school are Muslim. It's a Muslim community.'[67]

First of all, these 'religious rights' aren't absolute; Muslims can't use them at the expense of other people's humanity. We can't use them to advance prejudiced positions and expect to be respected. And secondly, the Quran reminds us to act fairly and equitably, rather than out of bigotry. 'Oh you who believe, stand out firmly for justice, as witnesses to Allah, even as against yourselves, or your parents, or your kin, and whether it be (against) rich or poor: for Allah can best protect both' [4:135]. At 60:8, it tells us to 'show kindness' and 'deal justly' with the people around us. It doesn't matter whether our opponent is a loved one or a stranger – we are accountable for our actions as much as we are for our inaction.

The Quran also speaks about the consequences of oppression: 'The unjust shall not have any compassionate friend nor any intercessor who should be obeyed' [40:18]. So the idea that we could use Islam to censor education about the existence of other communities is a real contradiction of our values. Protesting parents and their supporters should reflect on the capacity for potential injustice here; real harm, in fact, in preventing young children – especially those who are Muslim – from growing up understanding that sexual and gender diversity is normal. I delve into that harm properly in Chapter Five.

It's true that teaching about sex and relationships can be a sticky subject for some Muslim parents, but a number of distinctions need to be drawn. There's a difference between believing that the Quran disallows certain sex acts and assuming that the Quran condemns an entire group of people. There's also a difference between teaching kids about sex and teaching them about relationships and families. The 'No Outsiders' programme and its variants in other schools teach the latter, focusing on relationships and not sex.

I spoke to the Muslim head teacher of a Muslim-majority primary school in Manchester, who didn't wish to be named. 'It's ridiculous that a mob mentality has totally overshadowed what was actually being delivered [at the schools in Birmingham]. I feel that it's a few aggrieved parents and external fearmongers who have taken their disapproval to another level.' At his school, he explained, some parents also worried that they were going to 'promote four- and five-year-olds to be gay', but the school had already incorporated community concerns by delaying teaching about puberty until Years 5 and 6 instead of Year 4, agreeing the children weren't ready at that stage. So, the head teacher said, 'We told the parents that we won't hide that there are other forms of relationships, and that LGBT people exist and have a right to live their lives.' Parents accepted this.

Clearly then, balances *can* be struck. But it's difficult to do so when Western governments rarely come to the table with clean hands. It's necessary to mention that the 'No Outsiders' programme is part of the British counterterrorism strategy.[68] From 2015, the British government has required schools to teach 'fundamental British values' to students and acceptance of LGBT people plays a part in this. Once again, British values are weaponized against Muslims, though we aren't the first community to have objected to LGBT-inclusive teaching in schools. As a result, 'No Outsiders' is not just a matter of teaching young children about sexual diversity, but pulling Muslim children even further into the ambit of Prevent to save them from (their community's and parents') religious extremism. Time and time again, conversations about integration and values become exercises in defining what Western nations stand for and excluding Muslims from those definitions.

So what exactly are the criteria for integration? The Western demand isn't that Muslims fit in or respect certain social norms; we're expected to accept and replicate the superiority of Western culture, and erase ourselves in the process. This much is obvious from Douglas Murray's book, *The Strange Death of Europe*:

> If the newcomers were becoming 'as British as anybody else' – as government ministers and others insist that they are – then the pubs would remain open and the new arrivals drink lukewarm beer like everyone else who had lived on the street before them. It is the same with churches. If the incomers were indeed to become 'as British as anybody else', then they would fail to turn up to church most Sundays but would be there for weddings, occasionally christenings and most likely just once a year for Christmas.[69]

It's interesting that, by Murray's admission, Britishness hardly seems something worth upholding, consisting of little more than 'lukewarm beer' and church services nobody wants to attend. Echoing John Major's speech, it's an idea of Britishness that even long-standing residents of this country would fail to recognize. It's bizarre to forge an identity around religion and alcohol in a country where the take-up of both is falling, but I don't take this as a sign that Murray is simply out of touch. This is a construction of Britishness that is designed to exclude. After all, it denies belonging not only to Muslims, but also to white (non-Muslim) Brits who don't value the same pleasureless pastimes.

Moreover, Murray isn't simply out of touch because his whole argument is that Western Europe is committing an act of suicide. By the end of this generation, Europe will cease to be Europe and 'the people of Europe will have lost the only place in the world we had to call home'. Murray is using lofty notions about 'Europe's philosophically and historically deep foundations' to demand that Muslims pay a huge price for belonging. We should preserve European culture – by drinking alcohol, eating pork and going to church. We should stop being Muslim, because Muslims can only become European once we abandon Islam completely.

Logic of this kind has been a part of Western thinking for centuries and it is reappearing now in new and bizarre manifestations. In 2016, the Danish city of Randers made it compulsory for all menus in the municipality to serve pork. In 2017, a French court ordered a halal supermarket to shut down because it didn't sell pork or wine. In 2018, the Mayor of Beaucaire, a town in Southern France, scrapped pork-free meals, announcing that they were 'anti-Republic'. The obsession with eliminating halal meat, with forcing Muslims to eat pork, shows how assimilation is essentially the demand that Muslims 'whiten themselves'. We have to disappear, so argues the French political journalist, Edwy Plenel, 'in order to be accepted'.[70]

But Muslims cannot disappear. Against the backdrop of a white society and national identities constructed around white bodies, the Black and Brown body cannot help but stick out. And it's this inability to disappear that perpetuates the stereotype that we don't integrate and which subsequently cultivates violence against us. According to Défenseur des Droits, the independent body responsible for defending individual rights and freedoms in France, a French person of Middle Eastern or African descent is twenty times more likely to be stopped by the police than a white person.[71] Every year in France, between ten and fifteen people die within police custody; invariably they are impoverished young Black or North African men.[72] The case of Adama Traoré is but one example. In 2016, the French police stopped Traoré in Beaumont-sur-Oise, a town north of Paris. He later died in police custody. The police claimed that he died of a heart attack, but the family's autopsy report revealed his death was actually caused by asphyxiation.

Some of this behaviour is motivated by pure racism. But the rejection of Muslims, I understand, is also the result of fear. Periods of fast, profound change cause insecurity. When we fear losing ourselves, when our beliefs and ideals are under scrutiny, we hold on more firmly to our notions of identity, including our national identity. But exclusionary ideas of Western identity are utopian; they've never truly existed, not really. Unless we confront this disconnect and construct new identities, this crisis of confidence (that leads to our tribal and exclusionary tendencies) won't go away. We should create new stories about ourselves; ones that are reflective of what Western nations look like today. We can be proud to be from these countries, but we don't need to police the boundaries of Britishness or Frenchness to achieve that. We don't need to force Muslims to erase themselves in order to keep our traditions alive.

It's fair to say that Muslims who reject the West act out of a similar fear. Muslims have been attacked for our beliefs and practices over a long period of time. And as I described in my introductory chapter, this hostility encourages a culture of defensiveness; it stifles self-reflection and progress. Muslims fear the price of integration on Western terms. We fear loss – of ourselves, our culture, our customs, our way of life – in order to be embraced. It's only normal that we cling to our faith for comfort and identity. But sometimes, we end up clinging to the symbols of faith – things that will set us apart in the West – rather than faith itself. Symbols such as whether or not a person drinks alcohol, eats halal meat and avoids the consumption of pork are the flags of faith that we have become increasingly obsessed with. I'm not victim-blaming, but in the process, some of us end up living lives that feed Islamophobic assertions of Islam being incompatible with the West.

I recall my struggle to break free from these obsessions, how they imposed a good–bad binary upon me when I was younger; how I quickly became a bad Muslim if I resisted five-time daily prayer, but still good if I could manage two or even three. A better description of this is the observant–non-observant Muslim binary, given how swiftly we Muslims invalidate each other, especially when somebody fails to perform their faith in ways tradition- ally set out by Islam. I had felt myself become invisible to family and friends when I criticized eighteen-hour fasts during the long British summers, or when I argued that halal meat and the avoid- ance of alcohol didn't define whether or not we were *true* Muslims. I saw their expressions furrow with disapproval. Suddenly, what I said no longer mattered. I was informed that I was wrong, and then found myself excluded or ignored.

The irony of all this is that Muslims and Islamophobes share an obsession with these symbols of Islamic belief. That's the sad thing, really; how what Toni Morrison describes as the 'white gaze'[73] affects your ability to connect with yourself authentically; treating religion as a form of resistance, stripped down until it is no more than a series of practices, creates distance from true spirituality.

Religious puritans are guilty of incubating this attitude in our communities. They choose to fixate on a person's decisions about who we love (and when and how), what we consume and what we do with our bodies, rather than what is in our hearts. This fixa- tion isn't healthy. Strict observance isn't an indication of correct (or genuine) belief. How do you even identify a true Muslim? It's impossible. And who gave us the right to make this judgement? A person's relationship with God is intensely private. Our religious expression is only for us to determine.

When I was younger, I didn't know where I belonged (or where I was allowed to belong). I felt British and at the same time not at all comfortable with the label. I felt Pakistani and not Pakistani enough. I was Muslim, but constantly rejected it. I always doubted my place in the stories that the West tells about itself, I never saw myself in them, so when I was asked to account for my presence here, I had few answers.

Nobody provided me with that narrative. I sought it out and put it together piece by piece. I read about indigenous European Muslims in Albania, Bulgaria, Bosnia and Herzegovina, Poland and Lithuania. I learned about how, from philosophy to science, Islamic intellectual achievement helped to produce the Enlightenment. I visited the greatest cities of the Islamic world. And I slowly discovered how Muslim labour fuelled Britain's Industrial Revolution and how enslaved Muslims from West Africa literally built the United States and enriched the major European powers.

There are countless examples of the West's debt to the Muslim world. The narratives I uncovered showed me how the world is too connected for separation into East and West, Muslim and non-Muslim, no matter what the ideologues might say; and that the Muslim imprint on the West is too strong for those of us living here to be pushed outside of it. No wonder then that the more I learned about these points of connection and reliance, the more I entered myself into Western myths and stories, and the deeper my roots burrowed into the soil here. At some point, I stopped doubting myself and, when I did, my belonging in the West became stronger; absolute and unconditional. This is the point at which all conversations about integration need to begin; the place where Muslims have absolute belonging. As Imam Al-Hajj Talib Abdur-Rashid, the leader of a Harlem mosque, once said: 'We who have served in the armies of America as Muslim African-Americans since the American Revolution are not at odds with the West... We are the West.'[74]

Muslims are not going anywhere. The globalized nature of our world guarantees this. This means that we need to talk about integration honestly and realistically. Integration is about living in a harmonious society: we all want to be equal and to have access to the same opportunities; we want our cultures and beliefs respected, and to live with a sense of dignity, mobility and empowerment. Integration is not about control, subordination or assimilation. It is about freedom and compromise; it is empowerment, generosity and justice. Integration is no single community's burden and no side can exempt itself. We need to move away from using our values to punish and humiliate; we need to tell new stories about ourselves.

Within all of this, Muslim humanity must be centred. There's no space for essentialist, reductive stereotypes about why Muslims cannot live peacefully with others. But also, there should be no need to cite examples of Muslim 'goodness', because these are just as stilting and dehumanizing. Muslims require non-Muslim solidarity. Solidarity involves listening to our experiences and joining in the work of dismantling discrimination, but it also involves the creation of space. I want for citizenship to allow Muslims the space to fail, to make mistakes as other citizens are allowed to, and not have their behaviour scrutinized and belonging stripped, either through denunciation or worse.

To my fellow Muslims I want to say this. There is no tension between our duties to the Western nations that we're living in and our duties to Islam. Living here doesn't involve a necessary compromise with our Islamic principles. If anything, the comparative stability, justice and peacefulness of the West allows us to live closer to the ideals of our faith than we could manage elsewhere. This doesn't mean that we shouldn't strive for more – by all means we should. We should make full use of our citizenship and demand better – support, protest, contest – by calling for greater social and economic justice. We should feel free to develop our hybrid identities authentically, believing that there is no conflict. We belong.

2

'Islam Is Violent'

It was May 2011. The first time I ever travelled to the United States. Near midnight, I stepped up to the immigration counter at Newark Airport and found myself dispatched to a separate room for additional screening. The room was empty, lined with rows of orange plastic chairs. When the Transportation Security Administration official turned up, he asked me a series of bizarre questions – 'Have you ever travelled to Afghanistan? To Iraq? To Israel? Have you ever done military service?' – and I did my best to take them seriously. After a final, cursory question about Manchester United he let me collect my luggage from the carousel.

Three years later, in August 2014, I travelled to America again. The immigration official at Charlotte Airport, North Carolina took my friends' passports and stamped them without a word, but when I gave him mine, he stared at me and jabbed at his keyboard. 'What is the purpose of your visit? When did you last travel to Pakistan? What do you do for work?' I was halfway through a PhD at the time, so he confusedly followed up with, 'What kind of medicine do you practice?' I clarified that I was a lawyer and he fell silent. Eventually, he handed back my passport and I was permitted to join my friends.

Five years after that, I was 'randomly' selected for an additional security search at Cancun Airport. Though we were travelling back from Mexico via the United States, the additional search came as a surprise. It was my first in eight years. In that time, I had allowed myself to forget: additional security searches are still one of the many prices that Muslims must pay – seventeen years after 9/11 – as we try to live normal lives under the 'War on Terror'.

Ahead of a long line of people waiting to board the flight, I was signposted to a desk a few metres away. Behind it, a Mexican official looked at me impassively as she pointed at me and barked instructions. She asked me to remove my jacket, my belt, my shoes. She swabbed my bare arms, the pockets to my jeans, my ankles. Her hands tunnelled into my shoes to search – for what – explosives, weapons? I grew warm and sweaty under the inspection. I wiped my face and looked back to my travel buddy, who was waiting for me by the door that led to the plane. I smiled apologetically, as if *I* had caused him this inconvenience.

As the official plugged the swabs into a machine, I stared at a piece of paper on the desk, which listed the names of those selected for a search. There were five people on that list. Waiting in line, I had observed the checks for two others – a white man and a white woman – whose bags were opened and rifled through before they were allowed to board. I also had a bag, but the official barely glanced at it. Her only concern was me, and the threat of my Very Muslim Body.

I wonder what the line of white people saw as they boarded the plane before me. What label did they ascribe to me, to their glimpse of a Brown man darkened by the Mexican sun and roughened from two weeks without shaving? Criminal? Terrorist? All I know is that I boarded the plane feeling hot and humiliated and furious, but at the same time anxious about the consequences of being marked as different in such public fashion. Would somebody on the plane have an issue with me sharing this flight? There's a long history of white discomfort (by which I mean prejudice) being centred over minority rights and protections. All the possible scenarios ran through my head. In August 2016, three Muslim siblings due to fly from Stansted Airport to Naples were removed from an easyJet flight after a fellow passenger accused them of having ISIS material on their phones. One of the siblings had been sending text messages to her father about the Labour leader, Jeremy Corbyn. In another example, the Muslim student Khairuldeen Makhzoomi was kicked off a Southwest Airlines flight at Los Angeles airport in February 2018, then searched and interrogated for hours, simply for speaking in Arabic on his mobile phone.[1]

This is a tiny glimpse into the kind of treatment that has been meted out to Muslims since 9/11. Indeed, one of the less talked about legacies of that catastrophic moment in American history is the transformation of every single Muslim person into a potential terrorist. The stereotype that Islam is a violent religion has always lingered in the background of modern Western thought, linked to Christian projections that Islam was spread by the sword, or that Muslims were barbaric and less civilized. But the War on Terror resuscitated that stereotype and gave it a new lease of life. Post-9/11, Muslims weren't just savage and fanatical; we were suspects, threatening and capable of creating danger, needing to be monitored. For the last two decades, governments in the West have relied on this opinion – that Muslims are inherently violent – to justify a multipronged attack on our lives and liberties. This, our governments argued, was necessary to prevent terrorism. But in reality, the War on Terror was an ideological conflict – and not just in terms of the military operations to 'liberate' the people of Iraq and Afghanistan ('Operation Enduring Freedom' was the US government's official name for its post-9/11 counterterrorism response). The War on Terror enabled Western leaders to justify intrusive policies that actively harmed Muslim communities, with little consideration of how they contradicted Western laws and values.

Consider, for instance, how the War on Terror has targeted and stigmatized young Muslims engaged in the same activities as their non-Muslim peers, with little thought for the repercussions. In April 2010, seventeen-year-old Jameel Scott protested an event by

Talya Lador-Fresher, deputy Israeli ambassador to Britain, at the University of Manchester. Sometime after, the police visited his house and arrested him.[2] Lador-Fresher accused Scott of shouting antisemitic slogans, resulting in a charge of racially aggravated public disorder. The charge was dropped only when it emerged that she had fabricated the accusation; a security guard present at the protest contradicted Lador-Fresher's version of events. But the North West Counter Terrorism Unit (CTU) intervened. They contacted Scott's family and his school. They approached him and declared that he was at risk of radicalization. Citing his membership of the Socialist Workers Party and involvement with anti-racism group Hope Not Hate, they felt that he was too politically engaged and began a counselling programme for him, to continue for up to three years. Scott was banned from attending political demonstrations; the CTU pressured his family into ending his political activism altogether. They even tried to have the family relocated.

In another case, sixteen-year-old Rahmaan Mohammadi, a former refugee from Afghanistan, was questioned for wearing a Free Palestine badge to school and for requesting permission to fundraise for children in Gaza who were affected by the latest round of Israeli bombardment. In an interview with the *Sunday Times*, Mohammadi asserted that: 'When police come to your house and say, "I want to speak to you," with this massive folder with your name on it, that's intimidating. It makes you feel alienated.'[3]

The longer the War on Terror persists, the deeper it ingrains the stereotype that Muslims are violent. Muslims are understood to be predisposed to violence; Islam is said to make us more vulnerable to extremist behaviour; we are people to be feared. Thus, in 2011 Pew researched the characteristics most commonly associated with Muslims across Western Europe, Russia and the US: 58 per cent chose 'fanatical' and 50 per cent 'violent'. In 2017, it found that 41 per cent of Americans felt Islam encouraged violence more than other faiths (63 per cent of those who identified as Republican or

Republican-leaning); 35 per cent believed there was a 'great deal' or 'fair amount' of extremism amongst American Muslims.[4]

When I think about the effect of this stereotype on me personally, I return to my memories of those airport experiences, recalling how vulnerable, confused and defensive I felt. When I was first profiled at an airport, the practice of subjecting Muslims to additional security searches was widespread, but I still felt overwhelmed by stigma and shame simply for being Muslim. I was angry at being made to feel that way and all too aware that I didn't have the power to change or resist the characterization that I was intrinsically dangerous.

But what made this even harder to process was my fear that the logic behind this narrative might be correct; that surveilling Muslims was justified, even necessary. I didn't grow up in a household that approved of terrorist violence, but I didn't know what to think about the incidents covered by the news, where terrorists self-identifying as Muslims used Islam to rationalize their actions. I felt let down by members of my community who couldn't neutralize the interpretations that such violence is built on, who preferred to dismiss the terrorists' faith instead. And I was all too aware that in our communities we often communicate Islam using a language that is authoritarian; we speak of a God that is vengeful instead of loving, who punishes instead of forgives. The result is that I found myself pulled in two directions – both by Islamophobic slurs (variations on the theme that Muslims were violent) and the Muslim rhetoric (especially online) that appeared to confirm this narrative. I know that I am not alone in this. We are the children of the War on Terror. We've had our entire lives moulded by this narrative. We've had to advance our relationships with the scripture and our comprehension of the broader geopolitical forces that Muslims find themselves entangled within simply to make sense of the world around us.

*

From the very beginning, Western leaders sought to play down suggestions that the War on Terror was actually a war on Islam. They didn't want their response to 9/11 to be interpreted as the fulfilment of a long-theorized 'clash of civilizations' in case Muslim countries withdrew their support. So what followed was a series of PR exercises in which politicians engaged in linguistic and rhetorical gymnastics to avoid being accused of blaming Islam. For example, when President Bush referred to the American response as a 'crusade' in a speech and press conference on 16 September 2001, this was understood to be a catastrophic error. In a hastily organized event the following day, Bush insisted that Islam was peaceful. He would follow this approach when speaking to Congress, blaming 9/11 on 'a fringe form of Islamic extremism that has been rejected by Muslim scholars and the vast majority of Muslim clerics'.[5]

Most leaders might have been at pains to clarify that Islam wasn't the enemy; that there was a difference between Muslims and terrorists identifying as Muslim, but this distinction is meaningless. Islam *was* being blamed. Conservative and liberal politicians take different positions on the causes of terrorism (conservatives point to the failure of Islam to modernize; liberals blame terrorism on a distortion of Islamic principles), but they do not deny a common belief that Islam is the source of the problem.

And for all intents and purposes, the rhetoric didn't actually matter, since what followed in terms of policy was a two-fronted war against Muslims. Abroad, the West responded to 9/11 by bombing and bullying certain Muslim countries into submission. It invaded Afghanistan, then Iraq as it hounded countries like Pakistan into providing logistical support by declaring, 'You're either with us, or you're against us in the fight against terror.' (In his memoir, Pakistan's then president General Pervez Musharraf recounted being warned that 'if we chose the terrorists, then we should be prepared to be bombed back to the Stone Age'.)[6] At home, the West built an apparatus of counter-terror policies which has the surveillance and profiling of Muslim communities – and a disregard of our human rights – as its beating heart. With the passage of time, these policies have only become more sophisticated, more covert and ever more determined to monitor and control all areas of Muslim life.

Section 44 of the Terrorism Act 2000, for example, bestowed the police with powers to stop and search any person or vehicle without the need for 'reasonable suspicion' of wrongdoing. Although there were certain geographic restrictions, London's Metropolitan Police were able to stop and search freely across the whole of Greater London. The legislation wove discrimination into the fabric of the British legal system. Home Office guidance from 2004 made it clear that ethnicity would be a determining factor when exercising stop and search powers: '[S]ome international terrorist groups are associated with a particular ethnic group, such as Muslims' – not even hiding the fact that 'Muslims' as a general category were the primary target.[7] In 2005, Minister of State Hazel Blears, whose responsibilities involved policing and counterterrorism, said that Muslims should accept as a 'reality' that they would be stopped and searched more than others.[8] Between 2009 and 2010, an Asian person was six times more likely to be stopped and searched than a white person, a Black person more than eight times (Black communities already have a long history of being profiled in the West, on the basis of similarly reductive stereotypes).[9] This is a pattern that has not let up.

To monitor Muslims in the US, the FBI recruited informants from those communities to infiltrate Muslim spaces, e.g. mosques, community centres, even restaurants and shisha bars. The writer and professor Arun Kundnani has written a great deal about Muslims being forced into becoming informants; in Tennessee, for example, the FBI arrested a Palestinian man and threatened him with deportation unless he agreed to assist them.[10] Entire communities were indiscriminately surveilled. And when no terrorist threats were found, threats were manufactured. Shahid Hussain, a Pakistani immigrant, was forced to become an FBI informant. He targeted James Cromitie, an African-American man who occasionally visited the same mosque as him in Albany, New York. They became acquaintances; Hussain plied him with cash, compliments and free meals, and steered him into antisemitic conversations about attacking synagogues. Cromitie tried to lose Hussain, at one point pretending to relocate to North Carolina, but Hussain refused to give up, insistent that Cromitie needed to advance their 'plan'. Cromitie went along with this talk, although he remained inactive. However, when Cromitie lost his job at Walmart, Hussain offered $250,000, a holiday in Puerto Rico, a barbershop business and a car, as long as he agreed to bomb two synagogues in the Bronx. Cromitie appeared to agree (though he claimed in court that he had planned to dupe Hussain and flee with the cash) and was tasked with recruiting another three men. Later, Hussain drove them all to the Bronx to carry out the attacks, where the FBI caught them and accused the men of an attempted terrorist attack motivated by radical Islam. But radical Islam played no part in this scenario. The 'attack' was completely contrived.[11]

Some years into the War on Terror, there was a general change in Western surveillance strategies. Following the murder of Dutch film-maker Theo van Gogh in 2004 and the 7/7 attacks on the London transport system in 2005, European governments, led by the Netherlands, turned their attention away from external terrorist threats to the danger presented by home-grown terrorism. A lucrative industry grew up around it; experts and think tanks convinced governments that Muslim communities needed to be monitored for signs of 'radicalization' to help prevent further attacks. In the counter-terror landscape, radicalization became the new buzzword, a proxy for the idea that all Muslims were potential terrorists, all vulnerable to 'extremist' religious ideology.

In 2006, Britain launched 'Preventing Violent Extremism', a counter-extremism strategy better known as Prevent. From the outset, the vast majority of those targeted were Muslims, rather than, for example, white nationalists. Fearing that intelligence officials weren't doing enough to prevent terrorism, the government wanted to go deeper into the Muslim population, to identify and intercept those who hadn't done anything illegal, but were at risk of crossing the threshold. Early Prevent guidelines spoke of stopping the radicalization process by challenging 'terrorist ideology' and protecting 'vulnerable people'.[12] £20 million was made available annually for local authorities to establish programmes in England and Wales. The greater the Muslim population, the more money a local authority could command.

Channel, one component of the Prevent programme, emulated the Dutch counter-extremist strategy, which used the surveillance of Muslims to create a supposed 'early warning system' against potential extremists. It entered the so-called 'pre-criminal space' – i.e. before crimes were committed – to 'identify individuals vulnerable to radicalization and direct them towards the appropriate support'.[13] Channel was first piloted in 2007 and then rolled out across England and Wales from 2012. The Counter-Terrorism and Security Act came along in 2015 and placed a legal duty on all professionals in the public sector to report any and all suspicious behaviour. Public sector workers like teachers, doctors and nurses were pulled into the orbit of surveillance, responsible for ensuring (on the basis of whatever suspicion) their students or patients weren't being 'drawn into terrorism'.

Upon election in 2008, President Obama chose to emulate this European model. Obama had seen how toxic the War on Terror had become in the American public's eyes, due to the costly and protracted wars in Afghanistan and Iraq, and he wanted to break with that legacy. The attempted car bombing in Times Square in New York City appeared to reinforce the idea that the threat posed by Muslims domestically was greater than that from abroad. Thus, the Obama administration began promoting the 'Countering Violent Extremism' (CVE) programme in 2011, which it described as aiming to 'build resilience to extremism in Muslim communities'.[14] This was based on studies, like one by the New York Police Department (NYPD), which claimed that religious ideology was the key driver for terrorism.[15] The report argued that 'there is remarkable consistency in the behaviors and trajectory of each of the [terror] plots' it had analysed, which provided 'a tool for predictability' to catch would-be terrorists before they carried out an attack. The NYPD set out the four stages that Muslims passed through before carrying out a terror attack: 'pre-radicalization', 'self-identification', 'indoctrination', then 'jihadization'. Surveilling individuals for signs of these would allow officials to intervene before an attack was carried out.

The Black Muslim community has been at the forefront of this surveillance, a fact grounded in the decades-long surveillance of Black Nationalist, Black Muslim and the Civil Rights movements by intelligence agencies.[16] It was, therefore, no coincidence that the city of Minneapolis was chosen as one of three cities to first pilot the CVE programme – the state of Minnesota has the largest Somali population in the country.[17] A series of educational and professional grants and programmes were targeted specifically at the Somali community to prevent them from being recruited by groups such as al-Shabab and ISIS. These Black Muslims, who are already used to their Blackness being criminalized and brutalized, were thus doubly targeted, because of their religion too. In 2005, the *Seattle Times* quoted Imam Talib Abdur-Rashid telling the story of a young African-American Muslim who shared his experience of living in the US after 9/11. 'It's like being black,' he said. 'Twice.'[18]

Consequently, Muslims have found themselves effectively criminalized by programmes that claim to counter violent extremism. In Britain, 67 per cent of those referred to Prevent between April 2007 and December 2011 were Muslim. But if those who didn't specify their religion were to be removed, Muslims would constitute 90 per cent of the total.[19] Under the Counter-Terrorism and Security Act, figures soared even higher. Between April 2007 and May 2015, 6306 people were referred to Prevent. But in the twelve months between July 2015 and June 2016, 4611 people were referred – an increase of 75 per cent.

This is because surveillance programmes create links between Muslims and violence even where they don't exist. In some cases, identifying with certain political opinions or humanitarian causes has been interpreted as a sign of radicalization, but in others, the links are even more tenuous. This is clear when looking at the referrals that have come from schools, of which there are many. Between 2015 and 2016, 2311 children were referred to Channel, including 351 children less than nine years of age.[20] In one case, a four-year-old boy was almost referred to Prevent by staff at his nursery school for drawing pictures of his father chopping a vegetable with a knife. The child's slurred speech had led staff to assume that he was describing a 'cooker bomb' instead of 'cucumber'. His mother recalled being told, 'Your children might not be taken off you... you can prove yourself innocent.'[21] The academic environment should be a safe and stigma-free haven for learning, but as Rahmaan Mohammadi described, the duty of teachers to report signs of radicalization has contributed to a climate of fear: 'Prevent creates paranoia. In school... if a senior member of staff was walking past, we would whisper to each other saying, "What if they're listening to our conversation?" That's how paranoid it makes you.'[22]

But ultimately, Prevent is a surveillance strategy not a safeguarding strategy, which is why secret policy documents have revealed that public sector workers who contacted Prevent staff just for advice unwittingly triggered referrals to the programme.[23] It is also why counter-terror police store every single Prevent referral on a database; it doesn't matter whether you did something wrong or not, you will be monitored regardless.[24]

In 2018, fourteen of twenty-six CVE programmes under President Trump had targeted schools and students – some as young as five – encouraging them to report suspicious behaviour amongst their family and other students. Imagine how intimidating an environment this creates, how this would erode trust amongst Muslim children and families in the institutions around you. In some respects it brings to mind methodologies employed by authoritarian governments and their agencies, like the Stasi in East Germany or those which Japanese-Americans were subjected to under McCarthyism. As Western governments scour for leads on what may radicalize individuals in Muslim communities, the sad irony is that they refuse to acknowledge the possibility that their policies, particularly those responsible for othering Muslim minors, could be one of them.

Today, I'd wager that there isn't a single Muslim space that Western governments haven't tried to control, infiltrate or tamper with. In August 2019, it emerged that 'This Is Woke', a social media site aimed at young Muslims to engage 'in critical discussions around Muslim identity, tradition and reform' was created by Breakthrough Media as part of the British counter-terror strategy. SuperSisters, a similar site aimed at Muslim women, was also created by Breakthrough Media for the Home Office. According to a whistle-blower, at some points, there was only a single Muslim woman working at SuperSisters (who resigned when connections to the state counter-terror apparatus became apparent); the rest were middle-aged white men pretending to be Muslim women.[25] Some might argue that if Muslim communities have nothing to hide, they have nothing to fear. But revelations like these scupper even the most fragile Muslim confidence in public institutions and push our communities even further out towards the margins of society.

I know this first-hand. When I chaired a Muslim organization, a member of the Metropolitan Police turned up to one of our social events in 2012. After the event, the policewoman stayed behind and grilled my colleagues about the kinds of people that attended our meetings and spaces. She asked if she could come again. We feared that our activity was being monitored for signs of violent activity, that this was an attempt to spy on our members, so we chose to keep our distance, regardless of the consequences.

Two years later, when we applied for and were awarded charity status, this success came with an instruction from our members that we weren't to accept government funding associated with Prevent. At the time, the anger in our community had surprised me, but as my understanding has grown of the disproportionate focus of counter-terror work on Muslim communities and its effect upon them (under the hackneyed theory that 'all Muslims might not be terrorists, but all terrorists are Muslim'), I'm not surprised.

All this reminds me of how Muslim charities have also come under increasing scrutiny. In July 2014, HSBC closed down the bank accounts of several Muslim charities without notice. Finsbury Park Mosque, for example, received a letter stating, 'HSBC Bank has recently conducted a general review and has concluded that the provision of banking services to Finsbury Park Mosque now falls outside of our risk appetite.'[26] Islamic Relief, which is Britain's largest Muslim charity and is ranked amongst the world's top humanitarian organizations, also found its account shut down. There was no right of appeal.

HSBC refused to discuss what motivated these decisions, but the link to the War on Terror and its need to root out 'extremism' in Muslim communities is obvious. Muslim charities only began to feel the heat of this scrutiny when William Shawcross became the chair of the Charity Commission in 2012. It led Baroness Sayeeda Warsi to complain that there was a 'disproportionate focus' on Muslim charities, for which Shawcross was ultimately responsible.[27] Warsi's accusation isn't without foundation; before joining the Charity Commission, Shawcross was connected to the neoconservative think tank, the Henry Jackson Society – a key player in the Islamophobia industry. In April 2014, Shawcross gave an interview to the *Sunday Times* in which he declared that donor money was being used to fund terrorism.[28] These comments appeared to justify his crackdown on Muslim charities.

But there is absolutely no evidence that Shawcross was right. Between December 2012 and May 2014, 40 per cent of all enquiries made by the Charity Commission were into British Muslim charities.[29] But by 2016 only one charity was found to have links with extremists. Clearly, the threat was exaggerated. Muslim charities were suspected of extremist links simply because they were Muslim. The case of Finsbury Park Mosque illustrates this. Prior to the closure of its bank account, the mosque was the subject of a profile by Thomson Reuters, which accused it of having links to terrorism. The mosque refuted these allegations and took the news agency to court for libel, which it won. Thomson Reuters was forced to admit that it 'made the false allegation that there were grounds to suspect that the claimant had continued connections to terrorism'.[30] Like this, counter-terror policy has morphed into something more noxious than initially perceived; using the assumption of violence to control Muslims, and sort us into categories of either moderates or extremists. Neither government nor its institutions should be able to do that.

I would never attempt to deny that violence was a feature of Islamic history. I just don't believe it is a particularly unique feature of that history, as Islamophobes enjoy proclaiming. When I was fifteen years old, somebody on an online music forum that I used informed me that Islam had been 'spread by the sword' in order to dismiss my complaint about the post-9/11 profiling of Muslims. I continue to see this argument bandied about everywhere. In February 2018, for instance, Gerard Batten, then leader of the UK Independence Party (UKIP), asserted: 'It is factually and historically true. [Islam] was propagated by invasion, by violence and intimidation… [Muslims] believe in propagating their religion by killing other people.'[31]

But this is not factually true. Violence is not the reason for Islam's success, not in the Arabian Peninsula and not when it was taken up around the world. To begin with, Prophet

Muhammad only preached peacefully, though hostility in Mecca forced him to seek refuge in the city of Medina. Then after his death, Muslims only emerged from the Arabian Peninsula out of economic necessity, not a divine mission to convert people. All pre-industrial societies have relied on territorial expansion to obtain the resources needed to survive. Muslims were no different. Given the harshness of their landscape, Arab society couldn't rely on agriculture to sustain them, so expansion was vital to their survival.

Early Muslim leaders actively discouraged conversions to Islam. They saw Islam as an Arab religion, rather than a universal one. Conversions to Islam also meant that Muslim leaders would receive less money in the form of tax from their non-Muslim populace. Critics of Islam like to assert that taxing non-Muslims was a form of coercion for religious minorities to convert to Islam. It's true that the jizya tax is an outdated concept, but it's also true that the taxation wasn't a form of violence; it encompassed exemptions for the poor and elderly, and it was a far more progressive strategy than the oppression suffered by minorities under Christian rule. Looking at the agreement between the second Caliph, Umar, and Sophronius, the patriarch of Jerusalem, it's obvious that jizya was intended to be a system of protection that Muslims provided in return for payment:

> [Umar, the Commander of the Faithful] has given [the people of Jerusalem] an assurance of safety for themselves, for their property, their churches, their crosses, the sick and healthy of the city and for all the rituals which belong to their religion. Their churches will not be inhabited by the Muslims and will not be destroyed.[32]

Thus, non-Muslim populations living under Muslim rule were protected in a variety of important ways. Muslims weren't allowed to confiscate land, nor were they free to settle as they wished within conquered territory. They had to live in specially constructed garrison towns on the outskirts of the Muslim empire.

With regards to the actual pace of conversion that followed, there are a couple of important points of clarification. Firstly, Islamophobes intentionally conflate the growth of Muslim believers and the growth of Muslim territory; the two are not synonymous. Islam grew at a *much slower* pace than the empire. In *A History of the Modern Middle East*, William Cleveland and Martin Bunton explain this: '[F]or at least two centuries the majority of the inhabitants of the Islamic empire were non-Muslims.'[33] Muslims were such a minority (10 per cent of the population in Egypt, 20 per cent in Iraq) that mass forced conversions wouldn't have been possible. Indeed, it took many centuries for Islam to become the majority religion of the first Muslim Empire. For example, Muslims controlled all of Iran by 705, but in the middle of the ninth century, still only half of the population was Muslim. It would take another hundred years before the Muslim population stood at 75 per cent of the total.

Secondly, it's true that Islam spread fast, at least in comparison to Christianity, but this had nothing to do with violence. When I spoke to the author and scholar Reza Aslan about this, he clarified why:

> The ease with which indigenous tribes [and] cultures were able to simply absorb Islam into their already held belief systems – 'just do these practices, believe this sentence and you are a Muslim' – that had a huge role to play in how fast it spread. Christianity took a very long time to spread because its doctrine is unfathomably complex, whereas Islam's isn't.

So the fact that early Muslims could convert to Islam without any dramatic alterations to their existing practice made it incredibly attractive.

There are many racist assumptions that lie beneath the argument that Islam was spread by force, including one which uses violence to strip historical converts to Islam of their intelligence and agency. It's as if people can only be attracted to Islam through force or deception – which is exactly how medieval Europeans reacted to Islam when they first encountered it. And yet the message of Islam, the charisma and behaviour of Muslim leaders and the economic opportunities of adopting Islam are documented reasons that motivated the first Arab conversions.

Moreover, in West Africa, Islam didn't spread through conquest, but through trade. The trans-Saharan trade route between North African merchants (and scholars) and West African civilizations facilitated the introduction and spread of Islam. The great scholarly city of Timbuktu was first established as a trading post.[34] In South East Asia too, commerce encouraged the take-up of Islam, not the 'sword', and it was an esoteric, Sufi form of Islam that spread, which was attractive in its own right. So why is the stereotype of Islam being spread by force so popular? Reza Aslan told me that it was Christian projection:

> Christianity was an unsuccessful cult religion that was primarily the religion of the elite in the fourth century until it was adopted by Constantine for political reasons. All he did was decriminalize being a Christian; his successors made it the official religion of the Roman Empire. Once it became the religion of Rome, then that's it; you were either a Christian or were forced to become a Christian. That projection [is] common – we always see our worst faults in other people – you can understand where it comes from.

This is as revealing as it is damning.

As our appetite for Islamophobia grows, more recent examples of Muslim history are being dug up and reinterpreted as evidence of violence being endemic to Muslim cultures and communities. For example, the writer Pankaj Mishra explains that the Iranian

Revolution of 1978 is held up as an example of 'Muslim rage'.[35] But Iran didn't attack anybody; it simply ended Western imperialism and control of its oil resources by overthrowing the Shah. And it's inaccurate even to describe it as the 'Islamic' revolution, as is often the case in the West. When Iranians took to the streets in 1978, people of all backgrounds came together – secularists, nationalists, feminists and madrasah students – calling for equality of the sexes, democracy, political transparency and free speech. Iranians sensed that this was an opportunity for true political change. In a political calculation, they allowed Ayatollah Khomeini to lead the movement, believing that only a cleric could command support amongst the religious masses. He gave it a particularly Shia revolutionary zeal, with comparisons to Hussein's martyrdom. It was the invasion of Iraq and the hostage crisis in 1979 which emboldened Khomeini to abandon the ideals of the revolution and impose his ultra-conservative vision of Islam upon the nation.

The contemporary US–Iran relationship can also be viewed as an attempt to portray Iran as violent and volatile simply because it resists US domination. This has been most apparent during the Trump presidency. In 2018, Trump withdrew from the nuclear deal brokered by then president Obama in 2015, an agreement in which Iran had agreed to roll back parts of its nuclear programme in exchange for relief from some economic sanctions. Trump's rationale was that the deal was defective. As a result, the sanctions were reimposed and Iran went back to its enrichment of uranium. Then, after a series of skirmishes, on 3 January 2020, the US assassinated Iranian military commander General Qasem Soleimani.

The White House attempted to pin the blame on Iranian violence; it argued that Soleimani had planned an 'imminent' attack on US embassies – but no evidence has been put forward to prove this was true. Later, Trump justified the action on the grounds of Soleimani killing 'thousands of Americans over an extended period of time'. But far from exhibiting Iran's violent tendencies, Western violence towards Iran exposes much more about the

West than Iran, such as the American establishment's ceaseless appetite for war, especially one that might finally force Iran into submission.[36]

The other forgotten truth is that threats and interventions of this kind continue to undermine diplomacy and reform in the region. The nuclear deal took Iran and the US closer to peace than they have ever been in recent times; it was a deal that Iranian policymakers had taken much convincing to agree to. Trump's actions not only scuppered the hope of peaceful relations between the two countries, but also destroyed the fragile trust that had been building within Iran towards America.[37] It's worth noting that in the months before Soleimani's assassination, ordinary Iranians were out on the streets protesting against their government. After Soleimani's assassination, they returned to the streets for his funeral. They weren't expressing support for their government or even Soleimani, but for their country. In killing the second most powerful official in the country, the US had violated Iranian sovereignty – just as it has always done – and this hurt the dignity of the Iranian people.

The Israel–Palestine conflict is also too often presented – especially in America where Israel commands vociferous support – as a clash between the peace-loving, battle-averse Israelis and the fanatical, crazy Palestinians (who wish to eradicate Israel). But this conflict is also a colonial one. Palestine had been under Muslim control for over thirteen centuries until it came under British rule in 1917. Israel was created out of Palestinian land and it holds dominion over the land intended for a future Palestinian state.

The conflict admittedly has symbolic significance in the Muslim imagination. It represents the humiliation of Muslims (and indifference to Muslim suffering) at the hands of the West, which caused and perpetuated the conflict, and now refuses to act meaningfully to end it. After all, not only had Britain failed to manage the land that it carved for itself from the ashes of the Ottoman Empire, but European leaders supported the creation of a Jewish homeland in part to assuage their guilt over the Holocaust. The rights of Palestinians were always overlooked. This is why, days after the 1947 UN resolution to partition the land into two states, the scholars of Al-Azhar University declared a 'jihad' to defend the Arabs of Palestine. Eight thousand foreign Muslim fighters flooded into the territory. In 1948, five Arab armies joined in. Israel gained an emphatic victory, but more than half of the Palestinian population was displaced.

The Israeli occupation has worsened over the decades, but it's misleading to characterize it as the continuation of an age-old conflict between Muslims and Jews. This view has spread so widely it's become mainstream: responding to calls to boycott the Eurovision Song Contest hosted by Israel in 2019, Madonna said: 'My heart breaks every time I hear about the innocent lives that are lost in this region and the violence that is so often perpetuated to suit the political goals of people who benefit from this *ancient conflict*.'[38]

I object to that characterization. Jewish–Muslim relations have traditionally flourished; Jewish academics identify Islam's 'Golden Age' as corresponding with one for Jewish culture. This relationship undoubtedly declined, but in the fifteenth century, when Muslims and Jews were expelled from Iberia, many Jews went on to find refuge in the Muslim world.

Moreover, it's true that Islamophobes (and some antisemitic Muslims) look to the Quran for proof of Islam's historic enmity with Judaism. But the Quran doesn't condemn the Jewish *people*. It speaks, through revelation, to the Jewish tribes living amongst the Prophet. Judaism itself isn't the issue, but their abandonment of Jewish belief and practice. In verse 5:13, for example, the Quran criticizes these tribes for breaking their covenant with God, for being Jews in name only. Certain representations of Jewish–Muslim relations during Prophet Muhammad's lifetime also mask how the conflicts at the time were political and tribal in nature, not religious. Most Jewish tribes lived happily alongside Muslims and did so for many centuries. Therefore, it's an act of bad faith to instrumentalize Jewish–Muslim relations, either to show a Muslim tendency towards violence or Allah's condemnation of the Jewish people. Both are untrue. It's equally untrue to assume that these Quranic verses offer Muslims any instruction on how to interact with their Jewish siblings.

In the UK the grievances that lie beneath the Rushdie Affair are relegated in favour of citing it as yet another example of the Muslim thirst for violence. In 1988, the British-Indian author Salman Rushdie published *The Satanic Verses*. Part of the novel satirizes the life of Prophet Muhammad. Using the name Mahound – a direct reference to the name used during the Middle Ages to belittle him – the Prophet is depicted as sex-obsessed. He treats religion as a business and fabricates revelations according to his whims. In one incendiary scene, twelve women working in a brothel take on the names of the Prophet's wives to increase their earnings. Regardless of whether or not the novel was intended as a critique of Islam, it comes across as one, reproducing vulgar stereotypes that have existed in relation to Islam for centuries.

In the West, we dismiss the pain of having one's religious identity ridiculed and scorned, but when done by the powerful against the powerless, it's incredibly demeaning. At the time, Muslims were marginalized in British society and had little means of redress. Throughout the 1980s, British Pakistanis and Bangladeshis had the highest rates of unemployment, the lowest number of educational qualifications and were mostly found doing manual or low-skilled work at a time when Thatcherite policies were encouraging the collapse of Britain's manufacturing industries.[39] Up until 2003, Muslims weren't even protected from discrimination as a group under British law. So when Rushdie's novel came along, it provided fertile ground to voice frustrations that stemmed from their lowly position in British society.

British Muslim leaders began by complaining to the government and to Rushdie's publishers. They didn't want the book to be banned, but for a statement to be inserted in copies clarifying that it was a work of fiction. The publisher didn't respond, nor did the British government. Rushdie also dismissed the complaint, described by political theorist Bhikhu Parekh as treating the criticisms as the fantasies of 'illiterate fanatics who had neither read nor understood the book';[40] British Muslims moved on to a series of peaceful protests. These were also hopeless. But then on 2 December 1988, a small group gathered in Bolton. They burned a copy of the book. It gathered no interest. They tried again in Bradford on 14 January 1989 and tipped off the media beforehand. Armed with that image – the burning book – press coverage came to life, nationally and then internationally. This accelerated again one month later when Ayatollah Khomeini issued a fatwa against Rushdie ordering him to be killed. The fatwa was outrageous, indefensible and a major escalation of events; it suggested to British society that Muslims couldn't be trusted; we were loyal to a foreign Muslim leader and had the potential to carry out his violent proclamations.

Once the book-burning captured the media's attention, commentators began to criticize and deride the protesting Muslims. Writing for the *Independent* on 16 February 1989, the novelist Anthony Burgess said that Muslims had brought 'shame' on Britain 'through the vindictive agency of bonfires'.[41] When Muslim spokesmen were invited by newspapers to state their case, editors focused not on the source of their grievances, but on the danger to Rushdie's life (though our leaders bear some responsibility for this too). In 1990 Bhikhu Parekh wrote:

> The national press exacerbated the situation. It sent out correspondents to Muslim areas, especially to Bradford, where they interviewed leaders and even young and confused Muslim boys and girls with leading questions, and created the overwhelming impression that the entire Muslim community was seething with a bloodthirsty spirit of vengeance.[42]

When we resort to these caricatures of violent, barbaric Muslims, we fail to understand the Rushdie controversy in all its complexity. There's no doubt that the fatwa should have been condemned. It fanned the flames of a delicate situation, leading to several attacks and violent riots, in which fifty-nine people died, and led to the murder of the novel's Japanese translator. But we mustn't lose sight of the fact that Ayatollah Khomeini had several non-religious reasons for issuing it. The controversy bubbling in Britain provided him with an easy opportunity to consolidate his power over Iran and stake his own claim to global Muslim leadership in the face of Saudi Arabian silence. And whilst the media's objections to the book-burnings themselves were understandable, given the fascist connotations (a history, it's worth mentioning, Muslim communities do not necessarily share), it bears repeating that Muslim leaders did at least try to stem the community's anger by seeking diplomatic solutions first.

The academic Tariq Modood made it clear that the anger of British Muslims had less to do with religion and more to do with the shape of their rights in British society:

'[T]he Rushdie affair' is not about the life of Salman Rushdie nor freedom of expression, let alone Islamic fundamentalism or book-burning or Iranian interference in British affairs. The issue is of the rights of non-European religious and cultural minorities in the context of a secular hegemony. Is the Enlightenment big enough to legitimize the existence of pre-Enlightenment religious enthusiasm or can it only exist by suffocating all who fail to be overawed by its intellectual brilliance and vision of Man?[43]

Amongst the chaos of the Rushdie Affair, the threats made against Rushdie and the lives lost, we mustn't forget this. Indeed, in traditional discussions of the Rushdie Affair, the motivations of Muslims and the subsequent impact upon them are repeatedly ignored. In truth, the Affair represents a ground zero in Muslim/non-Muslim relations in the West. It set back those relationships by years. And it opened up the gates to a pile-on that has not stopped since. The impact on young Muslims was particularly pronounced. Many were forced to choose between their national and religious identities. In the 2019 BBC documentary, *The Satanic Verses: 30 Years On*, Imam Alyas Karmani recounted being blamed by his non-Muslim friends for the fatwa:

> I thought these friends understood and accepted me but now they were pointing fingers. The conversations went like this: 'What's wrong with you people? Why are you doing this? Why have you put a death threat on Salman Rushdie? What side are you on? Are you with us or against us?'

Growing up indifferent to Islam, these questions pushed Karmani towards it. He ended up embracing a puritanical version of Islam and even fighting in Bosnia. 'That's why I always say I am one of Rushdie's children. I was radicalized by white liberals.'[44]

I wonder how much of the anger directed at British Muslims by media commentators and their white peers was motivated by frustrations over Muslim impassivity. Were Muslims accepted only for as long as we acted as passive subjects without asserting our rights and grievances as citizens? Because when Muslim grievances are portrayed as irrational and fanatical, this inadvertently reveals contradictions in our societies about rights and entitlements. Who is entitled to be angry? Not us. Over the last few years, Western societies have tried to explain the societal anger that has produced Brexit, Trump and the rise of populism and the far right. But there is no impetus to understand Muslim anger, undoubtedly because Muslims are not allowed to be angry, let alone express that anger in the public arena.

*

Even in the War on Terror, the West exaggerates the role that Islam plays in motivating terrorist violence. We see this in the studies that have given shape to the theory of radicalization. Not only is the role of religion overstated, but experts are willing to distort their research results to fit Western policies that have pre-determined the threat posed by Muslims. For example, in 2009, Daveed Gartenstein-Ross and Laura Grossman examined 117 American 'jihadist terrorists'. They concluded that the terrorists' theological understandings 'were a relatively strong factor in their radicalization'.[45] But as Arun Kundnani has pointed out, the most commonly cited reason for the perpetrators' descent into violence wasn't religion, but 'the expression of radical political views'. Rather than admitting this openly, the authors stated that it would be 'crude' to deduce that politics was a more important factor for these terrorists than religion.[46]

Similarly, these studies fail to explain how an individual shifts from holding a particular view that is sympathetic to violence to carrying out that violence for themselves. Whilst blaming terrorism on religion, even the NYPD study mentioned earlier had to admit that not every person who subscribes to a radical Islamic ideology resorts to violence. This means that it must be something *other* than Islam that is responsible for the violence when eventually committed. In its own study of British terrorists, MI5 found that most of them were actually 'religious novices'.[47] This is why the French political scientist Olivier Roy has reasoned that 'the process of violent radicalization has little to do with religious practice, whilst radical theology, such as Salafism, does not necessarily lead to violence'.[48]

But ultimately, all counter-terror strategies are flawed. Racial profiling is an extremely ineffective way of protecting societies against violence. Focusing energy on people of supposedly Muslim appearance has allowed those who don't match specific racial stereotypes to slip through the net, such as Bryant Neal Vinas, a Hispanic-American recruit for Al-Qaeda, or Colleen LaRose, a blonde-haired, green-eyed white woman from Philadelphia. By 2008, MI5 had concluded that it was impossible to create a profile of the typical 'British terrorist'. Those who become terrorists 'are a diverse collection of individuals, fitting no single demographic profile, nor do they all follow a typical pathway to violent extremism', rendering radicalization theories obsolete.[49] It's no surprise that the American Civil Liberties Union summarized the achievements of the first decade in the War on Terror as: '[T]ens of thousands of Muslims questioned, thousands were deported for civil immigration infractions, and hundreds were subjected to secret and arbitrary detention and abusive interrogations' – all without a single public arrest or prosecution for a terrorism-related offence.[50] But these models continue to form the bedrock of Western counter-terror policy.

So if not religion, who or what is to blame? As the historian Mark Sedgwick has remarked, the Western concept of radicalization still 'emphasizes the individual, and to some extent, the ideology and the group, and significantly de-emphasizes the wider circumstances'.[51] Thus, racism, Islamophobia and imperialist politics are eschewed in favour of classifying Muslim men as the problem. But Dr Suha Taji-Farouki's research into Hizb-ut-Tahrir, a non-violent group that advocates for the establishment of an Islamic State, found that racism played a significant role in the group's popularity with young British Muslim men.[52] Most had grown up in the 1990s in a climate of racism, palpable in all areas of their lives and in all sectors of British society – housing, education, employment and security. This climate of racism and disadvantage has only intensified since the War on Terror began.

Politics is another important factor. The Yemeni-American Imam Anwar al-Awlaki described America as a 'nation of evil' not because he was opposed to Americans, but because Abu Ghraib and Bagram (where prisoners were tortured and abused by British and American armed forces) and Guantanamo Bay were the latest examples of Western abuse and disregard for Muslim life.[53] It always fascinated me in my early twenties, as the magnitude of the War on Terror became sharper in my eyes, how little we in the West understood (or wanted to understand) Osama bin Laden's motivations. Most of us swallowed the rhetoric that Muslim terrorists hated the West for its lifestyle and freedom. But when I was twenty-one, I stumbled upon a book of bin Laden's speeches on a sale shelf in Waterstones. I realized that the answers had been there all along.

In his 1996 Declaration of War, for example, bin Laden accused America and Israel of 'aggression, iniquity and injustice' against Muslims. He criticized the American military presence in the Arabian Peninsula, its interference in Saudi political affairs, its sanctions against Iraq, which led to many deaths (including of approximately 600,000 malnourished children), and its enrichment of corrupt regimes in Muslim countries.[54]

In the West, we wring our hands over the question of what causes a minority of Muslims to adopt radical ideologies (and sometimes violence). But the answers are often right in front of us. Appalling as they often are, Osama bin Laden's speeches contain truths that we'd rather not know, about how our violent and imperialist foreign policies dominate, destabilize and perpetuate the suffering of other nations. Why do we ignore this answer? Because ideologically, we can't allow the enemy to point a finger at us and be justified in doing so. As such, the West embraces the argument that terrorists hate what we *are* and we cannot change this, rather than admitting that they hate what we *do* and that we *can* change these practices, but don't want to.

Despite all this, and despite the condemnation of counter-terror policies by Muslim leaders, human rights organizations and even the United Nations, which warned that counter-extremism strategies isolate Muslim communities and violate their rights, Western governments haven't listened.[55] The official charge is that we are playing the victim. In his 2011 review of Prevent, Lord Carlile of Berriew argued that the 'dissipation of [a] sense of victimhood' is a 'proper and important part' of counterterrorism policy. He pointed to an event in East London organized to discuss the rise of Islamophobia in the UK and Europe as proof that Muslims were 'feeding assertions of victimhood'.[56] But this is ironic considering the government has refused to engage valid criticisms. Instead, its Commission for Countering Extremism has also 'played the victim', complaining that organizations engaged in Prevent work suffer from 'abuse, harassment and intimidation'.[57]

Nonetheless, Muslims don't have a victim complex; we are unfairly targeted. In January 2015, the French launched a campaign entitled, 'Stop Djihadisme'. As the name shows, the campaign not only targeted Muslims specifically, but also reinforced the idea that terrorism is rooted in religious violence, namely jihad. Moreover, the threat of violence from Muslim communities is treated far differently to others. In Germany, the programme to tackle far-right radicalization, 'EXIT-Deutschland', relies on self-referral, whereas the Muslim equivalent, 'Hayat' (Arabic for 'life'), requires Muslim communities to inform on each other. Why *is* far-right terrorism treated differently to terrorism committed by Muslims?

Finally, though it has become a cliché, with Islamophobes peddling it as proof of a cosmic justification of indiscriminate violence and certain Muslims invoking it as a divine commandment to enter into war, I want to address the concept of jihad. One preliminary thing to note is that Islam does not have a concept of 'holy war', as Christianity does and was able to invoke for the Crusades. Jihad does not mean 'holy war'.

Instead, jihad means 'to struggle'; the greater struggle is the one to achieve internal piety, and the lesser struggle refers to the (occasionally physical) fight for social justice. Jihad is, therefore, Islam's attempt to regulate conflict and minimize bloodshed through a series of ethical principles; a 'just war' theory.

In Islam, only defensive wars are permitted: 'Fight in the way of God those who fight you,' the Quran says, 'but do not begin hostilities; God does not like the aggressor' [2:190]. Thus, if a community is being persecuted, conflict is permitted, but to end the mistreatment only. In war, Islam prohibits the killing of women, children, the elderly or religious figures; it prohibits torture, the mutilation of the dead, sexual violence or the destruction of property.

Those seeking to reinforce Islam's violence will, nonetheless, quote a number of Quranic verses. When Islamophobes argue that extremists are acting in accordance with our scripture, they commonly cite, 'Slay polytheists wherever you confront them' [9:5] and 'Carry the struggle to the hypocrites who deny the faith' [9:73]. But these verses are aimed at specific characters and we can't read the Quran without referring to its context. By 'polytheists', God is referring to the Meccan tribes (namely the Quraysh), who forced Muslims out of the city and then hounded them in Medina. In some sections, the Quran actually condemns the Quraysh by name. The 'hypocrites' are those who claimed to believe in Islam and/or support the Muslims, but made clandestine agreements with the Prophet's enemies. In the same vein, verse 3:149 that begins, 'Kill the associators wherever you find them, and take them, and confine them...' is a reference to the tendency of the Prophet's enemies to renege on agreements. They feigned surrender on the battlefield, then started killing Muslims after the fighting had supposedly ended.

The application of these verses has been debated throughout Islamic history. In the thirteenth century, the scholar Ibn Taymiyyah argued that killing non-Muslims would violate the freedom of religion guaranteed in the Quran. At 10:99, for example, the Quran reminds us that God could have created the world's population under a single belief system, but chose not to: 'Can you compel people to believe against their will?' During European colonization, the Indian scholar Sayyid Ahmed Khan argued that imperialism couldn't fulfil the conditions for jihad because the British hadn't curtailed the religious freedom of Indian Muslims enough to constitute persecution. So when jihadists argue that they are fighting defensively against Western aggression and persecution, how can they be taken seriously? The scholar Chiragh Ali agreed with Sayyid Ahmed Khan and went on to say that the experiences of Prophet Muhammad had limited relevance for our current contexts.[58] The Prophet's community had lived under a perpetual state of war, which cannot be said for today.

Many pseudo-religious leaders and political groups have manipulated the Quranic verses to justify violence. It's not necessary to platform those ideologies here. I'd rather point to 'Open Letter to Al-Baghdadi', a letter signed by 126 Muslim scholars in 2014 (and many more afterwards), condemning the actions of ISIS.[59] Using classical Islamic theology, the letter is a brilliant point-by-point refutation of their violent tactics. And it doesn't just focus on warfare, but addresses the different types of violence that ISIS incorporated into its modus operandi: slavery, forced conversions, criminal punishment and the practice of declaring Muslims outside of the faith (takfir). The letter is available online; you should consider reading it.

So the theory of Muslim violence is ultimately a Western construct, albeit one manipulated by the likes of ISIS to justify their violent tactics. But what I cannot deny is that there remains an elephant in the room, especially for those of us who are Muslim. Saudi Arabia and its favoured sect Wahhabism share a symbiotic relationship with terrorism. I was surprised to have Reza Aslan spell it out for me so plainly, without an ounce of hesitation: 'Wahhabism is the theological source, the philosophical source, the financial source; it is the ground zero of what we refer to as modern Islamic terrorism' (though I must emphasize, obviously not all Wahhabis are terrorists).

Saudi Arabia was formed through a pact between the eighteenth-century puritan preacher, Abd al-Wahhab, and the founder of the country. Abd al-Wahhab opposed the cultural and ritualistic diversity that he witnessed in Basra, Iraq. He saw the practices of these Muslims to be nothing more than an assortment of superstitions that had little connection to Islam. When he returned to the Arabian Peninsula, he began a violent crusade to purge the faith of these supposed innovations and promote his own brand of puritanism. In one town he had a woman stoned to death for adultery and the horrified locals forced him to leave. He ended up in a neighbouring town where Muhammad Ibn Saud offered protection. But Abd al-Wahhab wanted more; he wanted Ibn Saud to wage war and purge the Peninsula of the Islam he disapproved of. In return, Abd al-Wahhab would provide his dynasty with an air of religious approval. Ibn Saud agreed and, in 1744, the two made a pact of loyalty to one another and set about establishing the first Saudi state. When the modern Kingdom of Saudi Arabia was established in 1932, the descendants of Ibn Saud and al-Wahhab continued to honour their pact. Wahhabism became the national ideology.

Wahhabism is highly simplistic. Anything that appears to interfere with direct devotion to God is bi'dah, an innovation (and innovations are *bad*, a deviation from the true path). Abd al-Wahhab's message isn't radical, but he himself was unique for his willingness to kill those who disagreed with him. But as the British writer and scholar Ziauddin Sardar points out, the violence of Wahhabi ideology is far greater than the sanction of death and destruction.[60] Wahhabis oppose critical thinking in favour of reverence for the Prophet and his companions. They favour literalist interpretations of the Quran and believe that history ends upon Prophet Muhammad's death. Nothing of significance happens after that, nothing after that can affect how we understand Islam. Sardar also claims that Wahhabism has no notion of ethics. Any action – no matter how violent – can be justified in the name of God.

And Saudi Arabia has used its petrodollars to spread these beliefs far and wide. Between 1987 and 2007 the Kingdom spent US \$87 billion on its propaganda, through charities, foundations, mosques and universities. Wahhabism is the national ideology, which it has bankrolled internationally to encourage Sunni

Muslims to treat the House of Saud as the de facto leaders of the Islamic world. Since the legitimacy of the ruling elite is derived from Wahhabi clerics, it cannot now go against Wahhabism for fear of weakening its hold over the country.

Alongside funding the Islamic right, Saudi Arabia is also responsible for nurturing it. The country harboured political groups seeking refuge from the rest of the world and indoctrinated them into Wahhabism. It bears responsibility for funnelling warriors into Afghanistan (with US support) to fight a 'holy war' against the Soviet Union. The legacy of this victory was the transformation of political jihadism into a global phenomenon. In its aftermath, many fighters returned home to fight against their governments. Thus, countless splinter groups developed, with their national and political contexts shaping their individual ideologies. One of these groups would become Al-Qaeda. And from the ashes of Al-Qaeda, ISIS would emerge.

A lot more work needs to be done to dismantle the stereotype that Muslims are violent. It's a difficult perception to shift since our governments and institutions are heavily invested in its continuation, as President Trump's 'Muslim ban' has shown. But the legislation, which in January 2017 banned Syrian refugees and the citizens of seven Muslim-majority countries from entering the US for ninety days, is completely superficial. It uses the stereotype of Muslim violence to score political points. We know this because Trump's justification for the ban – 'We have people out there that want to do great destruction to our country, whether it's 25 percent or 10 percent or 5 percent, it's too much' (alluding to a poll from the Center for Security Policy which found that 25 per cent of American Muslims believed violence in the US was justified as part of the 'global jihad') – has been thoroughly debunked.[61] In the same poll, 23 per cent of those surveyed said they were unfamiliar with ISIS and 18 per cent were unfamiliar with Al Qaeda. This led David Dutwin, executive vice president and chief methodologist at the research firm SSRS, to remark: 'The al-Qaida number seems entirely implausible and likely a canary in a coal mine as to the unrepresentativeness of this survey.'[62] The poll also contradicts a Pew survey from 2011, which found that only 8 per cent of American Muslims believed violence in the name of Islam was often or occasionally justified.[63]

This may seem quite high, but it's difficult to compare this figure since Pew didn't survey the followers of other religions to measure their support for violence – but then, why would they? Islam is the only religion ever considered violent enough to warrant surveying its communities. In the absence of comparable statistics, perhaps it's worthwhile to consider support for the Iraq war instead. Over the course of 2003, YouGov conducted twenty-one polls and found that an average of 54 per cent believed the UK was right to conduct military action in Iraq; according to Gallup, 72 per cent of Americans were in favour.[64] Or perhaps it's more appropriate to refer back to the Hope Not Hate statistics that I shared in Chapter One, where 21 per cent of British people said they would support a campaign against proposals to build a mosque near where they live, even if it became violent.

Returning our focus to the Muslim ban, it remains clear that the legislation doesn't serve the purpose it was supposedly created for. The Muslim countries subjected to the ban (Iran, Iraq, Syria, Yemen, Somalia, Sudan and Libya) have low rates of immigration to the US. None of them have produced terrorists that have attacked America, whereas those that have – Egypt and Saudi Arabia – are conspicuously left off the list. So yes, it's good to call out the ban for what it is – pure, unadulterated racism – but we should also remember that the ban is substantively disingenuous, intended to have more rhetorical than practical effect. It helps Trump appear 'tough' on terrorism whilst simultaneously doubling-down on Islam as the cause of it.[65]

But the question I keep returning to is what purpose this stereotype actually serves? Why is the West so keen to attribute violence to Muslims? What is it trying to hide? Well, for one, it deflects from the violence upon which the West is built and maintained, such as aspects of colonialism, capitalism and neo-imperialist policies. It obscures how easy it would be to characterize Europe as a bloody continent instead, and Western culture as inherently violent. One need only cite some obvious and celebrated historical examples – the Crusades, the endless pogroms against Jews, the colonial massacres across the Americas and elsewhere, and the Second World War (in which 85 million were killed, making it the bloodiest conflict ever) – to build a fairly convincing argument against the West's claim to peaceful, moral superiority.

The stereotype of Muslim violence also reduces complex issues to a simplistic narrative. We're fed playground tropes of good versus bad, victim versus perpetrator. But posturing of this sort that portrays the West as a benign victim and Muslims as the hateful, bloodthirsty enemy isn't new; the Cold War, the internment of Japanese-Americans, the historic xenophobia towards Germans, all of these issues confirm how Western nations (like many others) create and recreate ideological enemies for the same reasons that they create national mythologies: to shore up support for the national project and prevent criticisms that may arise from citizens properly scrutinizing actions carried out by the state.

But if we were to examine these stereotypes more thoroughly, we'd realize that the questions beneath them essentially concern the human condition. What drives people to violence? Is this a human impulse, part of our essential nature? When Islamophobes insist that Islam is sadistic or atheists claim that religions have brought nothing but chaos and division, I respond with my understanding that humans have the capacity for magnificent creativity and innovation, but we are also fundamentally violent beings. Our nations are formed from violence – and not simply the transition from agrarian to industrial societies – and we are engaged in a lifelong battle to overcome these impulses.

This is the story we need to tell. We also need the apparatus of the War on Terror, including Prevent, to be dismantled. Certainly we need to do more and expect more from our institutions because stereotyping Muslims as violent only serves to justify the reproduction of that violence against us at state and societal level. Thus, whenever a Muslim carries out a terror attack in the West, there's a corresponding spike in Islamophobic attacks on our streets. Whenever there's an attack against Muslims by white supremacist terrorists, several copycat incidents follow. Because Muslims are accused of being innately violent, violence against Muslims is taken less seriously. The result is that our suffering is rendered invisible. The death tolls under the War on Terror – in Afghanistan, Iraq, Pakistan, Somalia, Yemen, for example – are just some examples of how Muslim pain becomes an inconvenient fact (or otherwise justified) in the narrative of Western victimhood or heroism. Just consider estimates which suggest that 2.4 million people have died as a result of the 2003 invasion of Iraq.[66] How do we Westerners sit comfortably with that figure? Mostly through ignorance and erasure, it seems.

In March 2019, reports emerged that the newborn child of Shamima Begum, the British woman who travelled as a fifteen-year-old to live in Syria under ISIS, had died. The *Metro* broke the story on its front page: '"Too Risky" to Rescue Jihadi Baby'.[67] The mother's connection to ISIS allowed for no sympathy with the baby's death. But when the white supremacist terrorist Brenton Tarrant went into two mosques in Christchurch, New Zealand that same month and murdered fifty Muslims, the *Daily Mirror* put him on the front page with the headline, 'Angelic boy who grew into an evil far-right mass killer.'[68] The *Daily Mail* described him as a 'bullied school boy' who had been 'badly picked on because he was chubby'.[69] No Muslim terrorist would ever be humanized like that. No Muslim terrorist would be reimagined in terms of what he or she was actually *capable* of in an alternative environment. Rather Muslims are victim-blamed (as they were with the Rushdie

Affair), accused of creating the conditions of their own suffering. Commenting on the Christchurch shooting, the Australian senator Fraser Anning said: 'Let me be clear, whilst Muslims may have been the victims today, usually they are the perpetrators... Those who follow a violent religion that calls on them to murder us, cannot be too surprised when someone takes them at their word and responds in kind.'[70]

These words alone are enough to show how desperately we need to recalibrate our conversations about violence. In recent years, far-right extremists have murdered two European MPs: Jo Cox in Britain and Walter Lübcke in Germany. The Soufan Center found that between 2009 and 2019 73 per cent of all extremist-related killings in America came from right-wing radicals, 23 per cent from individuals identifying with Islam and 3 per cent from left-wing extremists.[71] The British counter-terror police revealed that a quarter of all terrorism-related arrests in 2019 were connected to the far right, who were also responsible for a third of all terror plots in Britain since 2017.[72] In 2018, for the first time since 2005, more white people (41 per cent) were arrested in Britain on suspicion of terrorism-related offences than any other ethnic group. In fact, between 2008 and 2016, the far right were responsible for twice as many terrorist attacks as anyone else.[73] All of this suggests that the greatest threat to Western civilization doesn't actually come from terrorists affiliated to Islam, as we're led to believe, but from extremist white supremacy. And yet Muslims continue to receive substantially more press attention – 357 per cent more, in fact.[74]

We in Muslim communities should continue our own work on violence. We should keep reframing our faith away from violence – the emphasis on condemnation, exclusion, sin and punishment – and towards love; the Islamist political parties, the terrorist groups and the families and communities who advocate for violence in all its forms tend to forget that Islam is underpinned by compassion and mercy. Nearly every verse in the Quran begins with the Bismillah, a reminder of God's beneficence and mercifulness. God even says so explicitly, 'My mercy embraces everything' [7:156]. So we need more space for love and healing. For the clearest example of this I look to the Sufi tradition, which, as the American professor Omid Safi remarked when I spoke to him, emphasizes love and justice:

> I see the love dimension as something that taps back into the Sufi understanding of Islam, with the rich dimensions of love, tenderness, mercy, and beauty. The dimension of justice I see as growing naturally out of the spiritual dimension, and addresses questions of gender equality, liberation, and anti-racist, anti-exploitative practices.

So, love is a matter of fairness and empathy.

There are reasons to feel positive. I see the work of Muslim scholars and activists trying to recentre the love in Islam all around me. Moreover, in August 2013, after engagement with religious scholars, the Egyptian Islamist group Al Gamah'ah al-Islamiya renounced violence, stating that 'stopping bloodshed is *the* religious obligation of our time and *the* form of religious devotion of our era', suggesting it is superior to any act of worship.[75]

Saudi propaganda is also beginning to fail. Corruption and political aggression; the gross wealth and lavish lifestyle of the ruling family; the murder of Jamal Khashoggi; silence in the face of Chinese persecution of Uyghur Muslims; and the destruction of Yemen have broken the chokehold. Many Muslims around the world are actively criticizing Saudi leadership, and even boycotting hajj in protest at their actions. As Reza Aslan told me:

> Things have changed dramatically. It's just not the case anymore [that people look to Saudi Arabia for religious leadership]. All you have to do is look at the actions over the last couple of years; the attempt to sow discord amongst Palestinians by supporting the most right-wing elements of

the Israeli occupations. This is a country that is rotted out from the inside. People like me have been saying it for a decade, but now Muslims are starting to notice it for themselves.

But if Western governments were serious about rooting out terrorism inspired by Islam, they would also begin with meaningful action against Saudi Arabia. Instead, as Adam Curtis's documentary *Bitter Lake* illustrated, the Western–Saudi alliance, which involves the sales and purchase of arms and oil in exchange for impunity over the promotion of Wahhabism, shows no signs of letting up.[76]

The argument that Muslims are inherently violent is the most cartoonish of all Islamophobic stereotypes. We need to move away from it. Violence begets violence, so imbuing every part of Muslim existence with a bent towards it rationalizes all the violence carried out against us – the violence of surveillance and detention; other punishments for 'would-be' and 'almost' extremists; the regulation and silencing of dissent; and, of course, physical harm and murder. But Islam as a religion, even when infused with the ambitions and grievances of many of its followers, is still no more violent than any other, as the reactionary and extreme factions of almost every religion illustrate. The faith has a long tradition of non-violence and, like all other religions, Islamic scripture seeks to limit the place for violence in our daily lives.[77] Our refusal to appreciate this renders all conversations around Muslims anaemic, the threat Muslims pose always lurking in the background, and the anger and frustrations of Muslim people constantly ignored. We can and need to do better, to understand Muslim lives without resorting to essentialist ideas about our innate disposition. We are children of the War on Terror, but we deserve understanding beyond that harmful narrative.

3

'Muslim Men Are Threatening'

One night in February 2019, I went out dancing with a friend. We got to the venue around midnight and gravitated towards the dance floor. At some point we took a break and drifted to the young man behind the cash desk, whom we knew well from our previous visits. We chatted, and when I noticed a blonde-haired woman approaching, we became quiet, assuming that she had a question to ask the cashier. I smiled, but she glared at me.

'You're so dodgy, you are,' she said.

'I'm not,' I replied, grinning as if it was some sort of joke.

'Well, you are.'

'Well, actually, I'm not.' I looked for signs of drunkenness. They weren't immediately apparent.

'Then why did you stop talking as soon as I got here?'

The cashier explained that we were discussing our plans for the weekend, but she ignored him and took a step towards me, moving her face closer to mine. 'You—' she said, pointing at my chest. 'You've got such an attitude problem.'

'No, I haven't.' I found her body language intimidating, but I refused to give in to the nonsensical accusation.

She edged even closer. 'No, but you have. Why are you being such an arsehole? You're being really aggressive.'

I took a step back. For a good few seconds, she glowered,

waiting for me to escalate the confrontation. When I didn't reply, she muttered something under breath and went out to smoke a cigarette. The three of us looked at each other in confusion.

'I'm so sorry,' the cashier said. 'I'll report her to security.'

We returned to the dance floor, where I promptly forgot all about it. But my friend couldn't. He looked agitated and was barely dancing. A few minutes later, he went outside to the security guards. He explained the incident to them and they promised to investigate. After a while, he asked the cashier for an update. Security hadn't done anything at all.

My friend came over and shouted across the music. 'I want us to leave after this song. I'm too angry and upset to enjoy myself.'

When I looked at his face, I realized that his sadness was the same sadness that I had encountered in my own life; the same sadness that legions of Muslim men had encountered before me. We tell ourselves that with every successive generation our societies are becoming more equal. We desperately want to believe in this idea, because that's what democracy is supposed to promise; prejudice falling until it disappears from our lives completely. But in my experience, this simply hasn't been borne out.

My friend had been failed, I believed, so I went outside to find the security guards. I saw two men standing by the barriers. Hoping for an update, I asked which of them was in charge.

'Who's asking?' barked the elder of the two. I described my friend. I mentioned the promise to investigate. (Incidentally, the cashier, who assured us that he would speak to security, hadn't done so either. Both sides failed to keep their promises.)

'How do you know we haven't already spoken to her?'

'We asked the cashier and he told us.'

They didn't like our interference with their work, they said. They'd investigate in their own time. I ignored them and repeated our story; my friend was upset because of the strange conversation we'd had with a young, blonde-haired woman. She'd made disparaging allusions to our race.

'But that's not racist,' the elder security guard said. The younger one agreed.

I made several attempts to explain how her words were racist, but each time the men talked me down. 'Please can I just finish what I'm saying?' I pleaded, but the third time I said that, no further along in my explanation, they'd had enough.

'Right, that's it. You can leave.'

This startled me. I was so confident that I could rectify the situation. Now I worried that I'd mishandled it. Other things went through my mind too: I've seen and heard enough about the violence inflicted by nightclub security guards to be afraid, or at least wary, of them. And after years of navigating racism, I know that not every battle needs be won. I told security that I would get my coat and my friend, and leave.

As we did, my friend went over and complained to the organizer – we knew him well too. He leapt off the stage and across the dance floor, racing out to confront the security guards. They denied ever asking me to leave. Humiliated enough already, we walked away.

Some readers may wonder how the woman's outburst was racist. But not all racism is explicit; racism has to evolve in order to survive. I know that the woman wouldn't have made her remarks if we were two white women standing by the cashier or, indeed, if we were two white men. It was the fact we were two *Brown men* (in a country where this is conflated with being Muslim) she had a problem with.

Besides, her words may have sounded innocent, but the meaning behind them was clear. When she accused us of being 'dodgy' she meant that we were threatening and behaving suspiciously; when she said that I was 'aggressive' and had an 'attitude problem', she meant to imply I was violent. It didn't matter what I said or did in that moment, this woman had decided who I was and what I represented.

In the weeks after the incident, it dawned on me that much of the Islamophobia I've experienced has been gendered. I've been slurred not just because I'm a Muslim, but because I'm a Muslim *man*. All through my adult life, I've had to bear the negative connotations of that particular identity. I've been accused of violence and aggression, of extremism and terrorism. Recently, somebody joked that I had joined a 'Muslim paedo gang' and I understood that this was a new addition to the pantheon of stereotypes and slurs that I would have to bear. When I criticized the joke, people rallied around the culprit, absolving him of racist intent, remarking that he wasn't a racist person and that his comments were simply in 'poor taste'. The response reinforced my impressions of the power dynamics that endure as we discuss racism. When a minority is on the receiving end of abuse, it is the racist who retains control. His or her sensitivities are centred (namely, their aversion to being branded a racist); he or she decides whether the racism will be recognized. The victim is expected to sit quietly with the abuse and its effect on their psyche. That need to hold on to power, to determine the response to racism, is something that people unaffected by it must learn to give up.

This is why I cannot write about Islamophobia and religious dogma without dedicating a chapter to masculinity. A blind spot exists in relation to how racism affects Muslim men. The tussle over Muslim women's bodies at the hands of Islamophobes and dogmatic Muslims is a very real one, and space must be reserved to discuss this. Racism is gendered and always has been. However, little attention is paid to how Muslim masculinity is stigmatized and has been since way before 9/11. Muslim men are viewed as the *real* problem – we are seen to embody many of the specific criticisms levelled at Islam. Muslim men are considered aggressive, violent and disrespectful to women (at its crudest, labelled as predators and paedophiles), and this has a profound impact on our relationship with ourselves. The idea that Muslim masculinity threatens the West has become a stereotype. Let us consider each of these 'threats' one by one.

*

Muslim men have always been stereotyped as having an aggressive temperament. As laid out in the Introduction, historically, Muslims were portrayed by Christian Europe as a people to be feared and despised because we were warmongering, savage, bloodthirsty and fanatical in the way that we approached faith. This presumption, that all Muslim men are aggressive – a disposition that we can't exorcize – has persisted through to the modern day. As Muslim populations in the West have grown and become more prominent, countless events have been seized upon to prove that all Muslim men possess a latent aggression.

This began with the Rushdie Affair, then continued through the 1990s and 2000s, when 'honour killings' were splashed across the media, cases involving Samia Sarwar, Ghazala Khan, Samaira Nazir and Sadia Sheikh. These murders were linked to the egos of Muslim men and their obsession with preserving their reputations through the control of women in their families. The riots in the ex-manufacturing towns of Oldham and Burnley in 2001, and across French banlieues in 2005, allowed politicians to portray the men as lazy, good-for-nothing layabouts filled with mindless aggression and criminality, described by then French interior minister, Nicolas Sarkozy, as nothing more than 'racaille' (which is translated as 'riffraff', 'thugs' or even 'outcasts').[1] In doing so, these men had their complaints stripped from them. But when young French men burned cars and attacked police officers in 2005, they did so out of despair, feeling like they had no other way of responding to a lifetime of police violence, poverty and societal discrimination. The 1983 March for Equality and Against Racism had been a response to the riots in a Lyon suburb that were triggered by a spate of racist attacks on African immigrants from the Maghreb. The riots of 2005 were sparked in a similar way.

With these stories, the media bears responsibility for perpetuating the image of the aggressive Muslim man. But it is Hollywood that has played a particularly crucial role, shaping how Muslim men are almost exclusively viewed as the 'bad guys'. The writer

Jack G. Shaheen studied over a thousand movies to find that Arabs, for example, are nearly always shown to be brutal and heartless villains.[2] Consider how Black men are portrayed as dangerous, or South and South East Asian men portrayed as sexless (imagine the multiple stereotypes that Black Muslim men must contend with, first labelled as 'gangsters' and 'predators' and now also as 'terrorists').[3] The effect is like finding yourself caught in an echo chamber of undesirability. Being a Muslim man and having a media narrative of violence reflected back at you – constantly – is overwhelming. It breaks your spirit, limiting the possibilities of masculinity that we see for ourselves.

When the 'War on Terror' came along, it only strengthened and intensified the connection between Muslim masculinity and violence, leaving no room for doubt that Muslim men were a problem. This is why Rutgers University associate professor Deepa Kumar asserts that 'the terrorist is, from the very beginning, raced and gendered'.[4] What she means by this is that Muslim men are not just associated with violence, but are considered to *personify* terrorism. It is carved on to our bodies. Close your eyes and imagine a terrorist. What do you see? A dark-skinned, 'Muslim-looking' man? Of course you do. We've been conditioned to think like this, to subscribe to the Western archetype of what a terrorist is supposed to look like.

This archetype underpins the entire system of counterterrorism policy. When the NYPD published its terrorism study in 2007, it placed Muslim masculinity at the very centre of its radicalization theory. It argued that imams and male converts to Islam were 'typical terrorists'. If a Muslim man behaved in accordance with 'typical signatures', such as by giving up cigarettes, gambling and urban hip-hop gangster clothes, instead adopting traditional Islamic clothing, growing a beard and becoming involved in social activism and community issues, it would indicate that he was a potentially violent threat.[5] But these kinds of responses to 9/11 and 7/7 were merely the progression of a medieval tradition, which believed that Muslim men weren't only violent, but were initiated in the way of violence by Islam. Counterterrorism policy took from these historical ideas and escalated them. Western governments believed – and still do – that a focus on Muslim masculinity will help them to curb terrorism.

Whilst there's no evidence that connects Muslim masculinity specifically to violence, the trope does serious harm to young Muslim men. The author and journalist Hussein Kesvani, whose work has explored expressions of masculinity amongst Muslim and non-Muslim men, told me about his experience. Hussein shared details of an identity crisis he had after 7/7 – not dissimilar to mine after 9/11, except instead of abandoning religion, he doubled-down on it. 'All of a sudden, I tried to be very religious, almost zealous in my faith. I was a really shitty person during that time, and I think a lot of that was a reaction to [being singled out].' Feeling torn between competing narratives within his religious and cultural community and broader British society, the only option he saw for himself was to embody what both sides wanted him to become.

But the harm isn't restricted to Muslim men being limited through government controls or suffering damaged self-esteems. As I explained in Chapter Two, stereotyping Muslims as violent justifies the reproduction of violence against us. Thus, on 4 June 2019, as millions of Muslims around the world celebrated the festival of Eid-ul-Fitr, three men were obstructed by German police at Cologne train station as they made their way to Eid celebrations. They were subdued and searched. An image showed the men wearing thobes and waistcoats, lying face down on the floor in handcuffs. There are far more violent examples I could share of how badly Muslim men are treated by Western state agencies – the case of Adama Traoré in Chapter One shows what happens when Blackness and class and Islam intersect – but this particular example chills me because it is such a transparent instance of racial profiling. These men were deemed dangerous only because they were dressed up in traditional clothing. As the Cologne police tweeted: 'We are checking men in white robes. They allegedly entered the station running, according to witnesses. The background is still unclear.'[6]

The picture and incident both remind me of my very first brush with the brutalization of Muslim men. In 1996, I was ten years old when I learned that the police had arrested several Pakistani men from my community. On this occasion too, it was Eid. The men were out celebrating along Manchester's 'Curry Mile'. One of the men was a neighbour and a family friend. Amer Rafiq, a twenty-one-year-old student and waiter, was so badly beaten by the police that his right eye socket was shattered and he lost an eye. However, the police claimed that he hit a piece of equipment in their van during the struggle to get him inside.[7] I have never forgotten the image of Rafiq's injured face looking at me from the front of our local newspaper. It haunted me.

So I cannot help but find the incident in Cologne – and every example of police brutality I come into contact with – incredibly distressing. I spent my late teens and twenties trying to mitigate how Islam (and therefore, danger) was also marked on my body. Before every flight, I shaved off my beard and, when I went through airport security, I made sure that there was nothing on me that would trigger the sensors. These are the kinds of decisions Muslim men have been forced to make for two decades now (our bodies rendered even more threatening under the War on Terror) – choices that are stress-free for others, but fraught for us. How long should our beards be? Should we have them at all? Should we wear skullcaps? Are we allowed to wear dashikis and thobes and salwar kameez and clothing that may identify us as Muslim? And if we do, what will the repercussions be? Never before have Muslim men had to deal with this specific cocktail of discrimination, one so explicitly linked to our faith and drawn from our appearance.

*

There's a long history of the West problematizing Muslim sexuality too, either by discrediting the comparative sexual permissiveness of our societies (and the sex positivity of Islam) or using Prophet Muhammad's relationships to dismiss his prophethood. Dominant societies have always used sex as a way of controlling how subjugated communities are perceived. European neoclassical artists like Jean-Auguste-Dominique Ingres and Jean Lecomte de Noüy painted Middle Eastern harems featuring white women kept as sexual slaves. The bestsellers of Victorian erotic literature, *The Lustful Turk*, *Night in a Harem* and *The Sheik*, depicted Muslim men as sexually aggressive. Today sex is used to advance another trope about Muslim men: that we are repressed sexual predators with no respect for women.

A salacious interpretation of Muslim history allows Islamophobes to make this argument. They use it to draw a line between Islam and the sexual misconduct of Muslim men today. Islamophobes hold scripture and religious tradition directly responsible for the behaviour of Muslim men, rather than their own agency. This is why the Dutch far-right leader Geert Wilders has called the Prophet a paedophile, alleging that he consummated his marriage with Aisha when she was just nine years old (having married her at age six). Other far-right leaders have made similar remarks; the slur is so common that you only need to read the comments section of any news story on Muslims or search Islam on Twitter to find the accusation rearing its ugly head. It hardly matters that Aisha's age is disputed, and that many scholars believe she was around eighteen to twenty-one years old.[8] The real issue is that nobody expects non-Muslims to justify historical relationships as Muslims are forced to. Nobody asks a white Englishman to explain why thirty-three-year-old King John of England married twelve-year-old Isabella of Angoulême in the twelfth century – five hundred years after Prophet Muhammad married Aisha.

This is because these examples serve to facilitate Western hysteria about Muslim men and our supposed inability to respect

Western moral codes about consent and female bodily autonomy. Muslim men, particularly recent arrivals, are held collectively responsible for sexual violence against white women. The goal is to inspire a fear of Muslim men and, by extension, of immigrants and of Islam in general, holding them responsible for a climate (more imagined than real) where Western sanctuaries for female agency are being eroded.

The Cologne sex attacks in 2015 captured these forces in action. The story began with an accusation on social media that the police had evidence (which it was refusing to make public) of mass sex attacks on German women on New Year's Eve. The mainstream press caught hold of the story. *Bild*, Germany's most popular tabloid, ran a story on it with the headline, 'Sex mobs across Germany'; *Die Welt* followed suit, claiming that anonymous police sources had revealed most of the attackers to be of Syrian extraction. In the midst of rising panic, police officials were forced to confirm that hundreds of women had reported being sexually assaulted whilst out celebrating New Year's Eve. Over subsequent months, dramatic figures were bandied about without proof – 1200 reports of sexual assault (600 in Cologne, 400 in Hamburg) and up to 2000 men involved – as accusations of a deliberate cover-up also mounted.

Many public figures laid the blame on Muslim men. Julia Klöckner, state president of the Christian Democratic Union party in the Rhineland-Palatinate region, argued that the assaults were an expression of the 'Muslim norms of masculinity'. The Dutch magazine *NRC Handelsblad* wrote an article questioning how Muslim culture had played into the attacks. The German magazine *Focus* carried a cover of a naked white woman dirtied by handprints with the caption, 'Women complain of sex attacks by migrants: Are we tolerant or are we blind?' A similar illustration appeared in a Polish magazine, of a white woman whose European-flag dress and blonde hair were being pulled apart by a series of black and brown hands. And the headline? 'The Islamic Rape of Europe'.[9]

The same moral panic has informed the framing of the 'grooming gang' cases in Britain. These cases are hugely significant, not only because of the nature and scale of the crimes concerned, but also because of the media coverage that resulted. By portraying them as examples of Muslim men attacking white British women, these cases have redefined how Muslims and Muslim men specifically are perceived in Britain. To be clear, I'm not disputing the genuineness and severity of these crimes; I am simply highlighting the way entire groups of people can be blamed for acts they had nothing to do with. Accordingly, these cases will continue to determine what our lives look like as Muslims living in the West, I believe, for decades to come.

For many years, the far right had claimed that South Asian men were preying on young white girls, but these accusations garnered little mainstream attention. However, in January 2011, *The Times* published an exposé, claiming to have separated cases of 'on-street grooming' from all other sex offences. It argued that 'criminal pimping gangs' were sexually exploiting 'hundreds of young British girls'.[10] Most of the victims were white and most convicted offenders were of Pakistani heritage. The story lit a fire in Britain, spurred on by the newspaper's decision to publish the story the same week that two men from Derby were convicted of rape and sexual activity with a child.

Since then, the story has only metastasized. More accounts have emerged of Asian, mostly Pakistani, men sexually exploiting young girls in towns and cities across Britain. The cases are only ever reported in racialized terms, in terms of Brown masculine violence against white femininity. For example, the Labour MP Sarah Champion wrote an article for *The Sun* in 2017 entitled 'British Pakistani men ARE raping and exploiting white girls... and it's time we faced up to it.'[11] In many cases, the failure to investigate matters sooner has been blamed on a culture of political correctness within British institutions, which concealed the racial character of the abuse.

In May 2012, nine men in Rochdale were found guilty of grooming and sexually exploiting young girls. Over 2008 and 2009, the gang of men had acted together, plying the girls with gifts, food, alcohol and drugs, and then forcibly having sex with them. The girls, often from broken homes or lost and forgotten in the care system, hung around kebab shops late at night where they befriended the staff and taxi drivers working late. There were forty-seven victims in total. Months of racialized reporting resulted in the far right picketing the court during the trial and clashes in the community where the abuse had taken place. Before the jury returned with a verdict, Nick Griffin, leader of the British National Party, tweeted, 'News flash. Seven of the Muslim paedophile rapists found guilty in Liverpool.'[12]

In this way, the sexual exploitation that occurred within the grooming cases has been seamlessly linked to Islam and its cultures. The British historian David Starkey accused the Pakistani men of 'acting within their cultural norms' and recommended they were taught about the emancipation of women in English history to become 'first and foremost English citizens and English men'.[13] Commenting on a series of convictions in Huddersfield, then Home Secretary Sajid Javid tweeted: 'These sick Asian paedophiles are finally facing justice.' When questioned as to why he made a point of singling out the perpetrators' ethnicities, he said:

Any normal person looking at the recent convictions of gangs that abuse children would have noticed that a vast majority are from a Pakistani heritage and we cannot ignore that... If you sit in a position of power like me and you ignore that, what you actually end up doing is fuelling the voices of extremism that are out there that will then prey on that.[14]

But rape and paedophilia are not Muslim or Pakistani cultural norms. We're not forced to have conversations about why white men rape, questioning which aspect of their cultural norms encourages them to prey on women. And when white men do rape and exploit, our media and politicians aren't compelled to specify their race. Stories about European paedophiles travelling to Gambia and Thailand are conspicuous precisely because race is rarely signposted (if these stories garner attention at all).[15] British celebrity Jimmy Savile's notorious sexual abuse of hundreds has never been analysed with respect to him being white. So by identifying when South Asian or Muslim men are the perpetrators, the media allows a myth to be perpetuated (which once belonged to the far right) that only these men are a menace to women, which we know is untrue.

Unfortunately, politicians and media commentators continue to disassociate themselves from the broader consequences of this particular narrative. They prefer to argue that 'openness' around the racial dynamics of the grooming cases will suppress extremist voices, but the opposite is true. Nazir Afzal, the chief prosecutor in the Rochdale case, warned that grooming is the 'biggest recruiter for the far right' and this is true; far-right figures demonize Muslim men, claiming that rape and paedophilia are forms of jihad.[16] We know that the far right has been remobilized not by silence, but by years of racialized commentary from public and political figures. After *The Times* published stories about a fifteen-year-old girl who had been groomed in Rotherham, the EDL carried out a large-scale demonstration in the town on 13 October 2014.[17] A total of fourteen demonstrations took place over the next four-teen months, capitalizing on the Brown faces in the media and the government reports (the 2014 Jay Report and 2015 Casey Review) that fed into the climate of conspiracy and hysteria.[18] Again, this is not to cast doubt on the veracity of the crimes reported; it is to show the very real impact of how they are framed and relayed to the general public.

Actively stoking the far right has resulted in hate crimes against Muslims. In August 2015, racists in Rotherham mur-dered eighty-one-year-old Mushin Ahmed as he walked to the mosque.[19] Before they attacked him, they accused Ahmed of being a 'groomer'. The cases have even captured international attention; the Christchurch attacker had 'For Rotherham' written on his ammunition. I've witnessed how variations on the phrase 'Muslim sex gangs' have become common parlance in British society, regurgitated as a knee-jerk response to any public expression of Muslimness. In May 2019, a friend shared a picture with me of a van owned by the Ramadan Tent Project, which holds public iftars (the meal where Muslims break their fasts at sunset) that bring communities together. The side of the van was daubed in graffiti with the phrase, 'Stop Muslim Sex Grooming Gangs Now'.

The emotional impact of all this on young Muslim men is neglected. According to a report by JUST Yorkshire on the impact of the Rotherham case on the Pakistani community, young Muslim boys found themselves being called a 'groomer' or 'paedophile' at school in the same way that I was once called a terrorist.[20] Similarly, when sociologist Joanne Britton conducted a study on Muslim masculinity in Rotherham she found that Muslim men aged between thirty and fifty were deeply affected by the grooming cases that had come to light there.[21] One of her interviewees said:

You know, it's the sort of innuendo comments from liberals, from people, from politicians to outright racist comments from bigots who don't know any better. But it's that sort of collective tarring of us all. And whenever I'm out and about, you know, it's odd, I always think, you know, what do other people think of me? How do they class me? Do they think I'm involved? I'm somehow a paedophile? Or, you know, that's, sort of, been the biggest impact for me personally. The idea that somehow we were all responsible, somehow we were all guilty or negligent, or whatever, and now we must all pay the price for that.

The consequences are particularly acute for the men who grow up facing a barrage of such political rhetoric with little ability to deconstruct the stories in the news or respond to the slurs levelled at them. Because it's not just the assumption that men have no respect for women; this stereotype has tentacles. It categorizes Muslim men as emotionally and sexually underdeveloped, lacking the ability to sustain relationships that are based on consent and intimacy. And these men witness the silence of the state and its institutions, its failure to protect them from violence and vilification, and lose faith in it.

All of these tropes stifle who Muslim men can be by inhibiting how we are portrayed and understood by wider society. The relationship between who we are and how we are represented may not be scientifically accounted for, but I believe it's a strong one. In the Introduction I wrote about how essentialist stereotypes left me feeling powerless and dislocated from both Britain and Islam. When, for example, Muslim men aren't allowed to be victims of violence – because the media gives little coverage to these stories – it stymies how we see ourselves. But if we were more invested in the emotional health of Muslim men, rather than in portraying them as a problem, it's possible far fewer would grow up assuming (and often acting in accordance with) that rhetoric.

Issues like these make it as important to explore the inner lives of Muslim men and our experiences of the world; to explore our masculinity and the absurd and dangerous ways it is essentialized. As I described above, Islamophobes project a series of negative images on to Muslim masculinity. Because these characterizations colour our interactions with the world, they end up shaping (and limiting) our identities and self-confidence. But it would be disingenuous of me to behave as if only one side is guilty of essentializing Muslim masculinity. In some Muslim communities, we're doing the Islamophobes' work for them. We often reduce masculinity to a series of stereotypes that men must fulfil, and I think we should talk more about this. We should consider how masculinity is shaped by Islam – or, rather, how Islam is used to scaffold the stereotypes that we expect men to conform to.

Some Muslims, I imagine, will have quite a guttural response to this. They might respond with the argument that Islam doesn't shape masculinity; that gender norms are innate, or that they come from wider society and the cultures to which we belong. But that's a half-truth. Almost every institution we encounter in our lives reinforces gender norms, and religion is no different. Moreover, religion and culture enjoy a close relationship; they support and give greater expression to the best parts of one another – and the worst. So a culture that is very prescriptive about how men should behave (as many cultures can be, both religious and secular) taps into religion to reinforce these stereotypes.

I have first-hand experience of this. For as long as I can remember, I have been reminded that I'm not the right kind of man. Especially when I was young, I distinctly recall feeling deficient. But that feeling didn't come from me. It came from the people around me. I knew that I was being treated differently to other boys my age – treated as somehow less – but I had no ability to change it. I was the kind of boy who read books and sang songs, who preferred painting and drawing to football and cricket. Unlike the boys who pulled girls' hair and ran away, I befriended the girls in my class, and this both bemused and concerned those in my world who believed (because religion dictated it) that boys should only play with boys and girls with other girls.

I was deemed not masculine enough. In primary school we always lined up in the playground after mid-morning break and lunch before going inside. We had to do this in a strict 'boy-girl-boy-girl' formation, and so, quite regularly, one of the rough young boys in my class would push in front of me with a sneer, commenting that I was out of place because I was a girl. I was such a sensitive child. I had no qualms with showing emotion. I cried when bullying of this kind began at age six or seven – the time that children begin to perceive difference and articulate the norms they have been taught about how boys and girls 'should' behave. I cried at silly things too. I remember once – I must have been no more than ten years old – my two best friends made fun of me when I sang a song that we'd been learning in the school choir, 'Never Smile at a Crocodile', with choreographed movements to go with it. 'It's such a stupid song,' my friends said giggling; my eyes stung and filled with tears.

That night I waited in the doorway for my dad to come home. My father is emotionally intuitive; I've inherited this trait. He took me in his arms and told me that their opinions didn't matter. My parents were pretty great (on the whole) when I was growing up, because they didn't try to mould me into somebody I wasn't. But everyone else did; my uncles mocked and laughed at the way I carried myself; my grandfather, on a visit from Pakistan when I was fourteen, remarked that I didn't walk 'like a proper man should' and implored my father to teach me. Gradually, I picked up on all the ways I was defective because I didn't behave as other boys did. I realized that boys didn't show emotion because boys were strong, and strength needed to be detectable from our bodies. Consciously or unconsciously, I began to move away from who I was naturally to emulate who I was *supposed* to be.

My desire to have a conversation about Muslim men is born from this experience. Growing up, I had two main problems with masculinity. One, that I was socialized to accept masculinity as a narrow set of traits and behaviours, with which my own masculinity was incompatible. And two, that the most stereotypically masculine men (and below them, many women) set themselves up as the guardians of gender norms and appropriate social behaviour, appropriating religion to give their domineering behaviour divine approval. I understand that whole communities and societies derive their stability from this system, but what is the point of it when it so often harms others? It harms men by creating unhealthy and unreachable standards of behaviour (how can it ever be worthwhile to suppress your emotions in order to appear 'tough'?). And it causes harm to those who are demoralized (and punished) when power is vested in the hands of a minority to decide how the rest of society is permitted to behave. Rather than accepting these systems, I want Muslim communities to think more about power and what happens when one group has too much power over another. Isn't that what Islam was supposed to correct?

I'm not trying to 'undo' gender and gender norms. My interest is in stretching the concept of masculinity so that it doesn't rely on domination and injustice, so that it's broader than the stereotypes that are used to bind us. If, for example, we as Muslim men refuse to examine how we benefit from a system that privileges the male sex and a very narrow concept of masculinity, how can we claim to be exercising our Islamic duties to be just and ethical in our lives? We can't. This is a conversation about how Muslim men can practise compassion and justice through the expression of our gender; how we can reckon with the power that we assume to judge and police others.

At the same time, I refuse to let this be a conversation that is co-opted by Islamophobes. I believe that we can reject how Muslim men are perceived from the outside as the defenders and benefactors of an oppressive faith and religion, whilst opening up a conversation about patriarchy. We can also reject the interpretation that Muslim men are uniquely bound up in rigid cultural norms and hierarchies whilst making space to reflect on how this might be true for some.

In *The Colonizer and the Colonized*, the French writer Albert Memmi observed how people belonging to minority communities are deprived of their individuality. Describing it as the 'mark of the plural', he argued that any act committed by a non-white person is treated as representative of his or her whole community, whilst an act committed by a white person is only ever reflective of that particular individual.[22] In a way, this book is about that phenomenon.

In the West, all forms of masculinity that aren't white and Western European in origin are deemed to be threatening – African, Caribbean, African-American, Eastern European – and men from those communities have been demonized accordingly. When Muslim men act badly, their behaviour is forced through the lens of Islam, offered up as some great wisdom on the short-comings of our faith and culture. Muslim men are stereotyped as aggressive, violent and predatorial. In 2007, Shakeel Ahmad Bhatt, a political activist in Kashmir, was photographed at a protest. An image of him screaming went viral. The accompanying memes made fun of the claim that Islam is peaceful; as a follower of the religion, he revealed the 'true face' of its aggressive and fanatical nature. On right-wing blogs, Bhatt was nicknamed the 'Islamic Rage Boy' and became an icon of Muslim masculinity in popular culture.[23]

But when white men behave badly, their aggression or anger is rarely examined through whiteness. This hypocrisy is visible in far-right groups, which rail against 'Muslim paedophiles' but count many convicted sex offenders and paedophiles as their members. Leigh McMillan, a 'senior member' of the EDL who was convicted in 2018 of sexually abusing a ten-year-old girl, is one example.[24] Would it be appropriate to view his crimes through his race also?

Instead, as I mentioned in Chapter Two, the source of white anger is given a depth and complexity that Muslim men are deprived of. The explanations offered by the media about the rise of populism in the West are proof of this. As recently as March 2019, a columnist for *Spiked* insisted that 'Brexit was a work-ing-class revolt.'[25] But much of this anger is steeped in whiteness. In her book *White Rage*, the American professor Carol Anderson explains how the anger that has emerged in the West is actually a backlash against the social progress of minorities.[26] Contrast that with Muslims. The socio-economic dimension of Muslim rage is actively ignored, even obscured. This is despite the fact that in

2019 the Office for National Statistics found workers of Pakistani and Bangladeshi heritage living in London to be the lowest paid of any ethnic group (up to 20 per cent less than white British workers).[27] In the US, Black Muslim households are more likely than any other Muslim group to earn less than $30,000 per year.[28] Class plays a huge role in the disenfranchisement of Muslim men. Poverty and poor social mobility (the UK placed twenty-first in the Global Social Mobility Index 2020) substantially contribute to their overrepresentation in the prison system.[29] Speaking to the *Intercept*, the French activist Abdelaziz Chaambi said:

In France, there isn't a door for young people born here to integrate into society... The riots in 2005 were about the frustration of people who have lived their whole lives without equal rights, dignity, access to jobs, or proper housing. They were a warning sign to the rest of society that things were getting unbearable for people in the suburbs.[30]

The class dimension of Muslim anger also came up in my conversations with Hussein Kesvani, but critically, he also connected this anger to the challenges faced by non-Muslim men:

We have this generation of young Muslim men who are dealing with the same things that other young men are dealing with. They have the same shitty job prospects, who are still going to be in loads of debt, who are never going to be able to afford their own property. We're never going to be afforded the same wealth as our parents did, who immigrated in the 1970s and 1980s.

Western societies are deeply uncomfortable with Muslim anger. They don't see us as entitled to it. It destabilizes their sense of control. And ultimately, because Western societies also fear the legitimacy of that anger, it's easier to portray it as dangerous and unhealthy. It's better to tie it up in religion than to reflect on where it might originate. But in refusing to accept responsibility and work to diffuse it, we unwittingly create the conditions for this anger to thrive.

The same is true for violence. Behaving as if violence is specific to a particular community derails the very necessary conversations that need to take place around it. Muslim men are stereotyped as terrorists, but we know from gun violence in America or white supremacist violence that terrorism has no faith. On the contrary, it is young men (regardless of religion) who are responsible for 98 per cent of all political violence.[31] Men are more likely to kill and more likely to be drawn to ideologies that offer absolutist solutions to the challenges of modern life. So we should be asking ourselves, why do masculinity and violence share such an intimate relationship? What is it about men, rather than Muslim men specifically, that makes them so prone to radicalization in the way of violence? Because let's be clear: this should not be a conversation that only looks at Islam.

'An act of violence is nearly always a complex decision, a confluence of personal, social and ideological elements,' wrote Benjamin Ramm, the editor-at-large of openDemocracy, in an article about the relationship between political violence and mental health.[32] The desire to be part of a group is one such motivation. The former CIA Operations Officer, Marc Sageman, linked friendship and violence, arguing that 'social bonds always come before any ideological commitment'. The FBI special agent and behavioural psychologist Kathleen Puckett argued that the same was true for 'lone wolves':

[T]here are people who want to be members of groups but can't affiliate or can't make the internal connections with other people well enough to become a member. The group rejects them or they reject the group. They're angry because they're stymied in their lack of ability to make connections that they want. If you're not in a group, how do you matter in the world? How do you make a mark? You have to do a societal level of violence – so the connection that they make is to the ideology itself...[33]

The Boston bombers, brothers Tamerlan and Dzhokhar Tsarnaev, were isolated, not by choice but circumstance, and they had this in common with white terrorists like Eric Rudolph and Ted Kaczynski. On social media, Tamerlan Tsarnaev had written, 'I don't have a single American friend.'[34]

Violence also appeals to men in a way that we cannot bring ourselves to acknowledge, even though it has appealed for millennia. Take the Crusades as an example. The Crusades offered the Franks an escape from a terrible life mired by plague, famine and flooding.[35] Some had apocalyptic ambitions and wished to hasten the coming of the end of the world. Others were motivated by wealth and adventure. Bohemond, the Count of Taranto, led the First Crusades because he wanted more land and more power; Hernando Cortés led the colonial expedition into the Aztec Empire dreaming of riches. Men today share the same intricacy of motivation when drawn to violence – Muslim men included.

This much is clear from *Fields of Blood: Religion and the History of Violence*, in which Karen Armstrong describes the restlessness that resides within some men that only the thrill of violence can fulfil. An outfit like ISIS speaks to that restlessness; it offers community, machinery and a taste of war; the chance of glory and personal transformation – from mediocre nobody to freedom fighter – and war spoils in terms of women as sex slaves. Martyrdom takes it one step further, offering glory, paradise and unlimited sex. We may struggle to relate to this, but we need to see cultural phenomena like ISIS for the narcissistic endeavours that they are, allowing people to rid themselves of their shortcomings and rebrand themselves as warriors. It's really no different to white nationalists who like to compare themselves to the medieval Knights Templar and hold egotistical fantasies of saving the West from immigration and multiculturalism. Brenton Tarrant, responsible for the Christchurch massacre in 2019, had even speculated that he would one day be awarded the Nobel Peace Prize.[36]

Within all this, it's fascinating to me how little we consider violence as a product of how we raise men. Many patriarchal societies teach men to suppress all emotions aside from rage, which they then channel into violence. Furthermore, we talk so little about how violent Western societies are that it jolts us when people push back against the notion that violence is ubiquitous only in the societies of the global South.

This also came up in my conversation with Hussein Kesvani:

Very few people want to talk about how young British Muslims who went over to Syria grew up in a country that venerates violence to a very high degree, that has a history of violence – especially in the East End. Like, these are British kids who grew up in a very British context.

Between us we reeled off the violence that is entrenched in the West, but often goes unnoticed: in our militaries, prisons, detention centres; in the overt and covert operations our governments execute in foreign countries; in the manufacture and sale of weapons which are used abroad by tyrannical regimes to suppress dissent – even in the annual Poppy Appeal. 'What we're actually saying is that war is good and we should cherish the people who go to war,' Hussein said to me.

Now I know that the Poppy Appeal is a controversial example. The campaign was established to support British veterans who fought in the two world wars. But the funds raised from selling poppies also support veterans from more recent conflicts. I recognize and respect that, for some people, the poppy represents the freedoms that were battled for on the fields of Belgium and

France. But we must also recognize that for other communities, like the Irish, or Muslims who have witnessed the conflicts in Afghanistan, Iraq and Libya, wearing a red poppy reads as an uncritical commemoration, even celebration, of British aggression. Perhaps this is why, in 2014, RAF veteran and activist Harry Smith tweeted that he was against wearing the poppy 'because it has been co-opted by politicians to justify our present wars on terror that are eroding democracy'.[37]

It's interesting to observe how dogmatic poppy wearing has become over the years. Voicing any dissenting opinion about the poppy's place in British society leaves one open to abuse. In 2017, the British Muslim cricketer Moeen Ali was criticized for not wearing a poppy in the England team's official photograph – though it later transpired his poppy had merely fallen off.[38] Piers Morgan, the journalist and television presenter, accused a peace campaigner who promoted wearing a white poppy to denote pacifism of wanting to honour Nazi soldiers and ISIS.[39] Colonel Richard Kemp, a veteran of the Afghan invasion, claimed that the wearing of white poppies 'was an insult to the war dead'.[40]

These comments made me think about how soldiers who have died on Western military escapades are received and buried with such pomp and ceremony, offered the kind of glory and martyrdom that disturbs us only when it is couched in religious vernacular. The reality is that we in the West cultivate and then celebrate certain forms of male anger, so why are we surprised when it finds other avenues of expression?

Inflated and misleading statistics also play a huge part in derailing important conversations about masculinity. In Sweden, for example, a spike in the number of rapes reported since 2015 was blamed on the country accepting young, male Muslim migrants. In 2017, Nigel Farage described the city of Malmö as the 'rape capital of Europe'. Then in 2018, the Swedish public broadcaster, SVT, added fuel to this stereotype by claiming that 58 per cent of all men convicted of rape were foreign-born, with the most significant proportion coming from the Middle East, North Africa and Afghanistan.[41]

But the SVT drew these conclusions from an analysis of 843 convictions – in a country where 8000 rapes are reported every year – so the figure is superficial and misleading.[42] According to a 2019 study by Sweden's National Council for Crime Prevention, there is no connection between Muslim migration and sex crimes. The municipalities with the highest number of reported sex offences weren't the same municipalities that had accepted the highest number of asylum seekers.[43] So the image cultivated by the media and far right – that dark-skinned men prowl the streets, ready to attack helpless white women – is simply untrue.

Fake statistics have also been conjured up to service the British narrative around grooming gangs and these must also be disregarded. In 2017, the Quilliam Foundation published a report claiming that 84 per cent of the perpetrators in 'grooming gang' cases were Asian, the vast majority 'of Pakistani origin with Muslim heritage'.[44] I interviewed Dr Ella Cockbain, an academic at University College London whose research focuses on child sexual exploitation, about this report. She had previously described it as a case study in 'bad science'. Her verdict was damning:

> If you look at the report in its entirety, it's full of really inflammatory language, really big, unsubstantiated claims that don't have any basis in their data, and them speculating but presenting them as hard fact. All the buzz words are in there; it talks about FGM [Female Genital Mutilation] and misogyny and honour killings and it creates this really powerful narrative of all the things that are wrong with Islam coming to get us. But it lacks a shred of credibility. The 84 per cent figure might as well be thrown in the bin because it's a bad stat, and bad stats are both worthless and dangerous.

Dr Cockbain warned against perpetuating the myth that South Asian or Muslim men are disproportionately involved in child sex offences. The data was nowhere near good enough to suggest this at all. The closest thing to a sensible sample came from an analysis of conviction data by Full Fact, the UK's independent fact-checking organization, which found no disproportionality at all.[45] The number of Asian child sex offenders was in line with the national population.

Moreover, let's put to rest the argument that the 84 per cent figure was formulated to buttress: that grooming cases are entrenched in a kind of 'reverse-racism'. These were not cases of Brown men preying on white girls because they were *white*. They were and remain cases of misogynist violence, of men taking advantage of girls who were *vulnerable*. In the sentencing of the men in a case from Newcastle, the presiding judge, Penny Moreland, confirmed that race had not been a determining factor in the abuse: 'In my view, and speaking in broad terms, these defendants selected their victims not because of their race but because they were young, impressionable, naive and vulnerable.'[46] So, on the grooming of minors, our conversation must begin with the acknowledgement that some men abuse their power to sexually exploit people – girls *and* boys, white *and* of colour, straight *and* LGBT, able-bodied *and* differently abled.

To do that, we have to be a little more honest about Western societies. When Islamophobes assemble to protest Islam, they accuse the West of importing a culture of rape or paedophilia from the Muslim world. In doing so, they behave as if Western societies are free of sexual violence, which they're not and wouldn't be, even if Muslim men had no presence in these countries. According to a 2014 study by the EU Agency for Fundamental Rights, an average of 33 per cent of women across Europe had experienced some form of sexual violence, including 35 per cent of German and 46 per cent of Swedish women.[47] A 2018 report from the Foundation for European Progressive Studies revealed that 40 per cent of British

women had experienced unconsented sexual touching at least
once in their lives; 86 per cent of French women had been sexually
assaulted or molested in the street.[48]

Needlessly racializing the narrative around the Cologne sex
attacks prevents us from understanding how mass gatherings
present men with opportunities to sexually abuse women. Thomas
Fischer, a German federal judge who writes for *Die Zeit*, reflected
on the New Year's Eve attacks in Cologne and pointed out that
sexual violence takes place on the same scale at Cologne Carnival
and Munich's Oktoberfest every year.[49] Furthermore, a YouGov
poll from 2018 found that 30 per cent of British women had experienced some form of sexual harassment or assault at a music
festival. Sexual violence is embedded within Western society.[50] We
should be talking about why that is the case, rather than engaging
in finger-pointing and worthless debates that cultivate rage but
do little to address societal problems. Dr Cockbain reminded me
that as horrific as 'grooming' cases were, focusing on them at the
expense of everything else detracted from broader issues that also
needed to be tackled:

> We know that, across the UK in 2016–2017, there were over
> 63,000 recorded child sex offences. That's huge. At the same
> time, this will be the tip of the iceberg because the vast major-
> ity of cases will never be reported in the first place. So we have
> this enormous problem [of child abuse]. If we're talking about
> an epidemic, that is the epidemic [and not grooming gangs
> specifically].

But when Islamophobes make interventions into child sex
grooming cases, it's not because they want to champion women's
rights. The paternalistic references to 'our girls' and 'our daughters'
uncover a great deal: that white women are worth saving above
Black and Brown women; that white women are nothing more
than possessions and white men their guardians; and that the

issue isn't that young girls and women are abused, but with *who* is abusing them. All other victims – all those who are not young, white girls – are erased from the narrative and the response.

Many organizations have tried hard to challenge this erasure. The Rotherham charity Apna Haq, which supports Black and Minority Ethnic (BME) victims of sexual violence, released a report in 2016. It warned that the British government and public authorities were 'not adequately safeguarding the rights of BME victims of violence or effectively supporting the service providers that support them'.[51] Shaista Gohir from the Muslim Women's Network has spoken out about the dangers of making non-white victims invisible: 'After Rochdale, I was going to meetings and no one was taking me seriously, because [Asian victims] don't show up in the statistics. I started looking for case studies – and they were there.'[52]

Asian victims are already more vulnerable – they are less likely to report abuse and face 'revictimization' by being disowned or forced into marriage, which makes their exclusion from the discussion on sexual abuse all the more problematic. So the need to reform our conversations is a desperately urgent one, because as it stands, our discussion of 'grooming gangs' is doing far more harm than good and is preventing us from making any meaningful improvements to the lives of young, vulnerable people.

Let me also take this opportunity to interrogate the argument that masculinity is clearly defined by Islam. For Islamophobes, Muslim masculinity is defined by aggression, violence and sexual predation. But for some Muslims, it is narrowly defined too, albeit in terms of the roles that Muslim men must play within their communities. In most Muslim cultures, after all, our sense of self is defined communally, not individually as it is in the West, in terms of hierarchies and our obligations to one another.

Muslim men, like most other men living in Western societies, are still expected to live up to some form of the patriarchal ideal. A man should be cisgendered. He's meant to embody confidence, aggression and emotional stoicism. He's meant to look strong, muscular and tall. He should perform the role of provider and protector, rather than caregiver. When a man fails to embody these traits, he becomes insufficiently manly. Hussein Kesvani and I talked about who we as Muslim men were expected to become. He pointed to certain figures in Islamic history that provided him with an archetype of the ideal Muslim man:

> During Muharram [a sacred month in which many Muslims commemorate the historical massacre of Karbala], you have ten, twelve days of listening to the stories of these rightly guided men who had to reconcile looking after their family and communities, whilst also being soldiers and warriors. I grew up with the stories of saint Abbas who would kill thousands of men with just one sword and one horse. There were vivid descriptions of how muscular he was, how beautifully chiselled his face was and how broad-shouldered and tall.

Even within Sunni tradition, the Prophet and his companions have historically had certain traits valorized and, as Hussein described to me, for many young Muslims these have reinforced the idea that Muslim men today should try to emulate their strength, leadership, resilience and stoicism.

But these are not just vague models of possible manhood. I see how Islam can be interpreted to promote an exceptionally rigid idea of masculinity. For example, verse 4:34 of the Quran is often translated to emphasize a husband's duty and responsibility to take care of his wife. But in more conservative translations, he is framed as a 'guardian' and protector, dramatically altering the marital relationship to one where the man is superior. This illuminates how Islam can be manipulated to reinforce patriarchal ideas around a man's right to dominate women.

This isn't just about interactions between the sexes. Islam is also used to add a celestial veneer to the policing of how men are permitted to behave. I'd even call it a form of religious blackmail. One memorable attempt is the Hadith in the Bukhari collection, which claims that 'Allah's Messenger cursed those men who imitate women and those women who imitate men.' In the modern day it has been interpreted with a lot of creative licence. For example, a commentary from the website, 'Islam Question & Answer' states:

> [F]rom the ones whom Allah has cursed are those men who imitate women… So any man, who softens their voice like a woman, sits like a woman, walks like a woman, plays on people's attention like a woman and even uses the makeup that women use is included in this curse.[53]

I've seen this verse in other places, offered as an apocalyptic warning, a sign that the Day of Judgement is near. In December 2008, the Kuwaiti government used the Hadith to invent a new crime.[54] Imitating 'the appearance of a member of the opposite sex' is punishable by up to a year in jail or a fine of over £1000 and has been used, for example, to crack down on the transgender community, whose identities are reduced to an act of imitation.

The fact that patriarchy can be wielded as a weapon against men to make them fall in line is important. As professor bell hooks writes:

> The first act of violence that patriarchy demands of males is not violence towards women. Instead patriarchy demands of all males that they engage in acts of psychic self-mutilation, that they kill off the emotional parts of themselves. If an individual is not successful in emotionally crippling himself, he can count on patriarchal men to enact rituals of power that will assault his self-esteem.[55]

The unspoken truth of gender then is how difficult it can be for some Muslim men to navigate the complex web that they find themselves in. On the one hand, they're offered certain privileges because of their sex, but on the other hand, they're weighed down with duties and limitations on how they themselves are permitted to behave.[56] I believe most men are struggling in some way with what being a man entails and what it demands of them. This is particularly acute today, when masculinity is being placed under increasing scrutiny. It can feel like masculinity is almost synonymously spoken of in terms of its toxicity, for example, in terms of the abuse of power that the #MeToo movement seeks to redress. This can be bewildering. Moreover, the gradual erosion of gender roles that has taken place over the twentieth and twenty-first centuries, to the point where even gender itself is being deconstructed, has only brought the issue of what masculinity entails into greater focus. All men are grappling with very difficult questions, but in the Muslim context, Islamophobic stereotypes and dogmatic readings of scripture complicate this further. Many Muslim men end up adopting very normative ideas of gender, based around obligation, gatekeeping and entitlement, using narrow, historical models as their examples. Too often these men have little exposure to less patriarchal alternatives, models that might be more authentic to them and more empowering.

To me, the story of Abu Abdullah Hasanat is the embodiment of this existential struggle. In short, Hasanat was a social media star popular for his brand of ultra-conservative (Salafi) Muslim piety. He was married to another social media star, Umm Abdullah, and between them they had over one million followers on Instagram. In many ways, Hasanat was the model Muslim man. He fundraised for Rohingya refugees and travelled across Europe to provide ruqya, Islamic exorcisms. He appeared to enjoy a devoted, yet playful family life as a husband and father. Together, they inspired young Muslims to believe that it is possible to combine life in the West with a commitment to traditionalist Islam. But in June 2019, Hasanat's social media credentials began to crumble. Multiple accusations were levelled at him; that he was an agnostic, had stolen hundreds of thousands of pounds raised in charity funds, that there were multiple former wives (never mentioned on social media), and that he'd assaulted, abused and even cheated on them. Muslim Twitter went into meltdown, having been fooled into swallowing the false image. I watched the fallout and wondered how Hasanat had gained so much clout in the first place. There are many obvious reasons, including the lack of role models for young Muslims to emulate. One acquaintance confessed to having been drawn in by his beautiful recitation of the Quran. It strikes me that it is all too common for us as a community to confuse outward performances of piety with an inward commitment to the faith. That's how weak our collective understanding of Islamic expression remains.

And yet, there's a great deal in the Islamic tradition that actually subverts traditional ideas of what a man should be. Despite conservative interpretations, the Quran doesn't try to define masculinity, at least not in accordance with patriarchal norms. As Mona Siddiqui, a professor of Islam, states:

> [T]he various themes of the Qur'an appear far less concerned in defining men and women in terms of the socially constructed gender traits of masculinity and femininity... It is a text far more concerned with the moral dimensions of people's relationships to each other as well as to God.[57]

So the Quran speaks of the duties that men and women owe one another, but that's only because pre-Islamic society functioned that way. The majority of people lived within the gender binary and mostly occupied traditional roles associated with men and women. It's hard to believe that, following this, the scripture endorses fixed, binary gender roles or that it precludes them from evolving. Why would it? God only cares about who we are as people and how we strive towards being good.

The same is true for Hadiths. So many of them are called upon to police masculinity and femininity, but we rarely stop to think about how unreliable Hadiths actually are, and what narrators stood to gain by linking stringent gender norms to the Prophet. Even in the eighth century, Muslims recognized the necessity to regulate Hadiths, separating true Hadith from false. After the Prophet's death, the number of comments and practices attributed to him had exploded. Many individuals were reverting to their pre-Islamic behaviours and creating Hadiths to support their actions. By the late 700s, around seventeen hundred statements were credited to the Prophet. But a hundred years later, there were hundreds of thousands of often-conflicting Hadiths in circulation.

So Muslim scholars developed a sophisticated system to evaluate Hadith authenticity. By examining the 'chain' of narration across generations, they sought to trace every comment or teaching back to the Prophet himself. Several of these scholars journeyed across Muslim societies to track down and collect Hadiths, which they then evaluated for their reliability. The first such scholar, Muhammad al-Bukhari, reduced his collected Hadiths from 600,000 to just 2762, which he then wrote down and published. Other scholars went through similar processes of collecting, evaluating and then discarding masses of false Hadiths. However, this doesn't mean that the Hadith collections that do exist are perfect. They were compiled, after all, by humans, and humans are prone to making mistakes.

For instance, the Hadith about 'men imitating women' may be used today to create red lines around how Islam permits men and women to behave, but traditional scholars never did this. They believed that it had a narrow scope, referring to a particular instance where a eunuch claimed to have no attraction to women and was found to be lying. As Mark Brustman, a contemporary researcher into Islamic concepts of sex and gender, has suggested, the Hadith isn't concerned with gender roles, but with deception; specifically men posing as women and women as men for material gain.[58]

Prophet Muhammad encapsulates a more fluid understanding of manhood than some orthodox narratives allow for. The

Prophet was a tender, shy and kind-hearted man, said to be so modest that you couldn't pick him out in a crowd. On a superficial level, yes, he had a beard – and conservative or patriarchal Muslim men seize upon it as an integral component of Muslim masculinity – but from the Hadith (and traditional biographies), we know that he also had long hair and lined his eyes with kohl.[59] He cried, as did Abu Bakr, his best friend, who once refused to lead prayers because the beauty of the Quran left him weepy. Few Muslim men would be eager to co-opt these practices into their idealized vision of masculinity; on the contrary, most Muslim men would consider them feminizing. But they are integral to being a man. I asked Omid Safi, a professor of Asian and Middle Eastern Studies at Duke University, about this. He said, 'When we look to examples of Muslim masculinity, we always see a combination of strength and nobility on one hand, and tenderness and mercy on the others. When the qualities of tenderness are missing from masculinity, we end up with a toxic masculinity.'

Traditional Muslim masculinity unites strength and tenderness, and it disrupts what we increasingly consider acceptable behaviour for men. It is a history of men writing poetry to celebrate beauty and love, playing musical instruments and singing, of wearing clothes and jewellery that we associate with the feminine, all in pursuit of a spiritual connection. Sufis centre love and compassion in their lives in an attempt to destroy their egos and become closer to God. Rumi, for example, used music, dance and poetry to express love for his mentor, Shams of Tabriz, and grief at his death. Amir Khusrau is said to have invented the sitar and is considered the forefather of qawwali, Sufi devotional music. His poetry eulogized the flora and fauna of India, and the welcoming nature of its people. These expressions of manhood are just as valid, just as Islamic as others and we need to reclaim them to expand our understanding of who and what men are allowed to become in our communities.

Writing across the twelfth and thirteenth centuries, the philosopher Ibn Arabi had a far more sophisticated (and dare I say spiritual) understanding of manhood than we do today. He described the Perfect Man as a union of the masculine and feminine, reflecting the way that God was an embodiment of both worlds.[60] This idea, that masculinity can't exist in its full potential without some femininity, found a more superficial expression too. I spoke to Leyla Jagiella, a German cultural anthropologist, about this. She explained that:

> ... the ideal of beauty in the early modern Muslim period was one of androgyny. So, nobody would have told off a young man for doing something 'feminine'. You actually see glimpses of that still in some less modernized parts of the Islamic world today. A rural Pashtun man can write poetry about roses and flowers and shed tears in ways that would see him being called a 'fag' in the US Midwest.

I would go further and argue that Islam encourages us to be true to our authentic selves, in our unique, personal concoction of masculine and feminine. At 17:82–4, the Quran explains that the goal of the text is to provide Muslims with healing and compassion, 'So say, "All act according to their own *shakila*, yet your Lord knows best who is on the most guided path."' The Arabic term shakila has been translated to mean according to one's own 'manner' or 'disposition', even 'personality'. All expressions, even those relating to our gender, are supposed to bring us closer to God. So if God is encouraging us to be true to ourselves, this, I would insist, frees us from the notion that we have to follow a certain script on how to be a man. The only script that exists is on ethics and ensuring that the kind of manhood we fashion for ourselves doesn't end up hurting others. I wish more men – regardless of their faith and culture – took account of this when considering what it means to be a man in the twenty-first century.

*

As conversation in Western societies grows around 'toxic masculinity' and its threats, what becomes clear to me is how undernourished masculinity happens to be. I believe that men are often failed by our societies. For example, we expect men to intuit many things about the modern world. We expect men to be able to understand consent, even as the concept evolves. But we do so despite taking no responsibility for teaching men about what this means, even as patriarchal structures continue to initiate men in the way of entitlement and domination over others. In the Muslim context, I think men are failed by the fact that sex remains such a taboo. By failing to talk about it, so many of us know too little about intimacy and mutual pleasure in relationships – curiously, this takes place in a faith tradition where much of the Prophet's sex life was spoken about and then documented in the Hadith as a way of guiding his (and subsequent) communities. When you have little knowledge of these things, it's easy to adopt stereotypical and patriarchal ideas about men's unparalleled right to sex and intimacy.

Talk about the emotional lives of men – particularly by men themselves – is also undernourished. We need to be thinking about how we can remedy that too. It's important to call men out on their oppressive behaviours and indicate an alternative path. But as bell hooks reminds us, we must also take male pain seriously. And there is so much pain. How else can we change society if we don't have solidarity and love for all? So love is at the heart of this chapter. Love is the ethical, spiritual practice that governs my conversation with other men.

I write with love to say that I don't believe that gender has an essential expression, that we can stretch and expand what our masculinity means to us. We men need to empower ourselves to develop a masculinity that feels authentic; that isn't constructed *by* or *at the expense of* others. But I acknowledge that men can only be empowered to shun oppressive, patriarchal ideas of masculinity if our societies take meaningful steps forward and structure themselves differently.

As societies, we need to move away from gender norms and stereotypes, both at a national level, and also within Muslim communities. We need to stop shackling men from certain communities to labels and characterizations. We only end up internalizing and adopting them or, even worse, hating ourselves. We also need to stop assuming that Muslim cultures and beliefs are entirely responsible for explaining why all Muslim people behave as they do, as if we are a product of nothing more than those two things. As we've done with Harvey Weinstein and Brett Kavanaugh and Kevin Spacey, when Muslim men do something wrong, we need to grant them their individuality – rather than treating them as proof that entire Muslim communities are bad – and hold them accountable as *individuals*. In pursuing the prosecution of the grooming perpetrators in Rochdale, that's exactly what chief prosecutor Nazir Afzal (a British-Pakistani Muslim man) has done.

We also need to create access to diverse forms of masculinity; we need to create alternatives to patriarchy as bridges for people who don't necessarily know better. We need to give historical role models their complexity, for example, allowing the Prophet to be tender and sensitive, as well as a provider and protector. We need to provide positive public representations. BBC documentaries like *Hometown* (about the drug trade in Huddersfield) and *Lost Boys? What's Going Wrong for Asian Men* may contain grains of truth, may even be well-meaning, but they trap Muslim men. 'Where are we telling these kids that they can be heroes in our stories?' Riz Ahmed asked in a speech to the House of Commons in March 2017. 'People are looking for the message that they belong, that they are part of something, that they are seen and heard and that despite, or perhaps because of, their experience, they are valued. They want to feel represented. In that task we have failed.'[61] So we desperately need contemporary role models.

From one perspective, the BBC comedy *Man Like Mobeen* provides one, with Guz Khan portraying a Muslim man who plays against stereotypes as a caregiver to his younger sister.[62] But what can seem progressive from one angle can fail on another. Talking to a prominent British Muslim journalist, she reminded me that the show was not challenging enough; it was a male-dominated show without adult female characters. So we need our role models to do even better.

I spoke with Magid Magid, a Somali-British activist and writer, about media representations of Muslim men. 'If *Newsnight* wanted a Muslim perspective, they would get some bearded Muslim wearing a salwar kameez. They would never approach someone who doesn't fit their frame of who represents Islam. But the idea of the normal Muslim man is changing and the media needs to reflect that.'

Magid shared with me his experience of breaking ground in his community:

I was always interested in things that weren't deemed culturally acceptable. When I was sixteen years old, I got involved in drama through the Crucible Theatre in Sheffield, but there was no way I would have told my parents or friends about it. They wouldn't have respected it or understood. There was always a narrative of what you were allowed to be. But I know this was because we never saw anybody doing anything groundbreaking or different. When I got involved in scuba diving and travelling, people were like, "That's what white people do", but after, they were asking me, "How did you do that?"

Magid is refreshing. As a former Member of the European Parliament for the Green Party and the youngest ever Lord Mayor of Sheffield, he defies many of the stereotypes attached to Muslim men, and even expands the boundaries of how Muslim men can exist in public life:

I just try to be a decent human being. There's a lot of young Muslims boys who are interested in politics or other things getting in touch with me – they feel we have a similar identity – and I always try to be supportive. I'm like, 'You *can* do these things. You don't have to subscribe to a set value system.'

Above all, we need to provide greater space for empathy and healing. Being a man isn't easy. As the social psychologist Roy F. Baumeister puts it, 'A few lucky men are at the top of society and enjoy the culture's best rewards. Others, less fortunate, have their lives chewed up by it.'[63] Patriarchy thrives on subjugating others, primarily women, but it also sees men, male power and labour as totally expendable, to be consumed so that a minority can profit.

To all those young Muslims struggling with what it means to be a man, I finish with some wisdom from Islam – invoking remembrance of our heritage once more. One day, Ali, Prophet Muhammad's cousin, was passing by a group of men who were deep in conversation. He asked them what they were doing. 'We are discussing manhood,' they said. Ali replied: 'Has not Allah Almighty sufficed you in His book wherein He said, "Verily, Allah commands justice and excellence" [16:90]? Justice is to have a sense of fairness and excellence is to prefer others to yourself. What remains of manhood after this?'

It is OK to struggle, but remember, being a man is about rejecting power and domination. It is about being kind to yourself and to others. It is about committing yourself to just and ethical behaviour. Indeed, what remains of manhood after this?

4

'Islam Hates Women'

I s Miley Cyrus a feminist? This was the question that captivated a community WhatsApp group I was involved with in 2013. Cyrus had just performed at the MTV Video Music Awards, triggering widespread controversy for twerking against her fellow singer Robin Thicke whilst wearing a latex bra and knickers. The young Muslims in the group – mostly young Muslim men – were discussing the topic fervently.

'How can she be a feminist?' one of them asked. 'She's so sexualized.'

Another chimed in, 'And what's so radical about taking your clothes off anyway?'

I trod carefully, not wanting to shame these men for their views, no matter how much I disagreed with them. I knew that a public humiliation wouldn't help to change their minds. 'I think if Miley Cyrus says that she's a feminist – I don't know if she has – then maybe she's a feminist and we should accept that,' I said.

The most vocal woman in the group dismissed me: 'I'm sorry, but to suggest that Miley Cyrus is a feminist is laughable. She's just a money-making tool for rich record executives.'

The men took this as validation: 'Exactly! She's using sex and her body to get attention. She shouldn't reduce herself to a piece of flesh.'

'But why is it so difficult for us to see women sexualize them-selves when men do it all the time?' I urged. I reeled off a number of examples.

The discussion took a strange turn. One of the men in the group expressed his bafflement at Cyrus's choices. 'You wouldn't leave your house unlocked, so why would a woman go out dressed like that?'

I grew frustrated. 'But that's such twisted logic,' I wrote. 'We compare women to unlocked houses when we want to talk about their safety, and jewels when we want to elevate them. But why do we speak of women like they're possessions, as if they only exist in relation to somebody else? What about what they want, what they think? What about their choices?'

The debate raged on.

A week later, most of us met up for dinner at a South African steakhouse. One of the young men brought up the topic. 'I'm so glad we had that conversation,' he said. 'It really opened my eyes. You're right, women should be able to choose what they do with their bodies, and we men have nothing to do with that. And you're right, there's a double standard to what we expect from men and women. It really hurts, you know, to recognize that you've been wrong, and so unfair.' His eyes shone.

This might seem like an especially smug and self-congratulatory anecdote, but I'm sharing it only because this young man's feminist awakening reminds me so much of my own. I can't remember mine with the clarity that I remember his. I just know that it was a signifi-cant consequence of my involvement with a grassroots activist group for Muslims. I joined when I was around twenty-one years old. Before this, I lived an incredibly sheltered life. I was so concerned with my own suffering, I had an embarrassingly poor understanding of how other people were oppressed. It was like I had spent my life until then in a dark cave; activism was my portal to the world outside.

I remember organizing events and realizing how little I knew about the specific needs of minorities: women, transgender people, people with disabilities, for example. I remember the conversations about inclusion taking place around me where I had absolutely no contribution to make. I had to wise up fast.

In particular, it was my interactions with female activists that were the most instructive. These conversations redefined my understanding of justice. I learned that they were fighting for the kind of liberation that is traditionally granted to men. I learned that my freedom was intrinsically connected to the freedom of others; I couldn't manifest the kind of liberation that I wanted for myself if others around me were oppressed. And I realized that to truly believe in equality, I had to first grasp what inequality looked like. I had to understand the fundamental ways in which men and women were and remain unequal. I had to appreciate how arduous the work to redress this imbalance is, given that gender inequality is so deeply embedded in our societies – though we might not see it on the surface.

I couldn't help but reflect on the systemic sexual inequality that existed in British society and in my faith community. Patriarchy may have taken different forms in those spaces, but I mapped them on to one another. I saw identical attempts to restrict women to the domestic realm. I sensed a scorn for female authority and leadership, both in secular and spiritual spheres. I noticed a similar obsession with women's bodies, not only with their sexual and reproductive rights, but also with how they clothed those bodies.

Since then, I've come to appreciate how Muslim women tend to be at the forefront of many different battles, in this case the battles waged by Islamophobes and dogmatic Muslims. The Western stereotype is that Islam is a misogynistic faith; it encourages the subjugation of women by men and approves only of women who are passive and meek. The result of this stereotype is that Muslim women face constant interventions into their lives by figures on both sides of the conflict. Take the veil. For Islamophobes, it's the ultimate symbol of Islam's disrespect for women's rights and, for dogmatic Muslims, it's a minimum standard for female modesty, used by some to justify denying Muslim women their individuality. Both sides are concerned with controlling Muslim women through their bodies – one side with the literal and metaphorical veiling of women and the other with their literal and metaphorical unveiling. On either side, there is little concern for how women think and feel. There is little understanding of how they are harmed.

That harm takes place in countless arenas and it does not discriminate against Muslim women on the basis of their religious convictions. Unveiled women aren't immune from Islamophobic attacks, nor are conservative Muslim women shielded from religious interventions. The obsession with controlling Muslim women essentially wishes to contain who or what they are allowed to be and represent. This much was clear from my conversations with the Muslim women I spoke to. First, I contacted the journalist Myriam François, who shared with me the complexity of working in an industry that allowed Muslim women to exist in only a narrow window, constantly expected to answer to minority subjectivities: 'The opinions that you are allowed to express are only those that confirm the existing assumptions about our communities.' Furthermore, because François was not born into Islam, but chose to adopt it in adulthood, her faith was treated as some kind of brainwashing, because 'no woman in her right mind would choose to be Muslim'. If you pay any attention to media representations of Muslim women, this would come as no great surprise.

Aware that social media has only multiplied opportunities to pillory Muslim women, I also spoke to Ruqaiya Haris, a freelance writer, about her experiences on Twitter. She talked about the abuse she regularly receives from Islamophobes and conservative Muslims. There exist, on platforms like Twitter, expressions of the 'hegemonic narratives of what it means to be a "good" Muslim'. Anybody perceived to fall outside of that paradigm quickly makes themselves open to abuse: 'That kind of hate tends to focus on superficial things in a sexist way, like [the] hijab as that's easy and visible enough to comment on, and call someone liberal and not practising, so you become a pawn in their game of proving your Muslimness.' Then she also receives sexist comments from Islamophobes, that she is 'oppressed' and that Islam is 'a barbaric sex cult'.

Of course, Islamophobes can't see the irony in telling a woman that she needs to be liberated from what she believes. Their solution to the perceived misogyny of Islam is to assert their own patriarchy. Well, patriarchy is far more palatable when the perpetrator is white. That sentiment certainly came across in January 2016, when then British prime minister David Cameron announced plans to spend £20 million on English lessons for women in migrant communities. With the initiative, he aimed to encourage Muslim mothers to develop language skills that would help them to curb extremism amongst their children. Privately, he blamed the vulnerability of young Muslim men to extremist narratives on the 'traditional submissiveness of Muslim women'.[1]

In a matter of days, the hashtag '#TraditionallySubmissive' went viral on Twitter. Spearheaded by the author Shelina Janmohamed, Muslim women took to ridiculing Cameron's comments. Women with a huge and varied range of skills and backgrounds listed their achievements: medical professionals, scientists, linguists, athletes and political activists. I saw pictures of Ibtihaj Muhammad, the Olympic medallist who was the first woman to compete in the Games wearing a hijab, and Doaa Elghobashy, an Egyptian volleyball player. 'We are vibrant, diverse, we're talented and we have opinions,' said Janmohamed in comments to the BBC.[2] 'The prime minister is always saying we need to take up British values, so I responded in the most British way I could – with sarcasm.' Comments like Cameron's are so inane and stupid – and repeated so often – that Muslim women have had to rely on thick skins and a sense of humour to deal with a pernicious stereotype that views them as powerless. But it's no laughing matter.

I asked Samia Rahman, director of the Muslim Institute, about this. She tried to rationalize the two-dimensional conceptions of Muslim women that exist in certain Western imaginations:

For those people who don't have direct, personal contact with Muslim women, you might imagine that we live these really oppressed lives where we've been forced into these situations by the men in our communities. And there's a lot of pity and a sense of 'poor them' and righteous anger on their behalf, and that's quite a widespread stereotype.

But Rahman went on to share how burdensome and exhausting it was, especially in social situations, to be compelled to disrupt and complicate people's assumptions all the time:

Sometimes you just don't want to have those intense debates with people who have no clue. I mean, there's so much Islamophobia being directed at people's internal subconscious, you expect people to have no clue, even other Muslims – often other Muslims are also surprised at the positions that I take. So there have been many occasions where I have made up my name or pretended that I have a different job to avoid getting drawn into those conversations.

Talking to Samia illuminated the complicated web of harm that Muslim women find themselves within. Harm from non-Muslims who are ignorant, even contemptuous of Muslim women, but harm also from the voices within Muslim communities that use patriarchal cultural codes and narrow interpretations of the scripture to assert their control. Samia described being raised in her early years in a close-knit Muslim community in the North of England. Her parents later relocated because they felt that 'for us to grow up there as Muslim would involve being policed in the way you dress, where you go, what you do'. Reflecting on who she would have been able to become if the family had remained there, she said: 'I think I would be, as a Muslim woman, less able to push myself into spaces where it wasn't expected for a Muslim Pakistani girl to be. But I know that depends on many other factors too.'

Yet, the truth is that even when Muslim women haven't directly experienced Islamophobia or religious patriarchy, they're still forced to position themselves in relation to those narratives. Samia agreed with me, stating:

> It's damaging because it narrows our horizons. It pushes on to us these ways of being and being understood that affects how we can feel authentic in ourselves. If society is constantly telling you what you are, you begin to feel like there's something wrong with you for not falling within those categories.

I know that this is true, but I wanted a better understanding of why. I asked amina wadud why there was so much insecurity and second-guessing amongst young Muslims, including Muslim women. wadud is an African-American scholar of Islam and an imam, whose pioneering work has inspired many Muslim academics and activists. She said:

> People who are working on issues with Islam have to grapple with a history of patriarchal interpretations. So there's often a bit of fear that maybe the Salafi, black-and-white version of Islam really is Islam. There's a little bit of concern about that. But that's because they've [the Salafis and puritans] always had the public space.

The result is that Muslim women are never free to simply be themselves, to work out, at their own pace, the kind of Muslim women they want to be. They are expected to locate and develop their identities with this albatross of assumption and expectation weighing on their necks. Psychologists have found racism, discrimination and stigma to have a negative effect on our mental and physical health, and there are suggestions that it leads to isolation from one's identity, i.e. internalized self-hatred.[3] Samia admitted to this in our conversation together: 'I grew up with a lot of insecurity and internalized racism and self-loathing, as we all do, so I pushed myself to feel confident in spaces that people wouldn't expect me to be in.'

In the days after our conversation, I thought about how blasé we have become about internalized self-hatred, as if it is a natural state that all minority communities must endure. We are left with no choice but to accept, even embrace, our traumas, because it's unlikely that we'll succeed in addressing the source of this strife. It shouldn't be this way, but since it is, we should also understand how and why.

The stereotype of Islam as a faith that hates and oppresses women has a particularly noxious history. It is a history in which the West has repeatedly appropriated feminist language to denigrate Muslim communities, whilst positioning itself as the saviour of Muslim women. The feminist critic Gayatri Spivak described this relationship as the insistence that 'white men are saving brown women from brown men'.[4] What the West has always done – as Cameron sought to do when announcing English classes for Muslim women in the same breath that he called them submissive – is use Muslim women's bodies to both hide and realize its political ambitions.

According to Professor Leila Ahmed and her groundbreaking work *Women and Gender in Islam*, in the 1800s European powers used feminism to create a new colonial discourse focused on Muslim women.[5] It was a narrative in which Islam was 'innately and immutably oppressive to women, [and] the veil and segregation epitomized that oppression'. It suited the West to argue that 'these customs were the fundamental reasons for the general and comprehensive backwardness of Islamic societies'. Thus, only by abandoning these customs – and Islam itself – could Muslim societies become civilized and Muslim women be truly free.

So the colonizers essentially invented the argument that Muslim women were oppressed to justify continuing and extending the West's occupation of the Muslim world, and the destruction of its cultures. Lord Cromer, the British controller-general of Egypt, claimed that the treatment of Muslim women was the primary reason why 'Islam as a social system' was 'a complete failure'.[6] Christianity preached a respect of women, he argued, but Islam debased them. He singled out veiling and segregation, arguing that they had a 'baneful effect on Eastern society'. Therefore, Egyptians needed to 'be persuaded or forced into imbibing the true spirit of the western civilization' in order to succeed. This line of attack has formed the backbone of Western attitudes to the veil ever since. Admittedly, during colonial times, the actions of the colonialists were rooted in a Victorian-Christian aesthetic. Today, the religious vernacular has given way to a more secular language, but the logic is just as self-righteous. The West continues to deploy pseudo-feminist statements to disguise its military zeal and verve for dominating the Muslim world. And because the West still views the veil as the marker of Islam's inherent backwardness and inferiority, it features heavily in its attacks on Muslim societies.

I spoke to Suhaiymah Manzoor-Khan about this, who pointed out that women have always been central to conversations about what our nations and societies stand for, since women are seen to be the bearers and reproducers of culture. 'So forget Muslim women for a second, whenever you try to form a sense of patri-otism, you focus on women and create this ideal of femininity for women to aspire to, both in a literal and metaphorical sense.' Subsequently, women become the plane on which civilizations are both constructed and destroyed. Frantz Fanon, the anti-colonial intellectual, made this clear when he described the French colonial strategy in Algeria. He wrote, 'If we want to destroy the structure of Algerian society, its capacity for resistance, we must first of all conquer the women; we must go and find them behind the veil where they hide themselves and in the houses where the men keep them out of sight.'[7]

In 1958, France organized a series of demonstrations to show the support for its continued colonial rule over Algeria. It staged mass 'unveiling ceremonies' in which scores of Algerian women were unveiled by French military wives in a show of solidarity and sisterhood. The unveiling was meant to symbolize the Algerian women's 'liberation' from the terrible Muslim patriarchy (as if the patriarchy that spearheaded colonization is kind and benevolent). And there are plenty of more recent examples of this. In February 2001, at a star-studded production of *The Vagina Monologues*, a play written by Eve Ensler, Oprah Winfrey took to the stage. She read from a new monologue entitled, 'Under the Burqa': 'imagine a huge dark piece of cloth / hung over your entire body / like you were a shameful statue'. As she finished, a woman in a burqa joined her on stage.[8] Oprah turned and lifted the material from her body. Zoya, a member of the Revolutionary Association of the Women of Afghanistan (RAWA), was 'liberated' to the rapturous applause of 18,000 people.

But when interrogated, the feminist credentials of these interventions fall apart. Lord Cromer was definitely not a champion of women's rights. He restricted women's access to education in Egypt and he was a member of the Men's League for Opposing Women's Suffrage. In France, it would transpire, decades later, that many of the Algerian women used in the demonstrations had never worn the veil before, and were pushed into participating by their colonial masters.

Moreover, it can't credibly be argued that the West's Afghan war has improved the lives of Muslim women, though this hasn't stopped the Americans from trying. In November 2001, First Lady Laura Bush gave a radio address to announce that the Taliban was in retreat across much of the country. 'And the people of Afghanistan – especially women – are rejoicing,' she said. 'Afghan women know, through hard experience, what the rest of the world is discovering: the brutal oppression of women is a central goal of the terrorists.'[9] Then again, in 2010, when support for the war across the West was flagging, the CIA advised European governments to use the 'suffering' of Afghan women to 'overcome pervasive scepticism in Western Europe'.[10] But the Western ideal of femininity, and the corresponding charge that Muslim women are oppressed, is ultimately just another tool to ring-fence the power of white men. It continues to be exploited to maintain political and moral supremacy over Muslim communities in the way that it has historically – Western concern about Muslim women, at least when it comes from our political leaders, is often not about feminism at all. This shouldn't surprise us.

The stereotype of Muslim misogyny has had to adapt to life since 9/11. Muslim women are not just ciphers for Muslim tyranny anymore. The fear that all Muslims are prone to radicalization means that Muslim women are now *also* considered capable of terrorism. This 'victim-terrorist' complex shows how Muslim women are still afforded little space by the West to be anything outside of this narrow paradigm.[11]

The much-lauded 2018 BBC drama *The Bodyguard* is an example of this. The series follows a British army veteran-turned-bodyguard, who is tasked with protecting the Home Secretary. The show aimed to subvert stereotypes; the screenwriter, Jed Mercurio, described the twist in the finale as his attempt to subvert perceptions of Muslim women as 'weak'. But in reality, *The Bodyguard* fed into these stereotypes. It wrapped the 'victim-terrorist' binary on to the only female Muslim character, Nadia Ali. She begins as a meek bride, shrouded in black, who is being manipulated into killing herself by her jihadi husband. She is 'saved' by Richard Madden's bodyguard character, David Budd. And in the finale, she is revealed to be the terrorist mastermind responsible for the attacks that take place within the series. One stereotype merely gives way to another.

The drama came under heavy criticism for failing Muslim women. Samia Rahman told me that she felt incredibly frustrated with it, even as she empathized with the writer's ambitions. In a series of articles, Shelina Janmohamed described it as 'lazy, unimaginative and a simple re-hash of almost every other story told about Muslim women being oppressed victims, and evil terrorists'.[12] She lamented the missed opportunity to portray Muslim women in a way that wasn't 'painfully derivative'. But what is most disappointing about *The Bodyguard* is that it grants Muslim women no agency; in both iterations, she is brainwashed and devoid of personhood, a vessel for somebody else's ideas.

The media's constant reinforcement of stereotypes of Muslim women has real consequences. With over 11 million people tuning into the finale, *The Bodyguard* was the most watched drama in over a decade. Some news outlets capitalized on the story to warn of 'the danger of underestimating female jihadis'. In an article for the *Independent*, Lizzie Dearden wrote, 'The character's transformation [...] mirrors warnings long sounded by security experts over the dangers of casting all female extremists as unwilling victims coerced by male terrorists, or "jihadi brides" living out a perverse romantic dream.'[13] Carving menace on to Muslim women's bodies is far from innocent, and the media is complicit in the violence enacted against Muslim women in public.

The statistics make it clear that women who are perceived to be Muslim from their appearance are the most vulnerable to Islamophobic hate crimes. A 2018 report from Tell MAMA found that 58 per cent of attacks recorded were against women.[14] The Director, Iman Atta, commented that, 'not a single year has gone by since 2012 when we started work, when the majority of victims of street-based hate crimes have not been women'. According to the Muslim Women's Resource Centre in 2019, 64 per cent of Scottish Muslim women had experienced or witnessed Islamophobia; 74 per cent had been subject to some form of hate attack.[15]

Consider the experience of thirty-four-year-old Samsam Haji-Ali. In August 2016, David Gallacher approached her outside a supermarket in Bletchley, Buckinghamshire. He racially abused her, saying, 'You come here with your fucking clown outfit on, you fucking people, you are the fucking problem in this place.'[16]

He followed her and her husband to their car, where he attacked them, kicking Haji-Ali to the ground. When she shouted out that she was pregnant, he repeatedly kicked her stomach and left her bleeding. Haji-Ali was pregnant with twins. She miscarried them both. In May 2017, Gallacher was jailed for just three years and seven months.

Often, abuse against Muslim women involves attempts to unclothe them. In July 2018, two assailants in Anderlues, Belgium, called a nineteen-year-old woman a 'filthy Arab' before they removed her hijab, tore open her shirt and used a sharp implement to carve crosses on her torso, stomach and legs.[17]

There are several reasons why Muslim women are at the forefront of Islamophobic violence. Firstly and most obviously, Muslim women who wear some form of head or face covering are the unambiguous representatives of Islam, and Islam is seen to belong somewhere 'outside' of Western societies. Secondly, because of television shows like *The Bodyguard*, their appearance is also increasingly associated with terrorism. Suhaiymah Manzoor-Khan reminded me of how the image of the veiled woman is suffused with negativity: 'A Muslim woman, wearing hijab or niqab, is also put next to any negative story about Muslims, so we've come to know that this means difference in a bad way.' I know this to be true; every time I stumble upon an image of a visibly Muslim woman in the media, my entire body tenses in anticipation of yet another anti-Muslim story. Thirdly, violence against women is a common way of demoralizing communities under siege; it is, after all, a tactic of war. And finally, visibly Muslim women are attacked out of a desire to punish them for refusing to abandon Islam and embrace the liberation that the West is perceived to offer them.

Shamima Begum is an example of how these complex motivations come together in violence against Muslim women. Begum was the fifteen-year-old girl from Bethnal Green who, in February 2015, travelled to Syria with two of her friends to join ISIS. In

February 2019, *The Times* found her living in the Al-Hawl refugee camp in Northern Syria.[18] Almost immediately, then Home Secretary Sajid Javid announced the decision to take away her British citizenship. Begum is not just reviled for her sympathy for ISIS ideology – even though she was essentially groomed whilst still a minor – she is also criticized for rejecting the freedom that life in Britain offered her, and failing to show sufficient remorse when she wanted to come back.[19] It wounded our national pride. This is why a Merseyside shooting range began using her image as a target. When criticized, a spokesperson for the shooting range cited Begum's lack of remorse as the reason behind their decision to supply customers with the image. But it's the reporting of this event that is most disturbing. There was not a single piece of reporting or commentary that appeared to condemn the event – at least nothing that came from non-Muslim women. MP Angela Eagle's response was tepid, saying only that she 'disapproved' of using people's faces at the shooting range.[20] By and large, the media appeared to accept the claim that using the image of a girl for target practice was a 'harmless bit of fun'. In doing so, they implicitly suggested that Begum deserved such treatment. They ignored how this dehumanized Muslim women, and how it legitimizes violence against women who look and dress like her.

The effect of this new and pervasive threat of violence is often overlooked. Women, who are hyperaware of the danger that men often pose in public spaces (and it's primarily men attacking Muslim women), are left feeling even more anxious and afraid, reluctant to even leave their homes. A report by the University of Birmingham in 2013 documented the effect of Islamophobic hate crimes on Muslim women. One woman who had been abused on public transport said, 'It made me anxious of travelling on the train again […] when I took the train the next time, I felt really cautious of the other people around me. I was very anxious where I was sitting and who was around me. I became afraid.'[21] Other women spoke of the feelings of rejection from British society. Some talked of wanting to leave Britain. Others spoke of a growing dislocation from their identity: '[W]hen things happen to you then the identity crisis comes in and you feel that you do not belong anywhere. You start to question your identity: am I a British Muslim or a Bangladeshi Muslim?'

These feelings are universal to women who have been victims of crime, but the truth is that Western societies assert their ability to liberate Muslim women whilst finding new ways to shame and denigrate them. It isn't Islam's alleged misogyny that is the greatest barrier to Muslim women and their empowerment, but the flourishing of Islamophobia in our societies, and the audaciousness with which people are willing to attack Muslim women.

Islam is not an inherently misogynistic religion. In fact, Islam has always affirmed sexual and gender equality. God establishes that men and women are different, but equal. To a society that didn't believe, Islam introduced the notion that all individuals possessed free will and sovereignty. Verse 4:124 of the Quran states, 'As for those who lead a righteous life, male or female, whilst believing, they enter Paradise; without the slightest injustice.' So men and women face an identical challenge to embrace goodness and avoid evil, and have the same opportunity to enter heaven if they're successful.

This gender equality proved attractive to the pagan Arabs. Many women fled Mecca to the early Muslim community of Medina (where the Prophet was political leader).[22] They wanted citizenship and access to new rights. In pre-Islamic Arab society, a woman was like property. When her husband died, his eldest son inherited her to dispose of as he wished. But under Islam, a woman could now inherit in her own right. She could divorce her husband and provide witness testimony. She was an equal before God. This was nothing short of a revolution.

But citizenship didn't mean that women only had rights providing they were silent. Muslim women were the exact opposite; they constantly sought out the Prophet for advice and challenged him on the substance of their equality. In doing so, they actively contributed to the revelation of the Quran. Some women, for example, complained that the revelation barely referred to them. The Prophet's wife, Umm Salama, relayed this to him and the lengthy verse 33:35 followed. In providing a sense of equilibrium between 'the believing men and the believing women', it emphasized, once again, that equality was at the heart of Islam.

In another example, Khawlah bint Tha'labah, a woman from Medina, brought a problem to the Prophet. Her husband was an ill-tempered man. One day, when she refused him sex after prayer, he flew into a rage and divorced her. Zihar was a form of pre-Islamic divorce, which was given verbally, and it was particularly harsh on women (as it permitted the man to remarry, but not the woman), so Khawlah rushed to the Prophet for a solution. The Prophet informed her that he was unable to help. Frustrated, Khawlah raised her voice to the sky and cried, 'Oh Allah! I complain to you!' She spoke of her isolation and grief at being separated from her husband. She warned of the impact that divorce would have upon her children. Almost immediately, the Prophet received a revelation: 'Allah has indeed heard the speech of the one who argues with you concerning her husband and directs her complaint to Allah. And Allah hears your dialogue; indeed, Allah is Hearing and Seeing' [58:1]. The subsequent verse set out her remedy. Her husband could reverse the zihar by freeing a slave, fasting for two months or feeding sixty poor people.

This merely provides a glimpse into why the Islamic scholar Fatema Mernissi wrote that Muslim women can 'walk into the modern world with pride, knowing that the quest for dignity, democracy, and human rights [...] stems from no imported values, but is a true part of the Muslim tradition'.[23] Islamic history provides us with role models of Muslim women who shatter contemporary stereotypes about misogyny and subjugation. For example, Khadijah, the Prophet's first wife, was an incredibly successful businesswoman and one of the wealthiest women in her tribe. The Prophet had been her employee and remained so even after they were married. His other wives, Aisha and Umm Salama, were renowned for their fierce intellects and the Prophet regularly sought their tactical advice before going into battle. Some women participated in these early clashes; Umm Umara fought in the Battle of Badr and Azdah bint al-Harith once led a female battalion.[24] When Zaynab bint Ali, the Prophet's granddaughter, was captured after the massacre at Karbala and taken to Yazid's court, she issued a blistering sermon in which she both humiliated him and held him accountable for the atrocities carried out in his name. Far from being meek and servile, the history of Muslim women is an inspiring one, containing many such examples of courage and ferocity.

And early Muslim women refused to be treated as paragons of virtue and patriarchal expectation. Aisha was known to be jealous, rebellious and argumentative with the Prophet. A girl unhappy about the marriage being forced upon her by her father complained to Aisha, with the result that the Prophet established that a woman was entitled to choose her partner. In the seventh century, Imam Husayn's daughter, Sukaynah, drafted a marriage contract in which she enshrined her rights; she could ignore her husband's commandments, deprive him of sex and prevent him from marrying another woman whilst they were together.[25] By contrast, the average Western woman in the Middle Ages had few rights within her marriage and wider society, and even fewer rights to divorce. The only way to transcend marital obligation was either by being born into wealth or joining a community of nuns.[26]

Muslim women asserted themselves not only in the social and domestic spheres, but in the spiritual domain too. The Hungarian Orientalist Ignaz Goldziher once suggested that up to 15 per cent of Hadith scholars were women.[27] Of course, the men would have outnumbered the women – these were still patriarchal societies – but the real percentage is likely to remain unknown because, as Islamic institutions developed and privileged male scholars, many women began to teach in informal frameworks of which fewer records remain. But this still does little to undermine the wealth of female scholars that have existed in Islamic history, are known to us, and who happened to be amongst the greatest religious minds of their time. As of 2007, the scholar Mohammad Akram Nadwi had uncovered a lost history of over 8000 female Hadith scholars.[28]

In the seventh century, women like Umm al-Darda were sitting in the mosque with their male counterparts, discussing faith and teaching Hadith and fiqh, the legal philosophy underpinning the Shariah. One of her students was the Umayyad caliph Abd al-Malik ibn Marwan. She wrote: 'I've tried to worship Allah in every way, but I've never found a better one than sitting around debating with other scholars.'[29] In the twelfth century, Zaynab bint Kamal was responsible for teaching over 400 texts on Hadith in some of the most prestigious institutions of Syria. In addition, Rabia al-Adawiyya transformed Sufism into a mysticism of ecstatic love. She pioneered Sufi practice to such an extent that legends were conjured up about her; that she could fly, that the Ka'bah in Mecca moved forward to greet her when she visited.

Even as Muslim societies evolved and grew, Muslim women found ways to thrive within them. Research into early-modern Shariah courts by historians like Amira Sonbol and Philip Mansel have found that women (and critically this includes non-Muslim women too) preferred to use Shariah courts over secular courts because they could better negotiate their marital disputes within them.[30] In eighteenth-century Aleppo, women were involved in 40 per cent of all property transfers. In nineteenth-century Cairo, they were being educated at the Al-Azhar University and mixing freely with men.

Thus, Muslim women have a rich and empowered tradition to inspire their work on achieving sexual equality in the modern day. They have never needed to, and are not now required to abandon Islam in order to achieve gender equality. Western women were able to embark upon the journey of dismantling patriarchy without erasing their cultures, so why wouldn't Muslim women be capable of doing the same?

Any doctrine that proposes to shake up the status quo is bound to come under attack. The declaration to pre-Islamic Arab society that men and women are equal in the eyes of God was no different. Muslim women were speaking up and defying patriarchal codes. They were using the message of the Quran to demand greater participation in public life and the same right as men to raid merchant caravans and earn their fortune. For some Arab men, who had only just been taught that women were not property, this was a step too far. They had adopted Islam, but they had not anticipated that the Quran's message of equality would involve women possessing agency and autonomy identical to theirs; they refused to accept this. Many began to fight back, demanding that the Prophet affirm male supremacy. In the final years of the Prophet's life, the issue became so tense that it threatened to splinter, even collapse, the Muslim community.[31]

Unfortunately, the Prophet died before the conflict could be fully resolved. In the years after his death, Muslim men attempted to claw back the power that Islam had taken from them. With every wave of attack, Muslim women found themselves debased and excluded. This is why it's so inaccurate to pin sexism in Muslim communities and societies on Islam. Religion has the potential to empower women in ways that reduce the influence of men, so men inevitably find means of asserting their control over faith, to manipulate it in a way that serves them, thereby allowing them to maintain their hegemonic status in society.

The actions of Umar Ibn al-Khattab, one of the Prophet's closest companions, provide a clear example of how women have been excluded from spiritual life and leadership in this way. Umar had always opposed women attending prayers at the mosque, despite the Prophet having no problem with it. When he became caliph, he insisted more vehemently that women should pray at home. Although men and women prayed in the same space under the Prophet, Umar instituted segregated prayer spaces and separate imams (who were only ever male). These choices would define how religious spaces operate and appear to this very day.

Later, as Muslims formed empires, these heralded different lines of attack on the position of women in society. In the Abbasid era, Muslim society grew dramatically in size, stature and wealth. Men emulated the practices found in the foreign cultures that they encountered, keeping harems filled with wives and concubines. These were cultural, not religious practices. In the same period, new converts also brought their particular baggage to Islam. Importantly, patriarchy in Muslim society didn't traditionally stem from a religious belief in women's biological inferiority. This came from Jewish and Christian converts, since Genesis 2:21–2 lays out that Eve was created from Adam's rib, and Muslim philosophers adopting Aristotelian beliefs.[32] By contrast, the Quran makes no mention of this pejorative image; it only says that Adam and Eve were created from a single soul [4:2]. But scholars took the seed and planted it into Islamic theology. The later Ottoman period saw the system of Islamic education becoming more formalized. As a result, Muslim women were pushed further out of the realm of spiritual and intellectual leadership. As I stated above, Islam has a strong heritage of religious scholarship by women, but only male scholars gained official positions in the Ottoman court. Again, this had little to do with religion; it was plain sexual discrimination.

The significant point is that, despite all this, Muslim women were always negotiating societal patriarchy and finding ways to thrive. Female scholars continued to teach, even without official positions, and as some scholars suggest, became even better scholars because they weren't required to satisfy their Ottoman patrons. Unfortunately, the legacy of this has been the marginalization of women as leaders and scholars equal to men. Even today, in our mosques, women are regularly excluded, conspicuously absent in all-male committees, their prayer spaces an afterthought.[33]

Colonization made this negotiation of societal patriarchy increasingly difficult. The colonizers presented Islam as totally oppressive – especially towards women – even as the colonialists themselves afforded few rights to women at home. The stereotype choked Muslim societies, stopping them from developing organic and indigenous discourses on sexual equality. Instead, women's rights were caught in the conflict between occupying forces and the nationalist intellectuals. Those intellectuals may have supported women's liberation, but any change or improvement in the lot of women felt like a concession to the occupying force, especially if the proposed change (i.e. unveiling) mirrored the feminist discourse that was taking place across the West.[34] So Muslim societies ended up defending the practices colonialists accused them of, which were hardly representative – like polygamy, which in Aleppo, Cairo and Turkey was barely practised over the seventeenth to nineteenth centuries – simply because the call for advancement came from the oppressor. In this way, conversations around women's rights in Muslim societies have always been a response to the West's assertion of supremacy.

The other consequence of colonization is that many elite figures within the Muslim world took it upon themselves to liberate Muslim women. They internalized the message that Muslim societies were inferior and that religion was almost entirely responsible for sexual inequality. But the Muslim men demanding that their societies cast off anachronistic Islamic practices failed to recognize the class dimensions of their attack; these were upper-class, Western-educated men already aligned with the West, preaching to the lower classes. In doing so, they ignored the key message of feminism – a woman's right to choose for herself – and how the lower classes had particularly suffered under colonial rule and would, therefore, reject any suggestion of emulating them. So when the Shah in Iran and Atatürk in Turkey sought to eliminate the headscarf and veil from public spaces, the veil didn't disappear. In Iran, a generation of women – whose veils were ripped off by soldiers' bayonets, but who refused to be seen without some form of head covering – was simply confined to the home.

Indeed, the veil is a good example of how Western interventions have led to strategies and narratives of resistance. It has become an anti-colonial symbol; an opportunity for Muslim women to affirm what Professor Leila Ahmed describes as the 'dignity and validity of all native customs'.[35] This remains true today; many women adopted head and face coverings in their various forms to oppose the stigmatization of Muslim identity in the aftermath of 9/11. 'It's gotten to the point where I felt this is my culture and my heritage. This is something I have to represent,' Lisa Hashem told the *Washington Post* in 2002. 'I have changed so much after 9-11, and I think a lot of young Muslim women who felt we were being called terrorists really found ourselves researching our own religion and wanting to wear hijab.'[36] In this way, as amina wadud reminded me in our conversation, the hijab became less an expression of one's piety, 'although for many who wear it, it is the same as modesty, and more a political choice'.

More recently, an article in *Glamour* magazine explored why some Muslim women are choosing to wear the hijab. Social media influencer and blogger Asha Hussain spoke of adopting it at the age of seventeen 'to become more spiritually connected' to Islam.[37] She said:

The first thing I noticed was that people listened more to what I was saying. I was coming to people as a blank canvas and that, as a woman, is both empowering and liberating. It's addictive. I am not my hair, I am not my beauty, I am not my body. I am me.

As a social media influencer, I feel attitudes towards hijab-wearing women can be polarising. You're either portrayed as an extremist, ISIS sympathiser or an extremely oppressed woman – I'm none of those things. In reality, the

only thing extreme about me is how late I leave it to return
books to the library.

In the same article, Muna Jama, a humanitarian campaigner
and former Miss Universe contestant, pointed to a flexible relationship with the hijab: 'I love wearing a headscarf on certain days
and, at other times, practice my modesty entirely differently. That
may be wearing a kaftan, owning the catwalk at Modest Fashion
Weeks around the world or simply by being a considerate and
compassionate person.' For most Muslim women, agency is at the
heart of their decision to wear the hijab.

Conversely, puritan movements have also grown in Muslim
communities and societies in resistance to colonial interventions.
Puritans, who view women's bodies as a tool to preserve Muslim
culture and tradition, end up introducing laws that are misogynistic misrepresentations of Islamic doctrine, and are much harsher
than anything we've known in Islamic history. For instance, when
General Zia-ul-Haq took control of Pakistan in a coup in 1977, the
country underwent a process of 'Islamicization'. In 1979 he introduced the Hudood Ordinances, a series of laws 'inspired' by the
Shariah. Adultery became a criminal offence. Whipping, stoning
and amputations were introduced as punishments.

As a consequence, it became exceptionally difficult for a woman
to have her rapist punished; she was required to provide four adult
(male) witnesses to the act. What makes this law so gross isn't just
the callousness behind it; it's also a clear distortion of Islam. The
Quranic edict [4:15] that was reworked aimed to protect women
against spurious accusations of adultery by forcing accusers to
bring forward four witnesses of good character. But this, too, is
part of the colonial legacy, since many of the crimes contained in
the Hudood Ordinances were directly lifted from the old colonial
legal system.[38]

*

Despite the difficulties, it's possible to strip Islam of the layers of patriarchy it has accumulated over the centuries and recover its original, equitable core. Muslim women scholars have taken the lead in peeling back these layers, and it is their work primarily that I lean on here.

Some patriarchal readings of the scripture are easy to remove. Both Islamophobes and conservative Muslims argue that Islam prescribes a veil on to Muslim women. In some cases, they use 'Islam' as shorthand for the (few) political regimes where women are compelled to veil. But no verse in the Quran commands women to cover their heads or faces. Instead, Islam urges them to 'guard their private parts' and cover their torsos, as some women in the Prophet's time appeared topless in public [24:31]. When it comes to Islam and its supposed dogma on female attire, terms are easily and deliberately interchanged.

The other famous verse, 33:53, is also misused. The word 'hijab' is interpreted as commanding women to veil, but the verse is actually referring to a 'curtain' or 'partition' in its differentiation of public and private spaces. The Prophet's house was positioned within the mosque grounds, so the congregation treated it as a public space. But God reminded them that it was actually a private space for the Prophet and his family, so when invited, guests weren't to outstay their welcome. Moreover, the verse reminded Muslims that the Prophet's wives were also entitled to their private space, away from the male gaze. Some men lusted after them and spoke openly about wanting to marry them when the Prophet died. Others recognized the wives when they were out using external sanitation facilities and tried to abuse them. Thus, the verse encouraged men to speak to them from behind a curtain, fostering a culture of respect and reserve: 'And when you ask [his wives] for something, ask them from behind a partition. This is purer for your hearts and minds.' After this verse was revealed, the Prophet's wives adopted the veil too, but we need not interpret this as an instruction upon all Muslim women to do the same. Instead, using our linguistic analysis, we focus on the fact that the verse is an attempt to teach good etiquette to the Arabs of the time.[39] We can also interpret the hijab more abstractly as a boundary – one which men should observe when interacting with women. After all, the duty of modesty is placed on men's shoulders first – which is why, in verse 24:30, men are warned to lower their gaze.

But this leaves unanswered the question of how veiling, in all its forms, became so deeply entwined with Muslims. Contrary to assumption, Islam didn't introduce the veil to Arabia and its adoption amongst Muslim women frequently had little to do with religion. Some women were simply emulating the Prophet's wives. Others were converts and were already familiar with it, since the practice of veiling was widespread across the Christian Middle East. In Persia, the veil was fashionable, proof of a woman's upper-class pedigree.[40] So as Arab Muslims grew wealthy, some women adopted the veil as a status symbol. Somewhere along the way, standards of modesty for Muslim women were wound up in it.

As amina wadud summarized to me, 'the Islamic head covering has become very, very politicized when we talk about the ethics of modesty'. But it has also become politicized in representational terms. It's worth thinking for a moment about how the media's and Muslim communities' preoccupation with hijab serves to erase Muslim women in their full complexity, including the diversity of their choices and expressions. Myriam François said:

> The media has contributed to the very narrow perception of what it means to be a Muslim woman, and a narrow percep-tion of what a Muslim woman looks like. Now when a woman is called upon on a panel, unless she's wearing a headscarf, she's not really considered to be a Muslim woman, is she? There was a time when it was the other way around. But now, if you want a woman to represent or comment on Muslims, if she's not wearing the headscarf, there's the whole, is she really a Muslim? Do we want her to speak/represent on our panel?

Deconstructing Hadiths that create a secondary position for women is relatively straightforward. Most, if not all, are products of seventh- and eighth-century sexism. Consider the Hadith, 'Those who entrust their affairs to a woman will never know prosperity.' It's an incredibly weak Hadith. Not only does it contradict the Quran, which refers to the Queen of Sheba positively, but Abu Bakra, its narrator (not to be confused with the Prophet's best friend Abu Bakr), was convicted of false testimony. As the scholar Fatema Mernissi rightly pointed out, since orthodox scholars like Imam Malik argued that '[I]gnorant persons are to be disregarded', the conviction would invalidate all of Abu Bakra's Hadith narrations.[41] The Hadith is also misleading, because the Prophet issued these words in relation to a change in power in Persia, not in relation to all female leadership. But Abu Bakra chose to recount his narration when Aisha (one of the Prophet's wives) had mounted a battle against Ali (the Prophet's cousin) in his hometown of Basra. The Hadith was his attempt to undermine her.

Other sexist Hadiths fail on similar grounds. Consider, 'The Prophet said the dog, the ass and the woman interrupt prayer if they pass in front of the believer.' When Aisha heard this, she confronted Abu Hurayrah, the narrator. 'Do you make us women equal to dogs and donkeys?' she demanded, recounting how often she lay in front of the Prophet as he did his prayers. Abu Hurayrah is another notoriously dubious narrator; a man who spent three years with the Prophet, but recalled more Hadiths than any other companion – over 5300. By contrast, the Prophet's best friend Abu Bakr is responsible for only 142.

Abu Hurayrah was discredited in his own lifetime: he was accused of financial corruption whilst the governor of Bahrain. Umar Ibn al-Khattab (the Prophet's companion mentioned earlier) called him the 'worst liar' and threatened to exile him to Yemen if he continued to narrate excessively (and it appears that he stopped until Umar's death, when he began again). It may stretch credibility to trust a man whose own attitudes to women were questionable, but we mustn't allow Umar's opinions on women praying in the mosque to distract us or interfere with his criticisms of Abu Hurayrah. He may have been patriarchal, but he still had many other virtues. In fact, Umar enjoyed a reputation for being a brave, honest and honourable man. Moreover, other close companions, including the Prophet's cousin Ali ibn Abi Talib and the Prophet's wife Aisha, both corroborated Umar's views. Aisha remarked, 'He is not a good listener, and when he is asked a question, he gives wrong answers.' For these and other reasons, Abu Hurayrah and his Hadiths lack integrity. This is not just my conclusion; it's the conclusion of many Hadith scholars throughout history.[42]

Recognizing the patriarchal attitudes of the Hadith narrators and recorders allows us to uphold the Quranic commitment to equality by dismantling the sexist trope that women aren't capable leaders or the pagan notion that women are impure (especially when menstruating). It invites us to look again at the sources of Islamic law we consider to be infallible – the Quran, the Hadith, jurisprudence, the Shariah – and consider how male scholars and leaders were consciously and unconsciously responsible for weaving patriarchy *into* the faith. For example, Imam Bukhari included both of those unreliable Hadiths in his collection, but if the narrators were disgraced in their lifetimes, then why did he? And why didn't he record Aisha's rebuttals alongside them? This alone teaches us that scripture cannot be taken at face value, especially if it has the effect of sanctioning the unequal treatment of others.

Let me explain what I mean by this. I accept the divinity of the Quran. However, as Professor Leila Ahmed points out, reading the Quran has always been an act of interpretation, even at the very beginning. Early Muslims were using a language that had multiple dialects and an Arabic alphabet that wasn't finalized. But this does not make the message of the Quran less sacred; if anything, it makes central to Islam the possibility of multiple interpretations (and truths) within a single ethical framework. However, it does mean that reading the Quran requires work, especially as 1400 years have passed since it was first revealed. If we put as much effort as we do into understanding the words of Chaucer (which were written when the English language was similarly unsettled) or Shakespeare to fully appreciate what they wrote, then of course it would take a similar, if not greater, effort to interrogate the meanings and intentions behind the verses of the Quran. This might be difficult – the Quran is uniquely structured and often written in a highly poetic register – but we do have a Quranic ethos to guide us, namely the duty to be compassionate and merciful, and to uphold justice.

Similarly, we assume that the Shariah cannot be disputed because it is sacred, derived from God. But it's worth remembering that the Shariah didn't exist during the Prophet's lifetime, nor in the decades after his death. The Shariah is entirely man-made, using the Quran and the Prophet's teachings only as a starting point. Contrary to common assumption that the Quran sets out a detailed way of life for Muslims, it actually contains very little hard law (of 6236 verses in the Quran, fewer than 9 per cent are of a legal nature), and the law that it does contain addresses a much simpler society. The same goes for the Prophet's teachings.

The task of creating a centralized legal system began in the eighth century, many years after the Prophet's death. It was formed, in large part, from existing customary practice of Arab society and the scholars' own intuitions. And as Muslim jurists and scholars embarked upon this process, they were far from unified on what constituted Islamic law. Different schools of law developed (around 135), each with a different approach to developing the correct Islamic rulings and different conclusions as to what those rulings should be. It was not until after the Mongol invasion of Muslim lands in the thirteenth century that conservative Muslim scholars – believing the invasion had been punishment from God for veering too far from tradition – began to argue that the Shariah should take precedence over other forms of religious expression. They went on to claim that it had existed since the beginning of Islam and came directly from God.

Finally, some Muslims also approach the Hadiths as if they're divine and infallible, but a little knowledge of their development (as I shared in Chapter Three) would show this to be mistaken. Even as they stand, the Hadith collections present several problems in terms of reliability. Bukhari's collection, for example, includes Hadiths that describe the Prophet performing miracles – even though the Quran is clear that there are no miracles in Islam, only the Quran itself. A Hadith cannot be true if it contradicts the Quran. Moreover, Bukhari only travelled across Persia and the Khorasan region, failing to collect Hadiths from the Arabian Peninsula where Islam was born. Too often, he and other Hadith scholars cite narrators who were children when the Prophet was alive. And because men were overrepresented in Muslim public life, narrations by women are rare. This last point is especially important. These scholars deprived us of many female voices from this time, whilst the Hadiths became a tool for the many men who wished to maintain the segregation of the sexes and their superiority over women.

So what does all this mean for us today? Many of us – both Muslim and non-Muslim – want clear, unequivocal answers on what the Islamic position is on certain matters. Some Muslims pine for a return to Islam's foundations, believing that it will resolve the conflict of differing interpretations. But this is based on misguided nostalgia for an imagined Islamic society. They want a society free of all the peculiarities of human behaviour (such as doubt, disagreement, division) that not only exist now, but also existed in the time that they want us to return to. There is, truthfully, no 'reset' button. There are no easy answers. But this doesn't mean that we should feel hopeless either. If we are serious about understanding Islam, then we should embrace its contradictions and complexities, rather than trying to reduce them. We should embrace the diversity of thought that is embedded within its consciousness. And if we as Muslims want to build an individual relationship with it, then we must remain confident enough to construct it in an image that best reflects (for us) the Islamic values of justice, equality and mercy. As the Prophet is said to have stated: 'The best form of worship is the pursuit of knowledge.'

Returning to the stereotype of Muslim misogyny, religious patriarchy infuses all aspects of women's lives, so there are numerous layers to lift away. I can't deal with them all here, but I can show how language and context can act as key analytical tools. On the matter of language, consider how legal systems in Saudi Arabia, Egypt and Jordan, for example, treat a woman's testimony as worth half of a man's. They rely on an orthodox interpretation of verse 2:282 of the Quran which, in its discussion of financial contracts, says, 'And get two witnesses out of your own men. And if there are not two men [available], then a man and two women, such as you agree for witnesses, so that if one of them [two women] errs, the other can remind her.'

But the Quran doesn't actually enshrine the worth of a woman's testimony as half of a man's. The operative term here is the Arabic word 'tadilla'. This doesn't mean 'err', as commonly interpreted, but 'forget'. So the verse isn't arguing that women are inferior, and therefore are prone to making errors, only that they could be forgetful. At a time when women had little experience of legal and financial affairs compared to the average man, the Quran was offering the opportunity for one woman to remind another woman should she forget, rather than making a pejorative statement about women's equality. Common sense tells us that this is the correct interpretation, because if a woman's testimony didn't have the same weight as a man's then the Hadiths narrated by them wouldn't have been recorded at all.

The scholar Asma Barlas asks, 'Why would a God who is above sex/gender and who promises not to transgress the rights

of others, as the Qur'an teaches, fall prey to shoddy sexual parti-
sanship or hatred by privileging men over women or advocating
the oppression of women?'[43] It's a fundamental question we must
all answer. The Quran may have first spoken to a patriarchal Arab
society, but that doesn't mean it agreed with its norms. amina
wadud provided the clearest answer when I questioned her about
the issue of patriarchy in Islam. She said, 'I determine that the
Quran as a book of justice and human dignity cannot be taken literally and instead needs to be conditioned upon whether or not it
will achieve its goal of honour and dignity, and therefore, whether
or not [the rules derived from it] are actually permitted.' Her comments shouldn't be taken to mean the Quran isn't also the word of
God. Indeed, it's because the Quran *is* the word of God (and God
is the true embodiment of justice and equality) that all interpretations can only be valid if they empower and do not oppress. And
yes, within that, we must accept the plurality of interpretations
(and that interpretation is an ongoing process).

This is how patriarchal interpretations of Islam have been
challenged across the Muslim world, by constantly re-examining
and redefining what equity and justice between the sexes looks
like in the modern day. In *Men in Charge? Rethinking Authority
in Muslim Legal Tradition*, for example, a group of Muslim feminist scholars (known collectively as Musawah) came together to
overturn a husband's authority over his wife, a father's custody
rights over a mother's and the male guardianship system.[44]
Others have mounted challenges to specific personal status laws
that constrain women's rights regarding divorce, inheritance
and testimony.

And there are signs that this pressure is working. In 2006,
Pakistan amended the Hudood Ordinances with the Women's
Protection Bill, which took rape cases from the Shariah courts
to the civil courts, doing away with the requirement of four witnesses. In Morocco, the 2004 amendments to the Family Code
made significant improvements to the status of women in the

country, including easier access to divorce and to custody of their children. It also set the minimum age of marriage at eighteen and repealed a law that enabled rapists to escape punishment so long as they married their victims. Tunisia has always been one of the most progressive Muslim countries on women's rights; as far back as 1956, it outlawed polygamy, made a woman's consent to marriage essential and provided a judicial route to divorce. In December 2018, it approved a bill that entitles men and women to equal inheritance. Some of these amendments are imperfect, but they show how Muslim countries aren't static on women's rights. When first introduced to pre-Islamic societies, many of the older principles actually raised the status of women, but as just our notions of equality evolve with time, Muslim societies are demonstrating the ability to follow suit.[45] It is true; in many countries, this progress is frustratingly slow. We have an incredible amount of work ahead of us – there is much work to be done on all sides – but these examples give me hope.

Once again, it is tempting for Western nations to claw these achievements up as evidence of the successful exportation of liberal values, but who 'owns' feminism? In France, for example, a woman could not vote until 1944, could not open a bank account until 1965; women had limited parental rights until 1970 and abortion was not legal until 1975. The progress of women's liberation is as contemporary and has been as incremental in the West as anywhere else.

Indeed, when Islamophobes or even well-meaning liberal Westerners wring their hands about the fate of Muslim women and express the need for the West to intervene and save them, they overlook this progress. In September 2015, members of Femen, the Ukranian radical feminist group, stormed a French Muslim conference and stripped off to reveal the words, 'I am my own Prophet' and 'No one subjugates me' emblazoned on their torsos.[46] It begs the question, why are they so focused on patriarchy in Islam when it hasn't been eradicated from their own societies?

These individuals cannot comprehend the fact that Muslim women aren't passive, nor do they need saving. They don't require such destructive, imperialist strategies of assistance. They are their own champions. And advancement in the domain of Muslim women's equality has not been the result of Western saviours, but Muslim advocates and organizations like Musawah and Sisters in Islam, which are engaged in the critical, delicate work of challenging restrictive laws that are cemented by patriarchal engagements with the scripture. Even in Saudi Arabia, the success of women getting the right to drive or travel overseas without the consent of a guardian belongs first and foremost to Saudi women – many of whom have gone to prison for their efforts – and nobody else.

Rather than helping them, Western interventions cause untold damage to Muslim women. I mentioned this before, but it bears repeating. For example, in November 2011 the head of Ofsted, Amanda Spielman, revealed that inspectors would speak to schoolgirls on their decision to wear the hijab, claiming that wearing the hijab 'could be interpreted as the sexualization of young girls'.[47] In doing so, she singled out the hijab (and therefore Muslim girls) and no other piece of clothing for its sexualizing effect, whilst also dismissing the possible non-religious reasons why a schoolgirl might want to wear hijab, such as the desire to emulate her elders, or even express something of her identity and heritage. Would it be appropriate for inspectors to question non-Muslim schoolgirls about why they choose to wear skirts instead of trousers; would the length of a girl's skirt warrant questioning?

France is the best example of Muslim women being used as ammunition in the broader assault on Muslim communities. There have been many years of moral outrage about how Muslim women choose to dress – outrage that is disproportionate to how Muslim women dress in reality. For example, in a country of 4.7 million Muslims, less than 0.01 per cent of the population (amounting to fewer than 400 women) actually wore the burqa and niqab when it was legal to do so in public.[48] In every Western country that has vigorously debated the burqa and maybe even moved to legislate against it, the threat is grossly inflated; only a tiny minority of Muslim women ever adopt some form of facial covering.[49] (Incidentally, a journalist tried to find out how many burqas were worn in Germany. He found two – which were being worn by white women in an S&M studio.[50])

In 2004, France banned religious symbols (including head-scarves) from schools and colleges, and followed this in 2010 by making face coverings (essentially, the niqab and burqa) illegal in public spaces. Since 2016, twenty French towns, including Cannes and Nice, have also banned the 'burkini' – a full-body swimsuit – from their beaches. French politicians and commentators justify their attacks on two grounds. First, they argue that all forms of head and face covering are symbols of patriarchy, regardless of a Muslim woman's agency in adopting it. For example, the former prime minister Manuel Valls likened the burkini to a 'political project' based on the 'enslavement of women'.[51] Secondly, they claim to offer something superior: laïcité, a secular doctrine that bans religious expression from public places and unites citizens under shared values, rather than affiliations based on gender, ethnicity or religion. Thus, in an article for *BBC News* in August 2016, the French journalist Agnès Poirier wrote that the burkini challenged 'two fundamental French values and traditions: women's emancipation and a desire to live together as one nation'.[52] These supposed values are undermined by the fact that Muslim women don't appear to have ever been consulted on these laws before they were introduced.

Comments like Poirier's ignore how Muslim women have been shamed and humiliated by French society, and how many Muslim girls have been expelled from schools and excluded from the main-stream. As Ndella Paye of the lobby group Mamans Toutes Egales ('All Equal Mothers') said, 'Little by little Muslim women are being pushed back indoors, where it is harder for them to integrate with the French population.'[53] In some cases, Muslim schoolgirls were expelled simply for wearing long skirts and headbands, exemplifying how these laws also encourage the excessive scrutiny of Muslim women's bodies (and how any accessory or item of clothing can become 'Muslim' simply by a Muslim woman's decision to wear it).[54] In 2019, the French Institute of Public Opinion revealed that around 42 per cent of French Muslim women – rising to 60 per cent of those who wore the headscarf – had been subject to harassment at least once in their lives.[55]

It's an irony that can't be totally lost on Western nations; in purporting to liberate them, these paternalistic laws only erode Muslim women's agency – the cornerstone of sexual equality – by taking away their right to decide upon their self-expression.

We can reject the blanket stereotype of Muslim misogyny because it doesn't reflect the realities of our scripture and because Muslim women are not the passive objects that they're commonly viewed as being. But I also reject the stereotype because patriarchy isn't exclusive to Islam. All the major world faiths have contended with centuries of male domination and must now reckon with that legacy. For example, female priesthood has been recent and hard-won, and remains far from the norm. In general, the Orthodox and Roman Catholic churches do not allow women to be ordained as bishops and priests. Many Protestant denominations do, but even their oldest traditions of female leadership – Quakers and Methodists have allowed women to preach for approximately 400 and 200 years respectively – are no older than Muslim equivalents. The Muslim community in China has a tradition of female-led mosques and female imams spanning more than 300 years.[56] Furthermore, in June 2019 the Dalai Lama agreed that a woman could succeed him as leader of Tibetan Buddhism, but only if she was attractive.[57] So even in the faiths assumed to be the most liberal, female leadership is still subject to sexist considerations.

Similarly, it makes little sense to isolate Muslim communities from their secular counterparts, as the work of Western feminists is far from complete. The West hasn't yet succeeded in eliminating sexism from its societies and is even facing a backlash to what it has achieved thus far. Islamophobes like to portray Muslim communities as particularly cruel to women, even as a pandemic of gender-based violence rages on in the West. According to national statistics for England and Wales, in the year ending March 2018, an estimated 1.3 million women had experienced domestic abuse in the previous twelve months.[58] Of the 1800 women killed in the US over 2016, over half were romantically linked to their killers – that's around fifty women per month being killed by their current or former partners.[59] In 2018, the Thomson Reuters Foundation included the US in a list of the top ten most dangerous countries for women (which, admittedly, also included several Muslim countries).[60] The World Health Organization points out that the prevalence of domestic violence ranges from 23.2 per cent in high-income countries to 37 per cent in the East Mediterranean and South Asia.[61] Coupled with the fact that Muslim countries like Morocco and Tunisia are actively legislating against gender-based violence and harassment of women, we must ask ourselves the question, how different are the challenges for Muslim women and their Western counterparts really?

The answer, of course, is not very much at all. Some feminists, and Islamophobes especially, would like to believe that Islam is somehow unique; that the fate of Muslim women is much worse than the sexism experienced by non-Muslim women in the West. But that's just not true. Consider how *CNN* named 2018 the 'Year of the Woman' in the United States because 272 female candidates stood for election to Congress out of a possible 964 places.[62] This was historic for that particular nation, but with women going on to make up 21 per cent of Congress, it's by no means impressive. The figure pales in comparison to many other countries, including Muslim ones. In Sudan and Tunisia, for example, women account for 31 per cent of all parliamentarians (down in Tunisia from 36 per cent in 2014), and Tunisian women account for more than half of all elected local officials. But that is even less impressive than

Senegal, where female representation in parliament stands at 42 per cent, one of the highest in the world.[63] By contrast, as of 2019, British women made up 34 per cent of the House of Commons – up from 32 per cent in 2017.

Moreover, in some parts of the West, women's rights are nowhere near progressive enough. Northern Ireland has had strict abortion laws in place for several decades, limiting it to situations where the life or health of the mother would be in jeopardy. In the Republic of Ireland, abortion was legalized in 2018 and then only after a referendum. In some cases, Western societies have seen women's rights rolled back. Over 2019, the states of Georgia and Alabama took significant steps to narrow their abortion laws. Consequently, abortion is permitted only in the first six weeks of pregnancy in Georgia. In Alabama, twenty-five senate members voted for a near-total ban. But as American commentators began to frame these laws as the 'Christian Shariah', many rightfully fought back. In a Twitter thread, Dartmouth professor Zahra Ayubi explained that most traditional Muslim scholars believed abortion is permitted in Islam for up to seventeen weeks of pregnancy.[64] Many Middle Eastern Muslim countries have abortion laws that are more permissive than those being reintroduced in America.[65] Even in Saudi Arabia, a woman is able to have an abortion if there is a risk to her life or health, or when the pregnancy has resulted from rape or incest. Given the fact that abortion laws have come under attack in other Western countries – Polish government proposals to introduce jail terms for women seeking abortion in 2016 were abandoned after mass protests (only to be revived again in 2020) – how could it credibly be argued that the fate of a Muslim woman seeking to terminate her pregnancy is so much worse than that of all women living in the West?

In truth, it cannot, so we must emphasize the points of contact that exist between the activism of Muslim and non-Muslim women, and the shared cause. Many forget that the feminist cause rose up more or less at the same time in the Muslim world as in the West (the late nineteenth century), and it began with an identical demand for education. Their language, or their context, or their tools might be different, they might disagree on the desired outcomes, but the objectives of all feminists are the same: the elimination of patriarchy and the preservation of a woman's agency and integrity. The #MeToo movement shows how much space Muslim and non-Muslim women share. In October 2017, the American activist Tarana Burke came up with the 'MeToo' slogan, subsequently launching a movement to raise awareness about sexual violence and its corresponding culture of silence. In 2018, the Egyptian feminist writer Mona Eltahawy followed this up. She coined the term #MosqueMeToo to shed light on her sexual assault whilst on hajj, and many Muslim women took up the hashtag to share similar experiences of sexual molestation in sacred spaces. Both hashtags are part of the same movement – an attempt to take power away from men, hold them accountable for their abuses and change the culture of male entitlement. In our conversation, I asked Myriam François about the tendency to distinguish the challenges faced by non-Muslim women from their Muslim counterparts. She provided the most brilliant summation:

> I experience patriarchy on a daily basis, in various forms and from different kinds of men. The only difference that I can see is that some of them have structural power behind them, which makes them feel that their positions are safer. And others may have weaker positions, but a sense of righteousness around women that resorts to dogma.

Thus, separating Muslim women from non-Muslim women, and patriarchy in Muslim societies from patriarchy in non-Muslim counterparts, makes no sense at all.

When I reflect again on the stereotype of Muslim misogyny, it's clear that, regardless of the ongoing challenge of addressing patriarchy in Muslim communities, the West needs desperately to alter its representation of Muslim women. To provide legitimacy to its claims, it has committed many grave mistakes. It has championed figures like the activist Ayaan Hirsi Ali, encouraging them to lead the charge against Islam even after it was revealed that she had lied about her account of forced marriage and domestic violence. It has curated stories that confirm its own prejudices. *Forbidden Love*, a biography by the Jordanian writer Norma Khouri, was incredibly popular, but when it turned out she had constructed parts of the story, her publisher, Random House, admitted that it had ignored warnings of errors because of the 'global post-September 11 demand for non-fiction, particularly books which perpetuate negative stereotypes about Islamic men'.[66]

The most striking example of this myopia is the story of 'Iranian ninja assassins'. In 2012, the Iranian-run Press TV shared clips of Iranian women learning ninjutsu, the Japanese martial art, in Tehran. Soon after, the *Telegraph* ran a story entitled 'Iran trains ninjas as potential assassins', declaring that the government was preparing the women for war. The *Guardian* and the *Atlantic* took pseudo-feminist angles, arguing that the women were 'fighting for sexual equality' in societies where their participation is 'arduous and painful'.[67]

The possibility that these women weren't 'Jihadi Janes' and weren't trying to break out of their misogynistic societies was apparently lost on Western commentators. It's only right that some of the women sued for defamation; these representations rob Muslim women of their humanity, stripping them down to superficial archetypes for Western consumption, bereft of agency and complexity. It's a kind of fetishization of Muslim women, a common colonial practice (harking back to when European photographers produced pictures of veiled Muslim women revealing their naked bodies) that has resurfaced with the popularity of 'hijabi porn'. Recently, a friend remarked that the 'problem' with Muslim women was how they made themselves unavailable to wider society. He could have taken it further and said that the problem is how the veil symbolizes Muslim women's unavailability to Western *men*. It's crucial to hold the male gaze to account in our conversations about Muslim women, particularly against the history of white men lusting after their 'exoticness', perceived availability and sexual permissiveness. In our obsession with ensuring that Muslim women are empowered, perhaps we could begin by reflecting on how our fantasies constrain them.

By refraining from reductive stereotypes, we can give Muslim women more freedom to work out who they are and want to be without reference to external definitions. And we will create space to look past religion and culture towards the historical and political reasons that often better explain the disempowerment of some women. It's significant that the American displacement of the Taliban in Afghanistan didn't improve the lives of Afghan women; it wasn't misogyny that disempowered them, but specific social and economic factors, namely decades of war, the fracturing of Afghan society and the poverty ensuing as a result.

At the same time, I don't deny that patriarchy exists within Muslim communities. We should acknowledge this and strive to eliminate it without behaving as if patriarchy is a problem that is inherent and exclusive to Islam. The work of realizing God's message of sexual equality is well underway. I've described some of that work above and elsewhere in the book. I also want to bring attention to the inclusive and female-led mosques that are cropping up in the Western world, such as the el-Tawhid Juma Circle in Toronto, the Inclusive Mosque Initiative in London or the Mariam Mosque founded by Sherin Khankan in Copenhagen. Since my mother was my first religious teacher – as our mothers tend to be – the idea that women would not have an equal right over religious interpretation and leadership is strange to me. amina wadud, one of the first women to be invited to lead a mixed congregation in prayer, reminded me of the strong ground for female spiritual leadership;

the Quran doesn't prevent women from leading prayers, nor does it specify that only men can become imams. Moreover, the Prophet once appointed a woman, Umm Waraqa, to lead the people of her area in prayer as the mosque was too far from them to travel to. As Sherin Khankan said in an interview, 'It's not a reform. We're going back to the essence of Islam.'[68]

To realize the true equalizing capacity of Islam, Muslim women scholars have argued (as I have above) that the Shariah is not sacred. It is not infallible. The rights contained in it are not divine. The notion of infallibility comes from the argument that our schools of law are essentially in agreement. But there were, and remain, significant divergences between the madhabs (the different schools of Islamic jurisprudence), which have massive consequences on women's lives. If scholars then couldn't agree whether the right to divorce belonged only to a man and whether he was unrestricted in his right to marry four wives, for example, why must we accept these ideas now?

In my conversation with Samia Rahman, I suggested that the Quran and the values it articulates should be the starting point for conversations about equality. Samia agreed: 'To be Muslim, to be practising, is an ongoing process. It's constantly building on the ideas of the past, taking the lessons of the Quran and applying them to your contemporary existence.' This was something that amina wadud expressed to me too: 'We're saying that that norm is historically, culturally limited and that we have moved on, and we have moved on to a deeper understanding of Islam and how Islam, as the tawhidic religion, therefore, makes a space for women's spiritual leadership.'

Islam as the tawhidic religion has been the intellectual and spiritual foundation for all of wadud's work.[69] Tawhid is the most important principle in Islam – the idea that God is One, the Creator and Sustainer of the universe. But as wadud explained to me, tawhid has many layers of meaning, including God's ability to unite what are seemingly disparate, disconnected opposites.

'So, in other words, if you believe in tawhid, you cannot believe in patriarchy because patriarchy is based upon a binary that necessarily must have one in charge or superior to the other.' It might be taking time for some Muslims to realize that inequality of any kind is irreconcilable with the key tenets of Islam, but the countless signs of change leave me feeling encouraged. As Mona Eltahawy emphasizes in her book, *Headscarves and Hymens: Why the Middle East Needs a Sexual Revolution*, our states and societies cannot prosper until women are empowered to prosper within them.[70] Full sexual equality is the only way.

5

'Islam Is Homophobic'

In 2008, I moved to Bethnal Green in East London. Like so many other parts of the city, it was an area of diverse cultures and narratives, a microcosmic world of East Enders and silk-weavers' houses, Bangladeshi shops and queer-friendly bars. I had chosen to live there for that very reason. I stayed in London for several years. In that time, I joined a group of Muslim activists and tentatively began to explore my conflicted relationship with Islam.

Around February 2011, reports started coming out, on social media at first and then in the local and national press, of homophobic stickers appearing on the streets of East London. In total, sixty-five were stuck to lampposts and walls; fifty in the borough of Tower Hamlets. 'Arise and Warn', they said. The area was a 'Gay-Free Zone'. Locals were cautioned to 'Fear Allah; Verily Allah is Severe in Punishment', citing verse 74:2 of the Quran.

Immediately, the stickers commanded public attention. They were compared to signs that had once designated 'Jew-free' zones in Nazi Germany. And as media coverage grew, the narrative rapidly took on an Islamophobic tone. Activists and journalists complained about the public's 'unwillingness' to blame rising anti-LGBT hate crimes in Tower Hamlets on the area's Muslim population. Journalists like Johann Hari fashioned a conflict between East London's LGBT community and its Muslim one, as did some LGBT activists.[1] But reading the Quranic verse more closely it's apparent that verse 74:2 isn't a call to arms for moralists and vigilantes. The previous verse begins, 'Oh you who covers himself with a garment,' making it clear that Prophet Muhammad is the one being addressed and reminded of his duties as God's messenger.

Eventually, the perpetrator was caught and fined £100. He was Muslim, an eighteen-year-old unemployed man living in Tower Hamlets. But before that, certain members of the LGBT community scrambled to respond. A group of six individuals quickly scheduled a pride march for 2 April 2011. They argued that LGBT people were being targeted once again. Their 'East End Gay Pride' would be a 'morale booster for the gay community'. The lead organizer, Raymond Berry, said: 'We want to send a message that this is actually a very friendly area. We're here, we're queer, so get used to it.'[2]

Berry claimed the event would celebrate the area's open-mindedness, but from the moment it was announced local LGBT groups had concerns. This march could be misused easily, scapegoating the entire Muslim community for the actions of a few. It was a reasonable fear: the national conversation was almost exclusively about homophobia and transphobia festering in Muslim communities. There were articles in the *PinkNews*, for example, that covered the unfolding story. The comment sections were filled with racist and Islamophobic abuse labelling Prophet Muhammad a 'paedophile' and expressing the wish for Britain to become a 'Muslim-free zone'. An activist friend would try to reply and neutralize the comments, but it was hopeless.

From the outset, the affected communities questioned the motives of the march. The organizers had announced their wish to make the pride march a 'politics-free' event and the community considered this impossible. All marches are fundamentally political. Disavowing any explicit political statements would not mean that the event would be absolved of all political narratives. If anything, it opened up the possibility of the event being appropriated by Islamophobes and used as a fascist platform to advance anti-Muslim bigotry.

These motives came under scrutiny once more when local groups tried to get involved and the organizers were unresponsive. It transpired that several organizers were not even from London and that they had failed to consult and involve local activists, undermining the claim that this was an event organized by and for the community. Moreover, discussions on a Facebook page created for the event suggested that coach-loads of people were planning to join the march from across the UK. This opaqueness and organizational slipperiness left local activists suspicious. Why would a pride march ignore its community and overlook potential misappropriation by anti-Muslim bigots? Why would the organizers ignore calls to tackle prejudice of all kinds? Why try to depoliticize an inherently political action? Perhaps they had ulterior motives.

As activists continued to push them for inclusion, one of my colleagues from the activist group that I was involved in started to investigate. Pretty soon he struck gold. My colleague, it transpired, was a member of the same transport workers' union as the lead organizer, Raymond Berry. He learned that Berry was a founding member of the EDL. He had been one of its leading proponents until changes to their leadership caused him to curtail his involvement. Berry was now working with other former EDL members on projects that had similar goals: to stop what they perceived to be the encroachment of Islam on British society. He also remained an active member of other anti-Muslim groups, including Stop the Islamisation of Europe. Berry's Islamophobia was indisputable. So too was the connection between the 'East End Gay Pride' and the far right.

We decided to reveal this information and, on 15 March 2011, issued a press release. It accused the organizers of exploiting the sticker scenario to spread anti-Muslim prejudice. The march would implicitly blame the Muslim community for the stickers and help solidify the idea of Muslim homophobia and transphobia in East London. The statement found its way into the national print and online media. That same day, Berry resigned as the event organizer. On 17 March, the march itself was cancelled. One of the remaining organizers, David Byatt, was unrepentant. He accused groups critical of their event of setting out to 'divide the community'.[3]

These claims couldn't have been further from the truth. When we chose to reveal Berry's fascist beliefs, the goal was not to protect fragile Muslim egos or undermine valid concerns about the LGBT community's safety. We sought to prevent the local LGBT community from being thrust into a conflict with their Muslim neighbours. The goal was to stop the event from being used as a cover for anti-Muslim bigotry. A march went ahead later, in September 2011. It involved and consulted with local groups, and it called out multiple forms of prejudice simultaneously, making it known that homophobia and transphobia were just as unacceptable as Islamophobia. I wasn't there on the day, but I saw pictures online; the atmosphere looked joyous and defiant.[4]

For me, being part of it all was fascinating as well as distressing. Once again, it demonstrated the duality of the struggle faced by Muslims. On the one hand, there was the Muslim individual who decided, using these stickers, to preach a form of Islam that excluded and condemned sexual minorities. For those of my friends who were queer, Muslim and had experienced similar exclusion, this was hard to swallow. But on the other hand, there was the insidious way this event was co-opted to make a grand statement about Muslim intolerance, and this was equally dispiriting. It doesn't matter whether it's LGBT rights, women's rights, masculinity, violence or integration – Islamophobes are constantly appropriating current affairs to discredit Islam. Witnessing this tactic first-hand was instructive; not only did it shape my awareness of the precarious situation that LGBT Muslims live in, but it went on to inform my knowledge of how LGBT rights could be used to stigmatize Muslim communities.

*

Regardless of the context, bigotry causes harm. Because mainstream interpretations of Islam assert that the Quran condemns homosexuality, in the LGBT Muslim context this harm is rooted in exclusion and erasure. It goes unacknowledged by imams and religious leaders, who lack the ability to deal substantively with the humiliation and exclusion LGBT people face. It is the harm caused when individuals are expected or forced to marry opposite sex partners – harm to the individual and harm to the partner, who finds themself (knowingly or unknowingly) attached to somebody not attracted to them and not capable of meeting all of their needs. It is the harm caused by those who advocate or carry out exorcisms or conversion therapy. It is the emotional and mental harm caused by secrecy, shame and stigma, and a lack of acceptance. It is the harm caused to LGBT people when they suffer violence from families and strangers, when they are made homeless or disowned. And it is the harm caused when LGBT communities fail to create safe, welcoming spaces for Muslims, or insist that being LGBT and Muslim is inherently contradictory.

For instance, Vanessa Taylor, a Black queer Muslim from Philadelphia, has written about the alienating experience of being a Muslim in mainstream LGBT environments:

> I have entered LGBT+ spaces conscious of how people watch me, as if they're waiting to see what I will do. I seem to exist only as ignorant ally, just dipping my toe, or as outright enemy, but I am never seen as having the capacity to be a valid member of the community... If LGBT+ Muslims are ever acknowledged, we are seen as modern discoveries instead of being regarded as members of communities that have long existed outside of the mainstream.[5]

I talked to my friend Urooj Arshad about all this. Urooj is a queer, American-Pakistani Muslim activist. She's on the steering committee for the Muslim Alliance for Sexual and Gender

Diversity (MASGD), a US-based organization for Muslims identifying along the LGBT spectrum. What kept coming up in our conversation was the dual nature of the harms faced by many LGBT Muslims, as I mentioned above. The stigma of being excluded by one's religious community was compounded by the current climate of anti-Muslim bigotry. 'The biggest issue is that people feel so isolated,' she said. 'And on top of that rejection from the community, you have a larger context of living in America and experiencing Islamophobia. You have people thinking that they really don't have anywhere to turn to for support.'

She singled out an individual from her community, a twenty-six-year-old gay Muslim who died some years ago. He had concealed his HIV status from his friends and family until he was hospitalized. His death was almost entirely due to internalized shame, and the feeling that he had no resources at his disposal, not amongst fellow Muslims nor amongst fellow LGBTs. It's heart-breaking, the way that shame and stigma collide and cause harm. As HIV activists said in the 1980s and 1990s, silence equals death.

Urooj's comments reminded me of the fact that, through my activism, I personally know of at least two young Muslim men who took their lives after battling with, amongst other things, their sexualities. It is poignant to consider that one of the essential functions of Islamic law and thinking is to prevent harm and protect life, and in too many instances like these, Muslim communities cannot manage either.

In 2015, the national press covered the story of Nazim Mahmood. Nazim was a thirty-four-year-old British Pakistani. He was, by all appearances, happy and successful; a Harley Street doctor who had recently opened his third medical clinic, a treatment centre offering Botox, dermal fillers and other injectables. He and his partner of thirteen years had just bought an apartment in West Hampstead. But three months after moving into this apartment, Nazim leapt from the balcony and died. In the initial reports, it was unclear why Nazim had taken his own life – the press focused on the details of his personal and professional success – but his fiancé, Matthew Ogston, soon came forward. Had he not, we might never have understood the pain and conflict that motivated Nazim's decision. Matthew revealed that Nazim had come out to his mother just days before his death.[6] She had rejected his sexuality, insisting that he see a psychiatrist to 'cure himself'. Nazim was crushed. With Matthew's media interviews, the tone of the coverage changed. The *Guardian* headline, for example, acknowledged the central conflict between Nazim's family and his sexuality: 'My boyfriend killed himself because his family couldn't accept that he was gay.' Matthew went on to set up the 'Naz and Matt Foundation', a charity dedicated to combating 'homophobia triggered by religion', and this also received substantial media attention.

Those years of activism taught me this: although many different Muslims are struggling, LGBT Muslims are the vulnerable, invisible heart of a growing conversation around Islamic homophobia and transphobia, and it leads them to experience a great deal of harm, both internally and externally. Their identities are fought over by gatekeepers everywhere. Within the LGBT mainstream, Muslims are shut out for belonging to a religion that appears to condemn same-sex love. Within the Muslim mainstream, sexual diversity remains a taboo. LGBT Muslims are regularly informed that their sexual and gender identities take them outside the fold of Islam. Both sides imply there is a choice – but the reality is, just as you cannot suppress or change your true gender or whom you love, you don't stop being treated as a Muslim by wider society even when you're struggling to identify with the faith. LGBT Muslims face intrusive questioning almost constantly; their identities are endlessly scrutinized. This takes an inevitable toll. LGBT Muslims must labour to find themselves within these competing narratives. Sometimes this can be too much to bear and we lose people because of it. It causes me so much sadness.

*

When I think back to the events relating to the East End Gay Pride, the organizer's right-wing sympathies no longer shock me, but back then I didn't realize how popular this would become. Now the connection between white gay men and fascism is far from new. But instrumentalizing LGBT rights to further xenophobic goals certainly is. It is worrying. Affinity with the far right is growing within LGBT communities. This rise is, in part, because of the way Islamic belief is seen to reject sexual diversity. Islamophobes continue to propagate the message that Muslims are opposed to LGBT equality. And because fascists also happen to be anti-immigrant racists, they use immigration and the visibility of Brown and Black bodies in Western countries to stoke existentialist fears. The implication is, if LGBT people don't stand up, Muslims will demolish their rights and freedoms, perhaps eliminate them altogether.

Google 'LGBT and the far right' and you'll find countless articles charting the rise in LGBT support for far-right movements. What makes this remarkable is that one would consider such support antithetical to the viability of the LGBT community; if anything, they have inherently oppositional identities. There is a long and uncomfortable history of far-right violence against LGBT people. This is highlighted by the 1999 nail-bombing of the London gay pub, the Admiral Duncan, by David Copeland, a neo-Nazi, or the 50,000 gay men who were imprisoned and 15,000 killed during the Holocaust. Nevertheless, in Germany, Alice Weidel, a lesbian, leads the far-right Alternative für Deutschland party, which, as of 2017, stands as the largest opposition party in the Bundestag. In France, Marine Le Pen has actively courted the LGBT vote, promising that a vote for her party will result in the protection of LGBT people from Islamist violence.[7] Le Pen is more popular than some LGBT people in France may care to admit: polling by gay app Hornet found that one in five of 3200 gay men were planning to vote for her.[8] It appears then that LGBT people in France are willing to support Le Pen in spite of her previous comments: that homosexuality was a 'biological anomaly' and that people with HIV should be forced to live in 'AIDS-atoriums'. The US presidential election in 2017 reflected a similar trend: 14 per cent of LGBT Americans voted for Trump, despite the fact that his running mate, Mike Pence, has consistently opposed LGBT legislative equality and supports 'gay conversion therapy'.[9] In the unholy alliance between fascists and LGBTs, Islam is always the common enemy. As one French voter said to Associated Press around the time of the 2017 French elections: 'Faced with the current threats, particularly from radical Islam, gays have realized they'll be the first victims of these barbarians, and only Marine is proposing radical solutions.'[10]

This argument has real power and it isn't just rhetoric; it has trickled down and had an impact on Western societies. On immigration, for example, UKIP has successfully dictated anti-immigration sentiment and policy in Britain. The most senior gay figure in the party, MEP David Coburn, used the safety of British LGBTs to justify clamping down on Muslim refugees: 'Many of these people, as we've heard, are ISIS,' he said. 'I don't know about you but I am a homosexual and I do not want to be stoned to death.'[11] In January 2017, when President Trump issued an Executive Order to ban the citizens of seven Muslim-majority states from entering the United States, the justifying rhetoric also cited the need to protect LGBT people from 'radical Islam'.[12]

To some extent, I can understand why this message is so compelling. The chosen evidence builds a convincing picture. Iran hangs gay men. ISIS throws them off buildings. Egypt pursues, jails and tortures them. It's not difficult to see why white men especially – who've gained the most from legislative advancements and changing social attitudes – are becoming increasingly aware that these rights are, in fact, unstable. They rest on societal and government acquiescence. The moment that either of them rescinds this tolerance, life as a sexual minority becomes much more difficult. It is easy for the far right to impress upon vulnerable minorities the idea that Muslims are powerful and malignant and must be stopped. It is easy to build a picture of Muslims, fuelled by their 'hateful' text, eroding British tolerance. To that, I have to briefly point out: Western societies do not need Muslim assistance in rolling back civil rights and entitlements. In many places, they are already doing so, entirely without Muslim interference. The situation in the US is the perfect example. President Trump's record on LGBT equality is abysmal. In his first year of office, the Trump administration refused to recognize pride month, tried to reinstate the ban on transgender people in the military and nominated to positions of power countless people with anti-LGBT records, both in the judiciary and elsewhere. Trump has rescinded Obama-era guidance issued to federally funded schools on the rights of trans students and revoked a similar Obama-era memo protecting trans workers against discrimination. His Justice department has argued in favour of the right to discriminate against LGBT people on countless issues, from bathroom usage to healthcare, and most recently in favour of allowing employers to fire their LGBT employees.[13]

Understanding why fascist thinking has gained popularity amongst LGBT people is important, as is naming the phenomenon. Let's call this relationship out for what it is: homonationalism. The theorist Jasbir K. Puar coined this term to highlight the intersection of sexuality and nationalism.[14] It describes how LGBT rights are used to shore up anti-Muslim or anti-immigrant bigotry. The West is cast as enlightened, egalitarian, inclusive and tolerant; Muslims as homophobic and transphobic. By claiming to protect LGBT rights and freedoms, far-right groups use them to whitewash their reputations. They normalize agendas of hate, shrouding them in benevolence. Homonationalism is sophisticated, painted as a defence of 'liberal values', but when used like this, it's just another form of Islamophobia, which treats Muslims as foreign, savage and uncivilized, and that is helpful to acknowledge.

Despite the growing platform in Britain for the far right to legitimize their views and reputations, it's important to resist their normalization. We have to challenge the way that fascist thinking is steering national conversations about race, identity, immigration and, yes, the LGBT and Muslim communities. It goes without saying that this alliance between sexual minorities and the far right is an exploitative one, one from which LGBT communities cannot prosper. There are two strikingly obvious reasons for this. First, fascists are not friends. They are not concerned with the interests of LGBT communities. At its very heart, fascist ideology is homophobic and transphobic.[15] It rejects LGBT people in exactly the same way as it accuses Muslim communities of doing. Should it ever succeed in its goal of driving Muslims and people of colour from Britain and other Western nations, fascism will turn its gaze to the same LGBT community that it now holds hands with.

Secondly, this alliance is inherently selective. It isn't concerned with protecting the freedoms of all LGBT people. Though LGBT individuals frame their decisions around a 'legitimate' fear of Islam, when they are drawn to fascist narratives, ultimately it is to protect whiteness – in particular, white masculinity. Otherwise, their conversations about LGBT equality would not erase LGBT Muslims. Like other queer people of colour, LGBT Muslims are ignored. Their existence is inconvenient. They are suppressed because Western concepts of homosexual identity are predominantly constructed around white gay men. Alternative constructions would only weaken the authority of white people in the LGBT community. This is why fascists and LGBTs are, to some extent, in agreement. They are both vested in protecting the same thing: the privilege of white people. Acknowledging this and identifying it allows us to deconstruct homonationalism, a supremacist ideology designed to demonize the 'other' (Muslims in this case) and protect the privileges of those at the centre of Western society.

This homonationalist narrative has unfolded many times. In 2015, the Swedish far right organized a pride march through a predominantly Muslim area.[16] Homonationalism was a significant part of the conversation that played out after the attack on Pulse in Orlando, Florida. I can't write about the stereotype of Muslim homophobia and transphobia without discussing what happened at Pulse. In June 2016, Omar Mateen stormed the LGBT club and murdered forty-nine people, injuring fifty-three. He claimed allegiance to Islamic State. The global and American media assembled its preset narrative: here was an Islamic extremist who targeted LGBT people. Or, as Urooj Arshad explained, here was an attack on sexual minorities that was 'motivated by homophobia and transphobia within the Muslim community'. In the hours after the attack, Urooj and other MASGD organizers were inundated with media requests looking for the LGBT Muslim perspective. We spoke about her experiences in coordinating this response: 'It was really important for us to get ahead of this narrative that Islam is inherently homophobic and transphobic. We are already constantly battling rhetoric that erases any kind of nuance around the fact that there are 1.8 billion Muslims in the world with various understandings of these issues.'

She argued that the post-Pulse narrative ignored homophobia within other faith traditions to focus disproportionately on the connection between the attack and Islam. The narrative also erased the needs of LGBT Muslims specifically, who, as Urooj said, 'are wanting to be part of both communities unconditionally'.

Since Mateen's wife was put on trial – wrongly accused of facilitating the shooting – we have learned that, contrary to this preconception, the attacker did not specifically target an LGBT club. Mateen had a history of domestic violence, he glorified the NYPD, he displayed a dubious understanding of religion (he claimed to have connections to both Al-Qaeda and Hezbollah, which is impossible given that they sit on opposing sectarian lines), and it turned out that his father had been an FBI informant for eleven years.[17] These and many other important factors in understanding Mateen's motivations were overlooked and undermined because of what Urooj calls, 'the gay versus Muslim framing'. Indeed, this oppositional framing informed the Pulse narrative from the outset. Journalists used reports from Pulse patrons and supposed friends of Mateen's to portray him as a 'closeted homosexual who used gay dating apps and frequented gay bars'. The implication was, of course, that Mateen had resorted to violence as a result of his internalized homophobia, informed by his Muslim upbringing.[18]

A protest group called 'Gays Against Sharia' now invokes the attack on Pulse as a reason for its activities.[19] When it demonstrates in cities across the UK, it does so against Islam, which it considers to be the real (and sole) oppressor of LGBT people. The exploitation of the LGBT movement here is plain to see. On social media, their event pages are filled with homophobic quotes from Islamic preachers, pictures of gay men being hanged and videos of anti-Muslim propaganda. One picture, a photograph of two white women kissing, was accompanied by the caption, 'Sharia law is not compatible with our way of life'. Incidentally, the group is organized by another former EDL member and founder of its 'LGBT division', Tommy Cook (who goes by the name 'Tommy English'). On his Twitter page, he describes himself as an 'Anti-Racist, Anti-Jihadi English Patriot'. Footage of him at an EDL protest shows English waving a rainbow flag on which is inscribed: 'United Together, Today and Forever. Help us Stop the Growth of an Evil, Hate-Filled Ideology'. But far from honouring the victims of the Pulse shooting, as the group believes it is doing, in these demonstrations the victims' lives are exploited to galvanize anti-Muslim feeling.

Historically, the Muslim view of sexual and gender diversity has not been one of blanket intolerance. From their very founding, Muslim societies have held complex, even sophisticated, relationships with queerness. In his day-to-day life, Prophet Muhammad encountered people of diverse sexual identities and he didn't condemn them. In fact, as the queer-identifying Imam Muhsin Hendricks points out, during the Prophet's lifetime there is no known instance where an LGBT person was prosecuted or punished simply for who they were.[20] Instead, we know that the Prophet and his wives openly interacted with sexual minorities; both eunuchs and mukhannathun worked within his household. Mukhannathun were individuals assigned male at birth who functioned in Arab society as women; eunuchs were castrated men who occupied an ambiguous, 'in between' gender status. As Scott Kugle explains in his book *Homosexuality in Islam*, in the environment of early Islam it was possible for those assigned male at birth to give up these gender roles; given the still-patriarchal nature of that society, this was less possible for those assigned female.[21] However, what is significant is that the earliest Muslims recognized gender diversity to be innate and unchangeable. Over subsequent generations these progressive attitudes did contract, but it's still valuable to know that as the initial Islamic empire grew, so did the power of some mukhannathun. Mainly, this was due to their unique ability to navigate segregated spaces. Some mukhannathun became singers, entertainers and comedians, and these positions enabled them to poke fun at and critique government authorities. Stories about mukhannathun were documented in the *Book of Songs* by al-Isfahani, a text focused on the lives of singers, poets and composers in tenth-century Muslim society. Later on, in the medieval period, a category would evolve for those born female to occupy male roles in society. Many concubines in the royal court became mutarrajulat, using gender-inversion as a sort of performance.

Even when scholars in subsequent generations began to argue that same-sex sexual relations, for example, were a crime, how exactly this was enforced depended on the society concerned and the Islamic school of law it followed. Today, there are eight main schools of law. The Hanafi school, to which the Ottoman and Mughal empires belonged, did not treat sexual relations as a serious crime. Punishments were at a judge's discretion. This meant that punishment was rarely, if ever, carried out. Countless studies of the Ottoman Empire and Mughal Empire have looked at the everyday realities of legal punishments. One such example is *The Age of Beloveds: Love and the Beloved in Early-Modern Ottoman and European Culture and Society* by Walter G. Andrews and Mehmet Kalpakli.[22] What becomes clear from these studies is that cases of consensual same-sex sexual activity were not brought to court and were raised only in instances of rape or abuse. For both Islamophobes and religious conservatives, who argue that Islamic civilizations historically punished homosexuality with death, an examination of these Muslim societies illustrates how same-sex attraction was fairly ordinary.

This 'ordinariness' is exemplified in love poetry, a popular form across Muslim societies. Poets like Abu Nuwas – whose homo-erotic verses were not suppressed and erased in Arab countries until the twentieth century – were able to express their same-sex attractions without adverse consequence:

My eyes are fixed upon his delightful body,
And I do not wonder at his beauty.
His waist is a sapling, his face a moon,
And loveliness rolls off his rosy cheek,
I die of love for you.[23]

Religious scholars wrote love poetry too. Abdullah al-Shabrawi was the Shaykh of Cairo's Al-Azhar University in the 1700s. Not only was his poetry homoerotic, he often named the object of his affections explicitly (though it isn't clear whether these people were, in fact, real):

Oh moon, you have let my heart taste the cup of love, so be generous and hold back the swords of harshness.

I am melting from love – enough harshness. Oh Ahmed, has my love not elicited your goodwill?[24]

Nonetheless, questions remain about how a scholar like al-Shabrawi could hold a position at the most eminent religious institution in Sunni Islam whilst writing and publishing this kind of poetry. Historical attitudes to sexual diversity cannot be mapped neatly on to contemporary ideas about sexuality as an identity, which only developed in the nineteenth century, but the answers rest on the way that Muslim societies distinguished love from sex. Aspects of same-sex intimacy – such as falling in love – and public expressions of that love were an accepted part of many Muslim societies. But when it came to sexual relations, things became testy; some acts were permitted, others forbidden.[25] As studies by academics such as Elyse Semerdjian, Thomas Bauer and Khaled El-Rouayheb show, clerics were mostly concerned with penetrative sex between two men and this is what was explicitly proscribed. This meant that other sexual expressions – as long as they were private – elicited relatively little cause for concern. In essence, what went on at this time was a form of 'don't ask, don't tell'.[26]

I asked Leyla Jagiella about this heritage. As mentioned previously, Leyla is a cultural anthropologist and the co-chair of Liberal-Islamischer Bund, an inclusive Muslim organization in Germany. We spoke of the importance of not trying to portray past Muslim societies as absolute havens for LGBT people; all pasts contain practices that are problematic and painful. 'But what our past teaches us,' she said, 'is that Muslims did not view same-sex attraction as inherently "sick" or "unnatural", but as something inherent in human beings.'

Equally important is the fact that clerics disapproving of certain sexual behaviours didn't result in these actions disappearing altogether. In the same way that we cannot portray Muslim societies as unequivocally tolerant, we cannot think of them as bastions of absolute observance either. In al-Shabrawi's time, for example, clerics also disapproved of playing backgammon and musical instruments, drinking coffee and smoking tobacco. But they remained important parts of the culture to which he belonged. Muslims possessed a multidimensional and nuanced attitude to religious doctrine – perhaps more so than in existence today. As the academic Khaled el-Rouayheb remarks, 'ordinary believers seem to have been able to acknowledge the religious authority of the jurists whilst at the same time resisting a wholesale adoption of their austere outlook and way of life'.[27] Thus, many Muslims simply paid little attention to what their scholars outlawed.

And so, across different Muslim societies, sexual minorities were able to assume positions of substantial power and authority. During the Mughal era, for example, eunuchs (who in South Asia were perceived closer to Western categorizations of non-binary or transgender women, or occupying an entirely separate, or 'third sex', category) did more than just guard the harem and serve the royal court. Many were involved in the administration of the state. One eunuch, Itibar Khan, became the Governor of Delhi during the reign of Akbar. Another, Khwaja Agah, was the garrison commander of Agra. A third, Wafadar, was sent by the Mughal Emperor Jahangir to govern the region of Gujarat.[28] There are many more examples of sexual diversity thriving in other pre-colonial Muslim societies, including the waria in Indonesia, the xanith in Oman and the yan daudu in Hausa communities.[29]

Across the Muslim world, these cultures of tolerance did not come under strong and sustained attack until the Europeans arrived. Early contact with the continent had led to the introduction of Western attitudes that saw sexual and gender diversity as indecent, even as a perversion. Then, when European colonization followed, these notions were forced on to Muslim societies.[30]

In 1858, the Ottoman Empire elected to decriminalize homosexuality. Just two years later, the Indian Penal Code came into force across British India. Drafted by Lord Macaulay, section 377 of the Code introduced the concept of sexual offences 'against the order of nature'. This outlawed same-sex sexual acts. By largely restricting the rights of colonized societies to legislate for themselves (with narrow exceptions), these Victorian social mores had an extensive impact, irrespective of religious affiliation. India is important here because most of pre-colonial India was presided over by the Muslim rulers of the Mughal Empire, and this territory contained a substantial Muslim population. All European powers tended towards imposing such laws on to their colonies, but Britain enjoys a particular heritage of exporting homophobia and transphobia given the breadth of its colonial endeavours: of the seventy-eight or so countries that still criminalize same-sex intimacy, almost half are former British colonies.[31] These include Muslim-majority countries such as Pakistan and Bangladesh (which have an identical section 377 in their Penal Codes), Malaysia (section 187 of the Penal Code), Sudan (articles 19, 20, 148, 151 and 152 of the Criminal Act 1991) and Gambia, where section 144 of the Gambian Criminal Code criminalizes as an 'unnatural offence' any person who 'has carnal knowledge of any person against the order of nature'.

Those uncomfortable with colonialism's noxious legacy will deny it. They'll argue that colonization is no longer relevant to the discussion around Muslim treatment of LGBT people. According to them, these societies are now free to organize and legislate as they wish. They can decriminalize homosexuality, just as Britain did. In July 2014, *Slate* magazine published an article entitled, 'Don't blame yesterday's colonialism for today's homophobia.' In it, the author called out the way 'gay hate in former colonies' is tacitly excused 'as an inevitable vestige of colonialism's anti-gay bent'.[32] But nobody is being excused. On the contrary, colonialism helps us understand the roots of legislative intolerance in post-colonial societies and the hurdles placed in the way of decriminalization.

The truth of homophobia and transphobia in post-colonial societies is complicated. There is amnesia on both sides. European colonial powers have erased their role in creating many of the laws that criminalize sexual minorities across the world. And post-colonial societies have forgotten the way that outsiders planted and nurtured this intolerance, both legally and culturally. We cannot overlook how, after independence, these legal systems have evolved to reject sexual minorities. Most post-colonial societies have uncritically accepted it as part of their culture. This is precisely why, when Western powers try to enlighten them on LGBT rights, formerly colonized countries perceive these interactions as evidence of sustained Western intervention. In 2011, for example, John Atta Mills, then President of Ghana, rejected British threats to cut aid if the country did not legalize homosexuality. Arguing that the UK could not impose its values on Ghana, he stated that our (then) prime minister, David Cameron, could not 'direct to other sovereign nations as to what they should do'.[33] An equally pertinent example is the decision of American diplomats in May 2011 to hold a pride event inside the US Embassy in Islamabad, Pakistan. When the Pakistani media reported the event, students and religious parties took to the streets to protest, condemning American intervention as well as homosexuality.[34]

Interactions between former colonizers and the formerly colonized are short-sighted. They're wrongly informed by an assumption that the conditions and challenges within Western and post-colonial societies are the same. But where Western societies have been stable enough – socially, politically and economically – to contemplate equality, Muslim societies have not. We forget that they're still trying to construct stable economies, political systems and societies. They're doing so in a globalized world far different to the one they were colonized in. As a result, many Muslim states are still faced with confronting artificially constructed borders, dictatorships, failing economies, resource competition and sectarian divisions, amongst other issues, leaving little space to address equality. The prospects of sexual equality seem limited in states where homophobia is easily weaponized. LGBT people become convenient scapegoats when political leaders want a distraction from their own failures. In countless post-colonial societies, challenging what is essentially the decriminalization of LGBT people becomes a peripheral issue – though it should not be – when 'more pressing' issues like the viability of the state and its political infrastructure demand greater attention. We should acknowledge that the future of liberation for LGBT people in Muslim societies is explicitly tied to broader notions of social and economic stability.

Moreover, it's not an act of detraction or defensiveness to discuss the role of colonization in helping foment current Muslim attitudes towards homosexuality. Only by exploring this can we begin to destroy the idea that homosexuality is foreign and homophobia indigenous to Muslim communities. It's a tool, one of many, to challenge not only Islamophobes, but Muslim gatekeepers who continue to insist that sexual and gender diversity is anathema to Islam; that 'there are no gays in Iran'; that homosexuality is 'un-African', as political and religious leaders are accustomed to declaring.[35]

At the same time, it provides context and insight into the complex task of decriminalization. In India, the battle to decriminalize homosexuality was long-fought. India isn't a Muslim-majority country, but it does have the world's third largest Muslim population. Moreover, as a former British colony, it's an especially pertinent example. Since 2001, section 377 has been subjected to a legal challenge. Initially, there was hope: in 2009, the Delhi High Court appeared to set aside the law. But in 2013, the Indian Supreme Court dismissed this decision and then opted not to decriminalize the law itself. In January 2018, the Supreme Court agreed to review the law again and in a judgement on 6 September 2018, it finally found that section 377 was unconstitutional – 158 years after it was first instituted.

What the Indian struggle teaches us is that the course towards enacting the necessary protections for LGBT people in societies with substantial Muslim populations – many of which are still haunted by colonialism – is far from straightforward. It will never be a journey that follows the route taken by Western societies. That's not to say we shouldn't push for decriminalization; we should, especially by engaging with activists at the frontline of these battles and supporting them in the ways that they want. But it's also fundamentally important that Westerners stop imposing their expectations on to these societies, and stop weaponizing these struggles to dehumanize the people who belong to these and Western societies simultaneously.

Contrary to the idea that LGBT people cannot exist within Islam, sexual and gender diversity can be reconciled with the faith. LGBT Muslims have begun to carve out spaces for themselves and reassert their right to exist within the fold of Islam. This right is constructed on a foundation of justice. As Kugle points out, the central principle of the Quran is to strive for justice in solidarity with the oppressed.[36] It is clear: justice is a non-negotiable facet of Islam. In verse 5:8 of the Quran, for example, Muslims are directed to be witnesses in justice: 'do not let the hatred of a people prevent you from being just. Be just: that is nearer to righteousness'.

Though the Quran commands believers to protect vulnerable minorities, this sense of justice is often disregarded when it comes to sexual minorities. Even sympathetic Muslims divorce themselves from duty in the LGBT context. Too often they abdicate responsibility, lamenting that LGBT Muslims are simply dealt a bad hand; God has given them a difficult 'test'. But what if the test was meant for Muslims who do not identify as LGBT? It could be a test examining their ability to uphold the dignity of the marginalized. Perhaps that reformulation would change how we view justice and sexual diversity together.

It is this reclaiming of the sacred text that, above all, allows me to believe in the potential for greater acceptance of sexual diversity within Muslim communities. But there is plenty of work to be done. The text is incredibly difficult to deal with; although theology and interpretation have always been contentious, Muslim societies, once led by clerics who saw diversity of opinion as a gift, no longer exist as they once did. The rise of Islamic puritanism across the world has also been well documented.[37] I have witnessed it within my own extended family – individuals who have abandoned our South Asian mystical interpretation of Islam in favour of the revivalist and austere Salafi movement. There are many complex reasons for this, such as Saudi foreign policy and the disaffection of young Muslim men, some of which I have outlined in previous chapters. But the most compelling reason for embracing the puritan narrative of a 'pure' Islam, where the scripture has only one possible interpretation, is that it provides certainty in a world of chaos.

It is easy to forget that Muslim-majority societies experienced European imperialism (in which European legal hegemony was imposed and the Shariah demoted) and modernity (in which they emerged far behind the West) as nothing less than a political and spiritual crisis.[38] As with other significant events in Islamic history, it precipitated a period of deep reflection. In trying to understand why the Muslim world had found itself so easily subjugated and how it should now move forward, many returned to the two fundamental questions at the heart of Islam: what does it mean to be a Muslim in the modern world? What should a community or society inspired by Islam look like? Once more, certain figures argued that the answer lay in greater political and spiritual unity, and in returning to the foundations of Islam.

'What is the appeal of puritanism?' I asked Reza Aslan. He replied:

> In all communities, the appeal is obvious: simple answers. There's no grey; things aren't complicated. There's an answer for every issue and every problem. It's a direct line to the source and you don't have to think about it. Diversity, on the other hand, means multiple views, perhaps even multiple truths. Puritanism in all religious traditions has always been enormously popular because it has the ability to set the mind at ease, as if that is the goal of a spiritual life, to live free of fear or worry or doubt.

Whilst I empathize with that, diversity shouldn't be sacrificed to set certain people's minds at ease. There's no justification for eliminating the right of all Muslims to direct their own beliefs.

Here, I am reasserting the right for Muslims to research the issues for themselves; to contemplate the texts independently, to navigate their beliefs personally, and to do so without the prescriptiveness of religious elites who believe that reflecting on the word of God is only a cleric's domain. Religious belief is not intended to be hierarchical. Denying all Muslims an equal right to examine the scripture is unacceptable.

I'm making two arguments here. First, Muslims and non-Muslims don't need to rely on mainstream interpretations to direct their understandings of the text. Delving into the scholarship of the past and the present can shed important light on the scripture that, for various reasons, has been overlooked. Secondly, there is no reason to deprive Muslims from developing personal relationships with the text, from finding independent answers that align with the equalizing spirit of Islam. Without strategies such as these, Muslim communities will be unable to address and counterbalance oppressive uses of theology. Muslims, young Muslims in particular, will not have the opportunity to be empowered by Islam, rather than dominated by it.

These strategies help challenge the idea that Islamic scripture explicitly denounces LGBT people. This work relies on historical scholarship and a personal relationship with the text, and it's important because dismantling the idea of Islam's inherent homophobia and transphobia isn't an absolute innovation – it builds upon a long theological tradition, many centuries old.

Take, for example, the story of Sodom and Gomorrah. As with Christianity and Judaism, in Islam it is generally interpreted as condemning LGBT people. In summary, the mainstream interpretation of Sodom and Gomorrah is that its residents were guilty of several 'transgressions', including the men having sex with other men. God sent Prophet Lot to preach to them, but they threatened to drive him away, and even tried to have sex with the angels. As a result, God destroyed the cities, sparing only Lot and his daughters.

I grew up with an uncritical acceptance of Sodom's association with sexual diversity, the Quran's condemnation of it and the severity of the punishment mandated. That the cities were met with fire and brimstone has certainly inspired laypeople, clerics and self-described scholars and religious leaders to argue that this establishes the illegality of sexual diversity, its immorality and the duty to punish – forever. These ideas seem outlandish to me now, particularly the tying of something as innate and innocuous as somebody's sexual or gender identity to what constitutes moral behaviour. And more of us need to challenge it.

More than a thousand years ago, Ibn Hazm, a jurist in Islamic Spain, discredited what is still somehow the common understanding about Sodom and Gomorrah. In his opinion, the Quran did not condemn sexual minorities with nearly the same force that it censured adultery or premarital sex between a man and woman. Accordingly, though he believed that same-sex sexual relations were a crime, he argued that this proscription didn't come from the Quran.

Rather than focusing on the sexual elements of the story, Ibn Hazm believed that the true moral behind Sodom and Gomorrah lay in the rejection of Lot's prophethood. If the destruction of Sodom had been motivated primarily by the conduct between men, then the women and children living there – including Lot's wife – should not have been destroyed too. Ibn Hazm also disagreed with the idea that Sodom legitimized stoning or other forms of the death penalty for same-sex intimacy. The stoning was God's punishment in this case; it was not a command for Muslims to mete out the same sentences.

Since then, contemporary scholars like Scott Kugle have expanded on this work. They have explained the crimes of Sodom in terms of male on male rape and paedophilia, just as Christian and Jewish scholars have done with their respective verses. This work takes the story of Sodom away from the explicit condemnation of LGBT people.

Given the frequency with which intolerant Hadiths are bandied about by inexperienced people (on both sides) with little understanding that, by their very nature, Hadiths are problematic and fallible, it is worthwhile examining them. A widely proliferated Hadith is the claim that the Prophet said, 'When the male mounts another male the angels are alarmed and raise a cry to their Lord...' This Hadith has been critiqued throughout history. In the fourteenth century the Hadith scholar Ibn Qayyim al-Jawziyya believed the authenticity of the Hadith was weak. A later scholar called it an outright fabrication. In the sixteenth century, Muhammad ibn Tahir Patani, an intellectual known as the 'King of Hadith Scholars', evaluated the Hadith using traditional Islamic methods. He also rejected it. Despite the extensive criticism, this Hadith is still cited indiscriminately by scholars and lay Muslims alike. In repeated publications of the Hadith, it has been stripped of the critique attached to it by some of the most respected scholars in Islamic history. There are other Hadiths used to condemn LGBT people and these have been historically discredited too. Yet they continue to circulate because these Hadiths bolster prejudices already present amongst some Muslims, prejudices we fail to confront when we ignore the intricacies of our own scriptural heritage.

Further subverting the idea of unequivocal condemnation, leaders and scholars including Muhsin Hendricks, the queer South African imam, argue that the Quran recognizes sexual diversity, in verses 24:31 and 24:60, for example, where it references men not attracted to women and women who will not reproduce. These strengthen the belief that the scripture recognizes, even celebrates, sexual diversity:

> Oh people, we created you all from a male and female and made you into different communities and different tribes, so that you should come to know one another, acknowledging that the most noble among you is the one most aware of God [49:13].

Developments within the Muslim world also highlight the evolution of theological interpretations, especially on gender. Take, for
example, the experience of Maryam Molkara, a transgender woman
living in Iran. It took her eight years to meet Ayatollah Khomeini,
then Supreme Leader of the country. In 1987, when she finally did,
Molkara explained to him that she was a transgender woman who
was marginalized in Iran because of her gender identity. Within
half an hour of listening to her experiences, Khomeini had consulted with his doctors and issued a fatwa. All transgender people
would be permitted to undergo gender reassignment surgery. As a
result, today Iran not only permits transgender people to change
their identity documents, but also subsidizes the cost of surgery.

Moreover, given that surgery is only one element of the transgender experience (and most often, not at all), it is heartening that
Pakistani scholars have used theology to address social, civil and
political rights. In 2016, fifty clerics issued a fatwa that protected
the inheritance and burial rights of transgender people. It stated
that harassing them was haram (forbidden).[39] The fatwa also
allowed transgender men and women to marry partners of the
opposite sex. Here, the fatwa was flawed. It focused too much on
external appearances and refused to extend these rights to inter-
sex people or those who 'exhibited outward signs of both genders'.
Nevertheless, it's a start.

Ali, Prophet Muhammad's cousin, pointed out that the
Quran itself is written in straight lines between two covers.
It does not speak; rather human beings speak on its behalf.
Speaking on its behalf does not mean thoughtlessly repeating
its content. It involves upholding its essence. I keep returning to
the idea that the essence of the Quran is in its commitment to
justice, equality and liberation from oppression. When trying
to understand the verses of the Quran, Muslim communities
should hold on to this essence, remembering that the scripture
by itself does not condemn a community. Condemnation comes
from the reader.

*

All this means that the high-handedness of Islamophobes and their argument about Muslim homophobia is difficult to accept. It's patently wrong, but it also contains a strong sense of irony. Throughout history, sexual minorities from Europe sought refuge in Muslim societies. European travellers to the Islamic world reported with disgust how local men openly displayed same-sex feelings. Muslims were seen as less civilized – sexually animalistic – for their sexual permissiveness. And now they are seen as less civilized for conservatism that was cultivated by the West in the first place.

It's also worth remembering that progressive social attitudes in the West didn't develop overnight. Up until the late twentieth century, LGBT people were subject to state-led persecution in Britain. Their rights were not granted or bestowed; they were won and hard-fought for. Section 28, which, from 1988 to 2000 in Scotland (and until 2003 in England, Wales and Northern Ireland), prevented the 'promotion' of homosexuality by local authorities across the UK, ensured an entire generation of LGBT people were stigmatized because of their identities. The psychological impact of this proscription was far-reaching. There's a great deal here that undermines Western arrogance regarding its recent record on LGBT equality, including harm to LGBT refugees and the rising statistics on LGBT hate crimes. Over 2017–2018, more than 1500 LGBT people in the UK reported homophobic, biphobic or transphobic hate crimes.[40] One in five LGBT people has experienced a hate crime or incidents of abuse connected to their sexual identity; that figure rises to two in every four transgender people.[41] According to analysis by the *Guardian*, between 2013 and 2014 and 2017 and 2018 LGBT hate crimes rose by 144 per cent in England and Wales. Everywhere, sexual minorities are vulnerable: at risk from the state and at risk from society.[42]

Brexit has also brought into focus British arrogance on LGBT rights. Shahmir Sanni is a British Pakistani who worked for the

BeLeave campaign in the run-up to the referendum. In March 2018, Sanni accused Vote Leave, the official campaign to leave the European Union, of breaking rules on election spending. Since Stephen Parkinson, the senior official implicated in the scandal, worked at Downing Street during Theresa May's premiership, it was the prime minister's office that assumed responsibility for responding to Sanni's claims. To deflect the accusations levelled against Parkinson, the Downing Street statement chose to 'out' Sanni as a gay man.[43] In doing so, it ignored the fact that sexuality is a private matter and the decision to come out is highly personal; by disregarding these, it displayed a fundamental indifference to Sanni's dignity. Moreover, it chose to overlook that publicly revealing his sexuality put him at risk of harm. It is not entirely absurd to feel, then, that a centre-right government has no interest in safeguarding the rights of LGBT individuals (or, for that matter, Muslims), and so long as this is the case, LGBT Muslims will find themselves doubly marginalized.

But there's an additional irony. Conservative Muslims, who often champion the earliest Muslim societies as setting out the correct way to live, are just as mistaken. They conveniently forget how, in many cases, these societies not only refused to persecute sexual minorities but protected them. Thus, embracing that heritage wholeheartedly actually involves championing sexual diversity.

With all that said, there is a gradual shift taking place in parts of the Muslim world towards greater acceptance of LGBT people. Aside from disrupting the idea of Muslim intolerance, it provides more reason to be hopeful. Progress is, admittedly, slow, but it shows the capacity of Muslim societies to legislate and move forward of their own accord. In February 2014, for example, Northern Cyprus decriminalized homosexuality. Albania and Kosovo have introduced laws prohibiting discrimination on the grounds of sexual orientation and gender identity.

In many cases, grassroots movements and organizations are driving this progress. In Lebanon, for example, the LGBT advocacy group Helem has led the resistance against article 234 of the Penal Code, which is used to mistreat sexual minorities. It has successfully challenged the police's arrest of several transgender men and women under the pretext of this law. In February 2017, the District Court returned a decision that found homosexuality was not a punishable crime.[44] Short of outright decriminalization, this decision has provided Lebanese activists with another important victory in the long road to equality.

In recent years, Pakistan has legislated extensively for its khwajasara, or transgender/non-binary community. Between 2009 and 2012, the Pakistani judiciary made a series of orders demanding that the government provide the community with greater recognition and protection, including access to medical treatment and education, and inclusion within the census. This has resulted in the Transgender Persons (Protection of Rights) Act, passed in May 2018, which consulted transgender activist groups, lawyers and even religious authorities.[45] The bill explicitly prohibits any kind of discrimination against the transgender community. Crucially, it allows them to register their gender identity (male, female or third gender) on all of their documents. In doing so, Pakistan is one of the few countries in the world to recognize the right to self-identify one's gender without the need for medical approval. Although the real test lies in its implementation, this bill marks a significant step forward, one many Western countries are yet to take.

In Britain, the decriminalization of homosexuality occurred across England and Wales in 1967, in Scotland in 1980, and not until 1982 in Northern Ireland. Even then, this decriminalization was, for many years, essentially partial. Only in the twenty-first century has Britain secured the rights of LGBT people to adopt, marry and serve openly in the military. Absolute equality remains elusive. Britain is still depathologizing sexual diversity, proposing to update laws on legal gender recognition that have forced transgender people to obtain medical diagnoses to legally change their gender (sitting behind Pakistan on this issue). At the time of writing, however, the Johnson government disappointingly looks set to abandon such plans. Nevertheless, British advancement towards LGBT equality is a relatively contemporary phenomenon and an ongoing process that reveals the hollowness of Western superiority on LGBT issues. There is every reason to believe that, with time, by directly confronting issues and with much stronger advocacy, Muslim societies could get there too.

Even today, I continue to feel hopeful. I believe that Muslim communities are moving towards greater acceptance, even when the Western media portrays otherwise. I think back to the incident in 2011, when homophobic stickers were plastered across East London. In his article for *Attitude* magazine, Johann Hari argued that, in an attempt to be tolerant, Britain had unwittingly 'allowed a fantastically intolerant attitude towards gay people to incubate' in East London.[46] He cited statistics; always, sophisticated anti-Muslim bigotry utilizes statistics, assuming that numbers and polls provide irrefutable evidence.

Personally, I am suspicious of the way Hari and journalists like him use statistics – and perhaps even of the statistics themselves – because data can so easily be manipulated when they're not scrutinized enough. As the French activist Pierre Tevanian has identified, statistics and opinion polls play a prominent role in both cultivating and producing a negative opinion of Muslims, where questions are constructed in a way that pits the Muslim community against Western society, and are interpreted to show that all Muslims speak with a single menacing voice.[47]

But when I look at those polls where care has been taken over sample size, methodology and questioning style, my optimism is vindicated. There is no way to deny that some Muslim communities have a problem with accepting LGBT people, which is consistently translated in the figures, but critically, the figures also show that things are changing.

In 2018, Ipsos MORI carried out an extensive survey into British Muslim attitudes, reviewing all existing research and uniting all information on British Muslim opinion.[48] It established that Muslims are, indeed, conservative on gender and sexuality. A majority disagreed with the legality of homosexuality (38 per cent strongly disagreed and 14 per cent disagreed). But the report drew two points of understanding: first, fewer Muslims appeared to hold a strong opposition to homosexuality compared to similar research conducted in 1993, when 50 per cent of those surveyed had believed that same-sex intimacy was 'always wrong' (although there are subtle but important differences in the language used by these two polls). Secondly, young Muslims were more likely to hold explicitly favourable views (28 per cent of eighteen- to twenty-four-year-olds and 23 per cent of twenty-five- to thirty-four-year-olds, versus 18 per cent overall). This is promising.

So, British Muslims are far from united on this issue. Their attitudes to sexual diversity are conflicted, complicated and, most importantly, changing. And it is this sense of division that has allowed hopeful spaces to grow within Muslim communities, both in Britain and elsewhere. As much as there is a desire to cling to a view of Islam as monolithic, Muslims also exist who are looking to discover an inclusive language and character to their faith. They just aren't given as much attention. In Britain, spaces created by the Muslim Institute, New Horizons in British Islam and the Inclusive Mosque Initiative, for example, have demonstrated a real commitment to the LGBT community. They foster LGBT-inclusive environments and work to address the struggle amongst some Muslims to accept sexual and gender diversity. Online too, forums and social media have allowed Muslims to not only connect with like-minded believers, but to obtain guidance on imbuing their practice of Islam with an inclusive and ethical character.

Still, I know that Muslim communities can and must do better. But better how? By rediscovering the ethical responsibilities to one another, something that informs the central tenets of Islamic belief. I like to describe this as 'doing justice', remembering that justice and equality are not simply about having 'good thoughts', but engaging in real, decisive action. Justice involves standing up for LGBT Muslim dignity. It involves creating spaces inclusive of LGBT Muslims. It means that LGBT Muslims should be allowed to negotiate their identities with self-direction. It means that they should be extended a hand of compassion – not condemnation – leaving all judgements to God. Muslim communities have to do this meaningfully, not with the kind of tacit tolerance that some religious leaders fall back on to avoid getting into trouble. When there are lives on the line, there is no virtue in obfuscation, in using playful language about accepting the sinner, but not the sin.

Solidarity is a part of the answer. The kind of solidarity necessary is for advocates to speak up for the unqualified acceptance and inclusion of LGBT Muslims within their Muslim communities. Ignoring or denying this need for solidarity would be naïve. Doubling-down on exclusion only makes one complicit in the oppression. After all, religion is not something that any of us own. Faith cannot be policed by anybody other than God. This reminds me of the *Free Speech* debate entitled 'Can you be gay and Muslim?' that was hosted by BBC Three in 2014.[49] There, a member of the audience verbally attacked Asif Qureshi, an LGBT Muslim activist. 'Why would you choose to be a Muslim? You can either be gay, or you can be a Muslim,' she said. In her mind, it was impossible to be both. In insisting upon this compulsory dichotomy, the audience member became complicit in the oppression Qureshi sought to address. The audience member was not entitled to force LGBT Muslims into choosing between their faith and sexuality, and it's objectionable that she saw herself holding such a right. Given that Islamic values are concerned with freedom, equality and human dignity, this kind of prescriptivism and judgement is not in keeping with the faith.

Today many Muslim thinkers and leaders are gradually turning to the scripture and finding a case for compassion towards LGBT people. In *Reading the Qur'an*, Ziauddin Sardar writes about how unjust it would be if God gave LGBTs no choice in their identities and simultaneously sentenced them to a condemned life. That kind of fate would be inimical to the inherent justice of the Quran.[50] Reading his book, especially his explanation of the story of Sodom as one of extreme excess – contrary to the Quran's constant call for balance and modesty – I thought of the way that many Muslim leaders call for 'private things' to be kept 'private'. It is true that Islam fiercely protects the right to privacy, particularly on sexual matters, but in this case, I think it's dangerous when Muslim leaders rely on the 'veil of privacy'. It allows them to ignore the harm that takes place within their communities. In that BBC Three debate, the self-described 'intellectual activist', Abdullah al Andalusi, did precisely this:

> The Islamic position is that we don't label people by their sexuality or their nationality or their race. This labelling was invented in the Victorian era. As soon as you assign some-body a label, you're discriminating them. The only thing in Islam that is judged is your actions – not your desires. And in Islam there are many actions that are sinful and many that are permitted.

When pressed as to whether he believed a queer person like Asif Qureshi was a sinner, he said:

> What he does in the privacy of his own home is not really my concern. However, we all commit sinful acts, but in Islamic theology, you're not allowed to express your sins. You don't say, 'I've done this or that,' you keep it to yourself. You shouldn't, therefore, say you want to come out of the closet. I don't tell everyone about my private life.

Under the pretext that what Muslims did in private was their own business, Andalusi totally disengaged with the rights and experiences of LGBT Muslims. Many other figures, with and without public platforms, use similar intellectual gymnastics to disengage with what justice looks like for them.

We should not support this line of thinking. Here, privacy is a noose that allows the mistreatment of LGBTs to go unchallenged. It is this kind of wilful ignorance and disengagement that should be left behind. This can only be achieved with more Muslims entering into a meaningful discussion about their ethical responsibilities to one another. After all, the exclusion of LGBT Muslims is emblematic of how many within Muslim communities broadly disengage with the duty to treat one another fairly. We cannot forget that liberation means liberation for all. Islam does not provide for selective application.

At the same time, it is the responsibility of wider society to help dismantle the idea that Islam stands in opposition to sexual and gender diversity. Not only is it patently untrue, but it is also causing a great deal of harm to young Muslims, particularly LGBT Muslims, who find their identities weaponized in the broader cultural war against Islam. We can condemn all of these dynamics equally. Healthy societies can only grow when there is cross-community solidarity.

Conclusion

The Muslim Problem

'Religion is far more about identity than it is a matter of beliefs and practices,' Reza Aslan reminded me when I interviewed him for this book. 'Taking part in religious rituals or mouthing religious professions of faith is not what makes one belong to a particular religion; it's a sense of identity, who you are, how you see yourself in the world, your point of view.'

I've spent a lot of time thinking about my identity; wondering who I would have become without the crisis of faith that crippled me when I was fourteen years old; wondering to what extent I would have resolved this struggle, had I not been forced to it in a climate of rabid bigotry. I have so many questions. Would I still be Muslim? Would I still believe in God? I would have been much more at ease with myself, that's for sure. When I think of my younger self, marching into a classroom and announcing that I was a pagan, I know that I was moving out of the faith, not towards atheism maybe, but away from organized religion.

And yet, I'm still here. I still identify as Muslim, perhaps more strongly than ever before. Islam plays a significant role in my life and at the same time it doesn't. There are moments when I'm completely ambivalent about faith. I look to the world and find inspiration, in nature, literature, music, activism, my work with migrants and refugees. Sometimes Islam complements, even enhances, my appreciation of these things. Other times, when my senses and vocabulary let me down, Islam is a comfort, a frame-work that I can fall back on to give meaning to what's happening around me. I have some choice in the role that Islam plays in my life and that is a privilege. But this freedom was hard-won and it came from my determination to carve a place for myself within the tradition. I am secure in my relationship with myself, with my religious communities and, now, with Islam and God too. I am secure in my understanding of what it means to be a good person. When other Muslims take issue with my spiritual expression, I'm not as easily displaced as I once was.

But I cannot tell you that this agency is absolute. The worst moments come when the choice is ripped from me, when I'm confronted by somebody's blind hatred or ignorance of Muslims, or worse still, when I encounter someone whose idea of a joke is calling me a terrorist or a paedophile. I have to engage and defend myself. And I'm reminded that my relationship with Islam doesn't belong to me, not completely, and doesn't seem like it ever will.

Minority identities are nearly always crafted under and in response to oppression; Blackness against white supremacy; socialism against the tyranny of class; feminism against patriarchal dom-ination. Muslim identities are no different; we're shaped by and in opposition to Western imperialism and hegemony. History lessons in our schools tend to focus predominantly on Western history, so it's easy to overlook what Muslims have suffered and what psychological consequences this might have for how we live our lives. Slavery and colonization shattered our societies. They stifled our religious expressions, malnourished our institutions and prevented our religious codes from evolving. They left us with generations of trauma. Post-independence, Muslim nations have faced repeated imperialist interventions (of which the 'War on Terror' is but one manifestation) from Western powers that claim benevolence, but are preoccupied with maintaining global dominance.

Muslims living in the West have not been immune from oppression either. From the 1960s and 1970s onwards, we resisted anti-immigrant racism by organizing in solidarity with other ethnic communities.[1] That solidarity was attacked and dismantled, and as part of it, Muslims were singled out as a nuisance. We were too different. We were constantly demanding rights – the right to halal meat, the right to wear the headscarf in public – and, as the Rushdie Affair showed, when we were angry, we refused to be silent, model minorities.[2] The media devoted countless column inches to condemnations of how difficult, how demanding, how foreign and how barbaric we supposedly were.

Then 9/11 happened and the discourse between Muslims and the West shifted into another gear. The Islamophobia being pumped out by the media, our politicians, government policies and public institutions went into overdrive. When the terrorism-related hysteria kicked in, every Muslim became a threat to national security. The War on Terror backed each of us into a corner; it pushed Islam on to us – regardless of our personal beliefs – simply because of our proximity to it. The assumption that we are all violent was a tool used to control us – and the narrative around us.

It's only to be expected then that Muslim identities would emerge from this moulded by the need to resist subjugation – resistance being an existential tool, one of the only ways humans can survive oppression. Islam as a form of resistance began in fractured Muslim nations, where people were rebuilding their self-esteems as well as their societies and religious institutions. It found its way into the West. Holding on to Islam even more tightly was a way of finding dignity in the chaos; of refusing to erase the parts of yourself that the oppressors had told you were rotten.

Every political crisis in Muslim history has been followed by a spiritual crisis, Muslims struggling with the questions of what it means to be Muslim and what an Islamic society should look like. Muslims returned to these questions in the modern day. As ever, Muslims failed to unite under a single position, sprawling out to connect with Islam in myriad different ways. But what gained a particular kind of force was an Islam (later promoted by powers like Saudi Arabia) that was rigid and uncompromising. Shorn of its eclecticism, it was held up as pure, unadulterated and true. As our lives have grown even more complicated, through nationalism and migration and globalization and the rapid development of technology, puritan Islam – an Islam that offers clear, unequivocal answers and spiritual certainty – remains attractive. Now puritan Islam isn't problematic in itself – it becomes so when it seeks to defeat all other forms and hold itself up as supreme. Muslims like myself who don't identify with an Islam that is narrow, singular and authoritarian are then forced into battle on a secondary front, fighting for the right to practise an Islam that is just, inclusive and pluralistic.

This sums up the process that took place inside me. As a young person, it felt like the world was telling me that I could only be safe from inner conflict if I stopped being a Muslim. But I rejected this message because I knew that the Western world was no safer, and renewed my resolve to make Islam work for me. We Muslims have found resistance in different Islamic spaces, interpretations and expressions; some in adopting the hijab, some in puritanism, some in ritualistic religious practice, some in affirming the inclusive spirit of Islam. We express our faith through art, literature, music, social justice, charitable giving and more. Some of us couldn't resist; we gave up on Islam altogether. We are all, consciously or unconsciously, shaped by the stigma and enforced shame of being Muslim at a time when it has become a liability. And though most of us end up acquiring the tools to negotiate anti-Muslim rhetoric and find peace within ourselves, the truth is that we shouldn't have had to. We deserve better.

Who would we be without all this? Without the slave trade? Without colonization? Without racial hierarchies? Without the West's hegemonic politics? Without the War on Terror? What would Muslim nations, communities and societies be capable of without all this? These are important questions, because the consequences of these policies on the psyche of Muslims everywhere is rarely considered, but came up repeatedly in my interviews. Suhaiymah Manzoor-Khan shared her belief that the War on Terror, for example, had left an entire generation of young people traumatized, with post-traumatic stress disorder (PTSD):

> I mean that in a very serious way because the first symptoms of PTSD are hyper-vigilance and paranoia. Young Muslim people, even our jokes reflect the trauma that we carry – haha, being stopped at the border; haha, not carrying a bomb. This is symptomatic of the fact that we have *had* to internalize – we've had no choice – and we have been socialized into understanding ourselves as an 'other' that is violent, that is a threat, that is an inherent danger.

Her comments made me think about how deep-rooted this trauma is. Our parents also have trauma, and not just from colonization and migration and war, but also from the racism that they faced in the West. For example, Altab Ali was a twenty-five-year-old Bangladeshi textile worker who was murdered in Whitechapel Park in 1978. One evening, as he returned home from work with bags of groceries, three white teenagers approached him and stabbed him in the neck. The murder was one of many racially motivated attacks that occurred at the time – 'If we saw a Paki we used to have a go at them,' remarked one of the assailants.[3] And though people of colour came together to organize against the rise of the National Front, the legacy of Ali's death and the death of so many others like him was the fear instilled into my parents' generation – and subsequently, their children – who were terrified that just stepping outside for work or groceries could endanger their lives. And it's only as I write this that I am beginning to process why my parents were afraid to let me go out alone as a teenager and young adult – and still are, to some extent – because they cannot forget the time when fascists openly combed the streets looking for Black and Brown faces to beat up.

And yet, this dynamic shows no sign of changing. The War on Terror goes on and Islamophobic hate crimes continue to rise. Rather than heeding Muslim criticisms of counter-terror programmes that disproportionately target our community or paying attention to figures that show white supremacist violence as the greatest societal risk to Western societies, we are still under the microscope. Western governments are constantly finding ways to infiltrate Muslim spaces, control and influence them, and obscure our ability to find our own answers.

The insistence that all Muslims are potential terrorists and therefore need constant monitoring reveals a great deal about Western paranoia and hostility, since surveillance programmes are proven to be defective, since the securitization of Muslim communities dehumanizes us, detaches us from our societies and erodes our trust in public institutions. What I find most depressing and infuriating, however, is that the generations younger than me will have fewer and fewer memories of 9/11 – it will be no more than a spectre on the horizon – but their lives will continue to be determined by it. It will frame how they move through the world, how they're perceived, the messages they receive from society about their self-worth and their future prospects. We need to find a way to break out of this matrix. We need to end the War on Terror and repeal its oppressive apparatus.

In 2019, the Transnational Institute published a report setting out an alternative to the War on Terror based on five key principles: democracy, evidence, human rights, community consent and peace. The report didn't suggest abandoning national security altogether. But its recommendations (for example, conducting a national audit of security needs, subjecting intelligence agencies to democratic scrutiny, making surveillance strategies accountable, ending support for states involved in human rights abuses, ending the separate legal system for terrorism-related offences and protecting academic institutions from being treated as arenas for intelligence gathering) involved creating a system to protect Britain from terrorist attacks without stigmatizing the Muslim community and attacking our basic civil liberties.[4] With a bold, radical approach like this, we could have a national security strategy that doesn't replicate the problems of the current system.

What depresses me even more, however, is how little some people care about racism. And I mean, truly care. Most people are prepared to at least declare that racism is bad. In an era of 'performative wokeness' and personal branding, there's cultural and financial reward to be gained from aligning ourselves with good causes. But public statements against racism also allow us to reject personal complicity. We can distinguish ourselves – the *good*, moral, anti-racist people – from the *bad*, immoral, racist people. Very few of us are willing to interrogate our personal attitudes (because it is a deeply uncomfortable, destabilizing process). Very few of us are willing to get our hands dirty in the work of dismantling racist structures. It is no great surprise. Indeed, as I said in the Introduction, racism has always had to evolve in order to survive; superficial alignment with anti-racism is one part of this evolution.

These dynamics around racism have been perfectly illustrated by a recent series of events. In December 2019, the British rapper Stormzy caused controversy by stating to an Italian journalist that racism still existed in Britain. Media outlets exploited this, reporting that he'd called Britain '100% racist'.[5] Stormzy was subjected to abuse on social media. The *Daily Telegraph* journalist Allison Pearson tweeted a survey that showed 'the UK was one of the two least racist countries in Europe'.[6] Consider, as an alternative, the response to Joaquin Phoenix's speech at the 2020 BAFTA awards about 'systemic racism' in the film industry: media commentators rushed to agree and praise him.[7] As always, the problem with calling out racism has much to do with *who* is calling the racism out.

Several weeks after Stormzy's comments, in January 2020, the actor Laurence Fox appeared on *Question Time* and refused to accept that Meghan Markle, the actress and wife of Prince Harry, was subject to racism. Britain was 'the most tolerant, lovely country in Europe,' he said. 'It's so easy to throw the card of racism at everybody and it's really starting to get boring now.'[8] When it was put to him that as a 'white privileged male' he might not be best positioned to understand the most insidious forms of racism, he responded: 'I can't help what I am, I was born like this, it's an immutable characteristic, so to call me a white privileged male is to be racist, you're being racist.' Fox's comments were warmly received by those who don't believe Britain has a problem with racism – people who I assume prefer to be comforted by an untruth than to interrogate the real reason for their uneasiness.

The Black Lives Matter (BLM) protests in the summer of 2020, sparked by the murder of George Floyd by police in Minneapolis, have also shown the lengths to which Britain will try to avoid honest conversations about racism. After protestors toppled the statue of seventeenth-century slave trader Edward Colston, public figures, including Tory MPs and even Prime Minister Boris Johnson, engaged in vociferous denial; by claiming a special role for Britain in abolishing slavery (which it absolutely doesn't have),[9] and by underplaying the racism of celebrated figures from Britain's past.[10] Such extreme polarities in the dialogue on race have only been possible because Britain is so disconnected from its colonial legacy. However, the problem isn't so much Britain's history, but the way it is selectively retold, parts valorized, the less salubrious parts suppressed and erased[11] to give the impression that those seeking a balanced representation of that history are either playing the victim or attacking the heart of what it means to be British.[12]

Elsewhere, media institutions have sought to describe BLM protests and fascist demonstrations on parallel terms; the latter are described as 'BLM counter-demonstrations' and 'anti-racist critics'; the media class creates a false equivalence between those protesting for an end to their oppression and those who have a problem with it – even as the latter sing 'Rule Britannia', urinate beside memorials and chant, 'We're racists and that's the way we like it.' Corporations and institutions have made a show of ceding ground: by taking the knee, offering statements of solidarity, culpability and promises to do better, pre-emptively removing statues and problematic television shows and movies.[13] These are only performances, revealing how shaken British society is by the demand for an end to Black oppression, how it will offer crumbs of distraction to stave off a painful reckoning with what it means to be Black and British today – anything to avoid substantive changes to the system. But rather than endless inquiries, which the government uses to brush legitimate complaints under the carpet, giving the public the appearance that it is taking such complaints seriously, Britain needs a truth and reconciliation commission, one tasked with confronting its racist past and present (and how this present is *informed* by our past).

With all that said, even if we're just paying lip service in Britain to the idea that racism is bad, it's infinitely harder to get some people to do even that, let alone care, with respect to Islamophobia. I've brought up Islamophobia in many conversations only to receive a mealy-mouthed reply. When that happens, I wonder how little people have considered the effects of hate on Muslim people or how little humanity they've been conditioned to afford to us. Maybe they've become desensitized to the deluge of media stories; maybe they've never considered that we also feel pain; that our self-worth also hinges on the ability to preserve a sense of dignity. My mentions of Islamophobia often cause people to fall silent, and I search their faces wondering what they're thinking about; are they feeling guilty, reflecting on the ways in which they've imbibed anti-Muslim messaging, or are they waiting for me to change the subject?

Getting people to understand Islamophobia remains a challenge. Talking about the hatred for Muslim people, their faith and culture is still relatively new, so awareness of its prevalence, its historic and structural roots, and its emotional consequences remains anaemic. Admittedly, Islamophobia is an imperfect term, suggesting irrationality, aversion, a problem with an ideology rather than with people. But it is still an effective term; one that Muslims have played a role in developing – outsiders to the dialogue should be mindful of that and respect it.

But the biggest hurdle to getting more people to take Islamophobia seriously is the evasiveness of our biggest institutions and their disingenuousness. Despite receiving cross-party support, the Conservative government has refused to adopt the All-Party Parliamentary Group (APPG) on British Muslims' definition of Islamophobia which, as I outlined in the Introduction, describes it as being 'a type of racism which targets expressions of Muslimness or perceived Muslimness'.[14] And though it never offered an explanation why, I find comments from Martin Hewitt, the chair of the National Police Chiefs' Council, incredibly revealing. Hewitt claimed to be 'concerned' that the APPG definition would challenge 'legitimate free speech on the historical or theological actions of Islamic states'.[15] Hewitt went on to argue that it could 'undermine counter-terrorism powers, which seek to tackle extremism or prevent terrorism'. I don't see how the APPG definition could hamper free speech or counter-terror work, unless this is an admission that Muslim communities *are* being targeted, and the right to do so should be ring-fenced. I suspect that this is the real reason why the government dare not adopt the APPG definition. Doing so would empower Muslim communities to hold it accountable for its Islamophobia. It's worth noting that Conservative voters have a Muslim problem. According to the 2019 Hope Not Hate statistics mentioned in Chapter One, 49 per cent of Conservative voters see Islam as a threat to the British way of life.[16] And since 2018, countless Tory MPs, councillors and members have been found making, or explicitly endorsing, anti-Muslim statements. The barrage of hatred coupled with the aversion to any meaningful engagement with complaints led Baroness Warsi to declare there were 'institutional' levels of prejudice within her party.[17]

And yet, the slippery Conservative Party dodges calls to investigate at every turn. During a television debate for Tory leadership in June 2019, Sajid Javid corralled his colleagues into pledging to hold an independent inquiry into Islamophobia. But once he became prime minister, Boris Johnson reneged on this promise. Instead, we were offered a review that examined the party's handling of all complaints of discrimination and prejudice. The review is to be led by Professor Swaran Singh, a figure who has actually defended Britain against charges of racism, ensuring that it inspires no credibility at all amongst Muslim communities.[18] The Muslim Council of Britain has accused the Conservatives of burying the problem: 'This appointment is at risk of being seen in the same light as the Conservative Party's customary approach to Islamophobia, that of denial, dismissal and deceit.'[19]

Similarly, the government has stalled on its review of Prevent. An independent review was announced back in January 2019, to be chaired by Lord Carlile again, who admitted to Parliament that he may 'be somewhat biased' given his strong support for the programme. But Carlile held on to the position until December 2019 after Rights Watch UK mounted a legal challenge. The government removed him from the role, maintaining it had 'full confidence' in his work. As of July 2020, the Prevent review remains without a chair, even though the government committed to completing the review by August 2019.[20]

All this raises questions about how the Conservative Party leaders actually view Muslims and Islamophobia if they keep refusing to give us the inquiries we deserve – especially when the Equality and Human Rights Commission is investigating anti-semitism in the Labour Party (and I am usually loath to draw comparisons between vulnerable minority groups). Is it that they don't think we're capable of handling the results of an investigation, or that they don't take us and our hurt seriously, or is it that the party leaders hold us in contempt like so many of their members? Is it that they view Muslim denigration as acceptable collateral in achieving and maintaining power, or are they just afraid of the results? I suspect all of these answers are to some extent true.

I'm also aware that the conversation on Islamophobia is taking place when other matters are capturing the world's attention. Brexit, climate change, rampant wealth inequality, the state of our health service, the rise of the far right – I am writing this in the midst of the coronavirus pandemic – these all seem like more pressing issues. It's hard to know which issue most deserves our attention and empathy. But when people argue that we mustn't talk about racism now and focus instead on coming together to fix more pressing matters, I must disagree. Islamophobia is a manifestation of one of many ills facing Western societies today. If we have any hope of creating societies that are truly sustained by democracy, equality and justice, we must address all those ills together, including racial prejudice. To solve these issues, we must recognize that they are connected. More than ever, those who believe in equality or have experienced oppression should recognize that our fates are intertwined. And rather than delaying it, I believe that we need this conversation now more than ever. The Prophet once said, 'Even if the end of the earth is upon you and you have a seedling in your hand, plant it.'

So Islamophobia is buried deep in the marrow of Western society and many people seemingly can't or don't want to talk about it. What do we do?

We mobilize. We deliberately create and enter into those conversations. We challenge preconceptions. We put a discussion of Islamophobia on to the agenda. The first stage in dismantling Islamophobia involves smashing the myths and stereotypes that were built over centuries. Arguments justifying the censure of Islam and Muslims will almost certainly grow more inventive, but they will never stray far from the elements that I set out in this book. Calling attention to Islamophobia also involves explaining the effect of these stereotypes on people's lives. The idea that one's humanity has to be proven or explained is a dangerous one and I'm not giving in to this idea. I'm not naïve enough to think that we can so easily overcome blind hate and the blanket denial of Muslim humanity. However, I do believe that many people are unaware of the pernicious effect of these stereotypes, how they trap and immobilize Muslims. Also, I can't ignore how little we talk about and acknowledge one another's pain. If we did a little more of that – if we forced people to stare at the repercussions of hatred and not look away – wouldn't it be that much harder to foster the already-rampant ignorance that exists?

In this book, I have provided the tools to dismantle Islamophobic rhetoric and explain the effect that it has on Muslims. I hope that young Muslims will be able to use these tools to navigate their worlds and resist the tendency to internalize anti-Muslim rhetoric. We have nothing to be ashamed of, no reason to doubt ourselves, no reason to believe in the stereotypes that the West has constructed around us. On the contrary, I think that we can look to our past with pride and confidence. We have just as brilliant and shameful, complex and contradictory an existence as any other community, and we're facing up to our challenges in the same ways as many others. It shouldn't take a book like this to make it obvious.

To all of us, I say this: we desperately need more sophisticated conversations about racism and Islamophobia. As it stands, those conversations waste too much energy on treating racism as some-thing that can and should be debated. We centre the perpetrators rather than the victims. We refuse to allow the victims to set the terms on which racism will be discussed. These are diversionary tactics, designed to avoid the possibility of change. I know this, but when I witness them in full flow, I lose all faith in the power of conversations to change minds. I lose sight of my objectives with this book. And yet, I return to communication because conversations are the only thing we have. They are the only way a movement can bring about systemic change.

To bring attention to the issues affecting Muslims, we need a shift in public consciousness and accountability. A consciousness that takes Islamophobia far more seriously than we do currently. We need to create a wellspring of public scrutiny to hold account-able the public and political figures, and the institutions, that are guilty of perpetuating the mistreatment of Muslims, ensuring there are consequences to an Islamophobic comment or policy. I turn to the public first and foremost because our press has let us down – our journalists and media have failed to hold to account the leaders who serve us. As US-based British journalist Mehdi Hasan describes his (now-celebrated) forensic style for interview-ing political figures: 'Most people ask the question and move on whether they get an answer or not. I don't.'[21] In many cases, those figures and outlets are equally guilty of seeding and harvesting anti-Muslim sentiment. In the absence of a rigorous press, we must show them what accountability looks like and encourage them to assume their responsibilities.

And once we capture the public space, we set out concrete demands.[22] Prevent is but one example of how we could begin dismantling systemic racism. An independent review of Prevent must be carried out immediately, led by a properly impartial figure. To have any credibility, that review must broaden its terms; as it stands, the proposed review has a deliberately narrow scope, focused only on the 'present delivery of Prevent', excluding how it has operated in the past. It must also respond to emerging research. For example, a report by the Youth Empowerment and Innovation Project found that 'generating positive psychology' by addressing social exclusion was more effective at challenging violent radicalization amongst young people.[23] And the outcome of such a review must be accepted. We have seen too many gov-ernment reviews that either legitimize oppressive policies or result in recommendations that go ignored. This cannot happen again.

As we call for the counter-terror apparatus to be dismantled, the government continues to strengthen it through longer sentences, instruments to expand the monitoring of individuals who haven't been actually convicted of any crimes – and lie detector tests.[24] Revelations that non-violent environmental and animal rights activists have also been referred to Prevent should emphasize the dangers of the programme to society at large. Because it is a tool that the government can employ to subdue and control any group and movement it feels threatened by; abolishing Prevent is in our collective self-interest.

So I ask you all to take these tools out into the world and hold people accountable for their ignorance and hatred. We should hold our families and partners accountable; we should hold our colleagues and friends accountable. We need to hold the systems and institutions around us accountable for creating environments that have allowed Islamophobia to flourish and Muslims to be mercilessly attacked and humiliated; our governments and their agencies, our politicians and their parties and ministries, our police departments, our newspapers, our journalists, our film-makers and television channels. Stop Islamophobia from continuing to pass the dinner table test. And when Islamophobes seek to evade our accountability, don't let them get away with it.

Many will be intimidated or even sceptical of the request to mobilize and make a stand. But we can draw inspiration from ACT UP, the organization founded in 1987 in the US to bring attention to the AIDS pandemic. ACT UP is probably the most successful social movement of recent times, using civil disobedience and public protest to force the Reagan administration into recognizing the pandemic and funding the development of a treatment.[25]

We can also learn a great deal from the perseverance of Doreen Lawrence, whose son Stephen Lawrence was murdered by racists in 1993. Without her tireless campaigning, we probably wouldn't have had an independent inquiry into the circumstances surrounding his death. Without the Macpherson report, set up in 1997 and published in 1999, we wouldn't have learned about the Metropolitan Police's mistakes in investigating the case; it wouldn't have been confirmed that the police force was institutionally racist.[26] And we wouldn't have had subsequent investigations into police corruption, or attempts by the Metropolitan Police to deliver on race equality.[27]

Our societies have long, stubborn histories of racism and Islamophobia that won't go away quickly or easily, but we shouldn't take this to mean change is impossible. Sometimes change is so incremental and small, we might not even notice it. After the white supremacist terrorist attack on a shisha bar in Hanau, Germany in February 2020, Chancellor Angela Merkel spoke of how it was motivated by far-right racism. Just her using the word 'racism' was incredible – no German chancellor has probably ever used it in such a way before – and a critical step towards tackling the problem. Such honesty by a German leader would have been unthinkable if it wasn't for activists in the country keeping the conversation on racism alive.

We Muslims are trying to do all this too, but we need your voices to help us. Only by calling the world to attention and forcing our societies to take Islamophobia more seriously can we start to make concrete demands for the kind of world we want to live in. Only then can we call for Muslims in the West to have access to the kind of life that certain others take for granted. But let me say this: I want there to be a day when Muslims are able to exist without feeling the external gaze bearing down on us at all times, watching us, scrutinizing. A day when every expression of ours is no longer pushed through the lens of Islam and essentialist ideas of Muslimness. A day when the state is not trying to set out what kind of Islamic belief is permissible. A day when our religion doesn't determine the kind of opportunities we will have access to in our lives. When we, as minorities, aren't described in terms of, or expected to answer to, the prejudices of the majority. A day when we are free to fail, a day when we are able to be human in the way so many others are permitted to be.

*

With every charge that is levelled at Islam and Muslim communities, the most valuable thing we can do (as Suhaiymah Manzoor-Khan also mentioned in our conversation) is query them and ask ourselves, what is the purpose of this accusation? Why is it being levelled? From this I have realized that the most significant part of the battle against Islamophobia involves the West addressing what it doesn't want to – its own crisis of confidence. I've come to understand that the growing appetite for anti-Muslim hatred has very little to do with Muslims. Instead, it represents a growing anxiety around Western identity. Whenever the West has suffered with this question in the past, it has lashed out at minorities. It is lashing out at Muslims, people of colour and immigrants today, but the crisis remains, prodding away. What does the West actually stand for?

I'm reminded of something that Toni Morrison once said: 'What are you without racism? Are you any good? Are you still strong? Are you still smart? Do you still like yourself?' She went on to say, 'If you can only be tall because somebody is on their knees, then you have a serious problem. And my feeling is that white people have a very, very serious problem and they should start thinking about what they can do about it. Take me out of it.'[28]

I pose similar questions to the West now. What is the West without an enemy? What is the West without the need to feel superior to others? What is it without the myths of its own supremacy? The West believes that it can only thrive by dominating others. It pushes a narrative on to its own citizens that, as the land of equality and opportunity, life is getting better for *everybody*. But as extreme disparities in income and wealth, austerity, the rise of populist leaders and exploding levels of depression, stress and anxiety show, this is a major deception (or as Toni Morrison labelled it, a manifestation of the 'profound neurosis' of racism) – life is not getting better; people are not necessarily happier.[29] As new political and economic powerhouses emerge and compete with the West for influence, as Westerners grow more discontent with their lives, as inequality and injustice become more pronounced in our societies and more difficult to deny, and as the illusion of our intellectual, moral, financial and technological superiority over the rest of the world begins to disappear, the West will need to find answers to these questions.[30] They are growing ever more urgent.

So I suggest that we don't have a 'Muslim problem' at all or, rather, that the so-called Muslim problem is a smokescreen for Western problems. The West's inability to face up to the evolving world. The West's rejection of reflection, healing and justice during periods of adversity and hardship. The West's need for superiority and dominance. The West being hurt by globalization too, in that it has exacerbated divides. But at some point, as Western citizens, we'll have to engage in all this. We'll have to heal our insecurities. We'll have to reject the path of exclusion and hatred. We'll need to invent new myths that fit changing realities. As it stands, our determination to dehumanize others, or our ability to allow it to happen, reveals a great deal about our society. Not its superiority, but the limits of its humanity. And the values it claims to hold so dear.

*

I was wondering how to sum up my thoughts on Muslim communities when Eid-ul-Adha came along and, with it, the answer: the mosque. After all, our mosques are at the physical and spiritual centre of Islam. I love going to my local mosque on Eid. I find peace and belonging there. I'm happy watching people dressed in their finest clothes, toddlers in miniature outfits running up and down the aisles. I've attended this mosque since I was a young boy. It's where I first learned to read the Quran and it's where my grandparents' funerals were held. It is home.

On this particular Eid, I was my usual contented self until the Eid sermon came. The imam started to remind us, yet again, of Prophet

Ibrahim's willingness to sacrifice his son out of his devotion to God. A familiar, bitter feeling came over me and I switched off. I stopped listening. I pulled out my phone and read the news and waited until he was done. I did so for several reasons: I'd heard the story many times before, I hated that the imam offered us the moral message of sacrifice, and was frustrated that his sermon was so far removed from our daily realities. When it was over and I got up to greet the people around me, I tried to stifle my annoyance and disappointment, feeling that we'd been short-changed with yet another sermon that had failed to touch upon the struggles we face in our lives.

Those of us who are religious should find ourselves in a particularly fortunate position to deal with these struggles; we should be able to tap into a support system that relates to our pain and finds ways to ease it. But in general, many of our communities, like our mosques, aren't rising to this challenge. Islam was once distinguished for its ability to adapt to changing social and political conditions, for its gift of developing innovative answers to the questions of the day. Many of us now are tossing that heritage aside. And some have gone on to obstruct those who *do* want to use our heritage as inspiration. I see a lot of injustice, a lot of gatekeepers stopping us from developing better relationships with God. And it's not just a question of spiritual guidance, but physical space. I can't talk about mosques without referring to the exclusion of women, who tend to be absent from committees and often lack equivalent spaces to worship in. When they do, these spaces can be cramped and decrepit, where they can barely hear the imam. Our mosques have lots to address too.

It goes without saying that I'm not arguing that all mosques and all communities are failing to rise to the challenge of modernity. But there's no denying that the most transformative and sacred spiritual spaces I ever experienced were the ones that my colleagues and I co-created. Those spaces rejected gender segregation and affirmed sexual equality. They encouraged horizontal leadership and refused to elevate one figure above others as the repository of all religious knowledge. And they understood that spiritual spaces were incomplete without the opportunity to socialize and connect outside of prayer. In doing all of this, my fellow activists and I encouraged the entire congregation to shape and articulate our collective spiritual expression. We gave dignity to Muslims, many of whom had been alienated and demoralized by existing religious spaces, and dignity to their desire for more authentic, more organic religious expression. I asked two friends for their memories of those spaces. One of them said, 'When I used to go to mainstream mosques, I didn't feel like my voice could be heard, nor was there a space for me to feel comfortable. Our spaces – where everyone was equal regardless of gender, race, sexuality or ability – made me feel like I belonged.' The other agreed: 'It was like a spiritual awakening. Seeing women leading prayers and giving the call to prayer, it felt like an equal setting for the first time. I felt free, safe, empowered and enlightened.' Since I left my grassroots activist project, I'm not sure if those spaces exist in quite the same form.

When I imagine what my ideal mosque would look like, I take from that work, which built on the work of Muslim activists who taught and inspired me. I also take from the tradition of Black Muslim theology, which has used Islam to address anti-Black racism and oppression in the US and South Africa.[31] I also latch on to an image of the Nigerian mosque that sits around the corner from mine. On Eid, as I make my visits to my uncles and aunts, I catch the congregation in the courtyard. They're all dressed in brightly coloured prints, men and women laughing together and children playing around them. There's the smell of meat sizzling on the barbeque. The communal spirit, the *ease*, that's what I want more mosques to encourage. Mosques once played multifaceted roles in the lives of Muslims, a place not just for prayer, but for our congregations to socialize and connect. That certain aspects already exist in some religious spaces gives me a lot of confidence that it's both entirely possible and right to encourage our mosques to be the beating hearts of our communities.

I'm encouraged that some mosques are changing. The Muslim Council of Britain's 'Women in Mosques Development Programme', which began in 2018 to accelerate the development of female leadership, is one example of the kind of work being done within Muslim communities to diversify religious leadership.[32] I also continue to be inspired by the Inclusive Mosque Initiative. Not only does it nurture female spiritual leadership, but it organizes important social and educational events, some celebrating Muslim heritage (Rumi's birthday, for example), others tackling contemporary issues (like climate change, sexual diversity, disability access, Islamophobia and gender justice). I have met the new generation of young imams, activists and creatives who are taking up spaces in our religious institutions to change them, and creating new spaces that better suit our needs.

With the mosque as my lens into the state of Muslim communities, I can say with confidence that there's enough happening for me to stay hopeful. But I'm also not going to deny that the challenges ahead of us are momentous. If we are to stop young Muslims from feeling like they are being pushed around or excluded from the faith by puritan narratives, we need to assert more strongly the diverse and inclusive spirit of Islam. We need to evolve our spaces. Our religion has always prescribed very little in terms of hard doctrine, which means that it can encompass any number of relationships and approaches to faith. So why are we restricting it?

I'm conscious of urging Muslim communities to work at the necessary improvements at a time when we are being heavily criticized from the outside. During the course of writing this book, I've had to assess whether it's truly possible for us to confront and resolve our greatest challenges when we're under siege from Islamophobia, both in the West and increasingly in Eastern nations such as China, Sri Lanka, Burma and India. Even the coronavirus pandemic didn't stop Muslims from being treated differently; as vectors of infection, infantilized through videos telling us to stay at home during Ramadan and on Eid by institutions and media outlets that were far less critical when white masses gathered for Victory in Europe day parties and appeared on the news dancing together.[33]

From our conversation together, Myriam François's words ring in my ears: 'It's very difficult to evolve in terms of your thinking as a community when you live in a constant state of embattlement. That's the state that we live in.' Many of us feel wounded and vulnerable; even those of us willing to have difficult conversations are wary of having our statements exploited by Islamophobes. Can the two conversations around religious dogma and Islamophobia take place simultaneously, I asked Myriam. 'I think it's very, very difficult to have them simultaneously,' she said. But critically, she acknowledged that they were taking place, albeit in closed quarters. Muslims are creating spaces in magazines and podcasts and conferences to have the conversations that are important to us. It's hard, but we must keep having these difficult conversations and creating spaces for them to take place. If we refuse, we risk being unjust to the people who are being damaged by the status quo.

So where do we go from here? What do these conversations look like if you're new to them? First, I believe that Muslims must decide what it is that Islam stands for. To do that we need to go back to the scripture, reassert our values and make all Muslims aware of what principles we are subscribing to when we decide to belong to Islam. Secondly, we need to take back our diverse history from the people who wish to erase it. We have to reserve the right to extract from it the wisdom that we want. Remembrance is political, a tool for our survival. Thirdly, we must face up to the ways in which existing interpretations or approaches to Islam hurt people, and work to eliminate those structures of oppression. The sooner we realize that past Muslim generations have always used Quranic principles to interpret and reinterpret their religious responsibilities, the sooner we accept that Islamic law has always been flexible and has adapted to changing times, the sooner we will accept that we are also free to do the same.

*

My final words are for the Muslims reading this who've been hurt, discouraged and disenfranchized by faith. Hang in there, you can find a place for yourself within Islam. It's worthwhile to keep trying. For you, I asked my interviewees for their advice on resolving religious and spiritual conflict. I collected their suggestions (and my own) to come up with the list below. Consider it a manifesto.

1. The Struggle Is Real

You might assume that only a small number of Muslims struggle with faith, specifically those who find themselves marginalized by narrow interpretations of the scripture. But this isn't so. None of my interviewees found belonging to a religion easy or straightforward; faith ebbs and flows, growing weaker or stronger in contract with the rest of our lives. Struggle is more common than you think.

I know that it's hard to get a sense of this: our spiritual practice is driven by perfection, and we don't acknowledge how perfection is impossible to achieve. And there aren't any Muslim figures in the public eye willing to articulate alternative relationships with faith. Instead, we have conservatively inclined Muslims taking up too much space. But I know that struggle and doubt is integral to Islam. The Quran acknowledges doubt by continually providing evidence of God's existence and the veracity of the Quran as God's message [2:1–7]. Let this legitimize your struggle and your journey. As the scholar, Al-Ghazali once said, 'Doubt is the beginning of faith.' Explore what you feel; the payoff could be huge.

2. Take Responsibility for Your Journey

'Read,' began the first revelation to Prophet Muhammad. 'Read in the name of your Lord' [96:1–5]. Here, at the very outset of Islam, the duty begins for Muslims to use their critical faculties to engage with the world and enrich our spiritual practice. Over and over again, the Quran refers to 'signs' in nature of God's existence aimed at those with the ability to think and reflect.

If you're looking to develop an independent relationship with Islam, you have to take responsibility for your own journey. Educate yourself and do not be discouraged by the gatekeepers who insist that you're not capable of understanding historic Islamic scholarship. You have every right to probe that work; all scholars, regardless of their pedigree, are human and may have been restrained in their abilities by the time in which they lived or their biases. You will have a lot of decisions to make: What to do with the Shariah? How to approach Hadiths? How to use Islam to resolve very modern questions around climate change or eating meat or sexual identity? There are books and scholars and organizations to help you, but don't indulge in the tendency to make these people your infallible icons and authorities. Remember that the choices are yours. You have to be comfortable with them. We are all on personal journeys with faith and each of us is separately answerable to God.

3. Get to Grips with the Basics

Ground yourself in the core values of Islam. What is Islam? What does it mean to be a Muslim? It's good to define yourself against the things that you don't believe in (authoritarianism, misogyny, racism), but what about defining the things that are important to you? When I was younger, my father taught me that Islam centred around social justice, that no edict could be compatible with the religion unless it preserved human dignity and uplifted society. That has framed my conversation with Islam ever since.

Identifying Islam's core values will provide you with a moral compass to navigate a route through the faith. I particularly appreciate the scholar Farhana Mayer, who looks to the Ninety-Nine Names of God as the source of Islam's values. The most important names anchor Islamic belief and behaviour; they cannot be superseded. Mayer cites the Quran to support her argument, which tells us that God's character 'is the eternal religion but most people do not know' [30:30]. Names like 'the compassionate', 'the tolerant', 'the just' and 'the impartial' not only guide us, but also have the radical potential to tackle oppressive interpretations and behaviours identified with Islam. As my dad says to me constantly, if there is no mercy, no kindness, no fairness in your practice of Islam, then it is not Islam that you are practising.

4. Know Your History (Context Is Everything)

History is a source of pride when we read of the many Muslim achievements through the ages. History can also be a guide in so far as the religious practices of previous generations enable us to imagine life free of puritanism and Islamophobia.

But most importantly, history gives context. It allows us to interrogate the motives and character of our Hadith narrators, and the attitudes of scholars that we have been taught to uncritically revere. Reconnecting the Quran with its history also lets us look at it again with a fresh pair of eyes. After all, most of its legal verses were responding to the specific problems of early Muslim society. This raises the very important question of whether Allah intended for those edicts to remain with us for eternity or for the principles behind them to guide future societies. I would argue the latter; so do many other scholars. Remember that the Quran is a historical, as well as spiritual, text.

5. Acknowledge the Constructedness of It All

Islam, as a system of beliefs and practices, isn't infallible; it is constructed. Puritans would like us to believe in its sacred nature, so that we don't challenge their specific interpretations. But the truth is that Islam has been shaped by humans, whether it's the figures who decided how to standardize the pronunciation and meaning of Arabic words, the figures who decided the revelations should be ordered to form the Quran as it exists today or the figures who decided from which region Hadiths should be collected and which ones should be documented.

Recognizing how the Quran came to exist in its current form doesn't take away or undermine its sacredness. As I have said before, I believe the Quran is the word of God; but I also accept responsibility for interpreting it and the possibility that other readers will find their own truths (that do not violate the fundamentals of Islam). Nor do I treat the Shariah or Hadiths with the same reverence. It's only when you acknowledge the role of ordinary, non-Prophetic humans in constructing Islam, you understand that you are free to shape it for yourself. These humans may have been closer to the Prophet or may have had greater knowledge, but they don't know your reality better than you. They were no more entitled to contribute to Islam then than you are today. As amina wadud explained to me: 'I determine a definition of Islam for myself. I construct Islam. And when I finish constructing that Islam, I promote that Islam. I am not responding to Islamophobes or neo-conservatives. I am continuing to promote a construction that I think would be the most amenable to the world.' Let this be the beginning of *your* conversation with God.

6. Follow Your Heart

Islam is also meant to be easy. When we are conflicted or struggling, we lose sight of that. Don't. Avoiding hardship is a critical part of the faith. The Quran repeats this several times, 'Allah wishes to make things easy for you, and not to make things difficult' [2:185] and 'We did not place difficulty in this religion' [22:78]. Even Imam Bukhari developed a whole section in his Hadith collection entitled, 'The Chapter of the Religion Being Easy'.

Now this might appear simplistic. It might seem as if I am failing to engage with the struggles of those who are plagued by stubborn doubts or crises of faith. But my broader point is that whilst Muslims may believe that life is a test, Islam doesn't have a doctrine of suffering like Catholicism does. There is no redemption in misery. It will not send us to Heaven. It might also seem like I'm ignoring the very real suffering that exists in the world. But the principle of ease refers specifically to religious doctrine – simply put, God doesn't wish for religious matters to increase our misery.

But how does one make religion easy? Start by being kind to yourself and others. Take your time to work things out. Practise and believe in what feels authentic to you. Find pockets of joy and revel in them. Find a community to support you. Don't lose touch with spiritual and religious practice, even if it's just meandering through the Quran, in your native tongue, at your own pace. If you're struggling with a particular decision, follow your heart. Myriam François does: 'In my life, I am more reliant on my heart. I ask myself, is this to serve my ego, or am I recognizing that in my reality, it's a struggle?' Leyla Jagiella reminds us: 'God loves even the small and simple things we do.'

I believe this: every religious person is taking a leap, a risk in order to believe in something. That is what faith is all about. Deciding to adopt the simplest, easiest solution to your problems is also a risk, and it is not that much different. So choose the gentler path and remember, God is beneficent. If one of Islam's key messages is of God's infinite mercy, then we must fully embrace it and what that could mean for the choices we make, for our well-being and happiness.

7. Prioritize Healing

Pay attention to your pain and make time and space for healing. The Quran can heal some hurt, as can some of the more beautiful

Hadiths and works of scholarship. But don't be afraid of therapy or other types of healing and self-care. As Samia Rahman remarked:

> Why do we aspire to ritualistic perfection? Why not seek perfection in love and healing and therapeutic ways, perfection in terms of self-improvement and figuring out the best ways to interact with each other and bringing out the best in each other? That's where our priorities as communities need to lie.

Begin by prioritizing healing for yourself.

8. You Are Muslim If You Say You Are

Finally, your right to belong to Islam cannot be stripped from you. Some will claim the right to takfir (declare somebody a non-Muslim), but they are wrong. Many scholars, including the initial 126 scholars mentioned in Chapter Two who wrote to condemn ISIS through the scripture, don't believe that ordinary Muslims can strip somebody's faith from them. As Reza Aslan said to me:

> There is no body, no authority, no institution that has the power now, or has ever had the power, to define who is and who is not a Muslim. That's what is so unique about Islam. We've never had a high priest. We've never had a pope. That has never existed, not a single authoritative figure who speaks for all of Muslims, in 1400 years, for now what is 2 billion Muslims. Think about how extraordinary that truth is. What is a Muslim then? Who gets to say what a Muslim is? No one.

Remember this as you pursue your individual journey. Do not let a person come between you and God, between you and your identity as a Muslim. Decide what kind of Muslim you want to be and stick with it. Good luck.

Notes

Introduction

1. Whitaker, B. (24 Jun. 2002). 'Worst impressions', *Guardian*; Ahmed, S. and Matthes, J. (2017). 'Media representation of Muslims and Islam from 2000 to 2015: A meta-analysis', *International Communication Gazette*, *79*(3), pp. 219–44; Saeed, A. (2007). 'Media, racism and Islamophobia: The representation of Islam and Muslims in the media', *Sociology Compass*, *1*(1), pp. 447–62.
2. Ibid.
3. *Telegraph* (4 May 2015). 'Prophet Mohammed cartoons controversy: Timeline'.
4. Littlejohn, R. (8 Aug. 2006). 'If they hate us so much, why don't they leave?' *Daily Mail*.
5. Sheikh, F. (7 Mar. 2018). 'Voices of young Muslims: Building a society free of Islamophobia', Jawaab.
6. Halliday, J. (22 Jun. 2017). 'Islamophobic attacks in Manchester surge by 500% after arena attack', *Guardian*.
7. *BBC News* (24 May 2017). 'Manchester attack: Morrissey criticises response of politicians'.
8. Hooton, C. (26 May 2017). 'Katie Hopkins to leave LBC "immediately" in wake of Manchester attack "final solution" comments', *Independent*.
9. All-Party Parliamentary Group on British Muslims (27 Nov. 2018). 'Islamophobia defined: The inquiry into a working definition of Islamophobia'.
10. Webb, E., ed. (Aug. 2019). 'Islamophobia: An anthology of concerns', Civitas.
11. For example, the Australian author Hal G. P. Colebatch argued that Islamophobia was 'among the most purely dishonest expressions in modern politics'. He cited Islam's 'oppression of women', 'ongoing massacres of Christians in the third world' and Iran and ISIS, to argue that 'it is hardly "Islamophobic" or irrational to criticise all this'. See Colebatch, H. G. P. (11 Mar. 2017). 'The inquiry into a working definition of Islamophobia', *Spectator*. See also comments made by Richard Dawkins: Flood, A. (24 Jun. 2017). 'Richard Dawkins event cancelled over his "abusive speech against Islam"', *Guardian*.
12. Massoumi, N., Mills, T. and Miller, D., eds. (2017). *What is Islamophobia? Racism, Social Movements and the State*, Pluto Press, pp. 3–8.

13. Izzidien, R. (23 Jan. 2018). 'Higher insurance if you're called Mohammed? That's just the start of institutionalised Islamophobia', *New Statesman*.

14. Home Office (24 Feb. 1999). 'The Stephen Lawrence Inquiry: Report of an inquiry by Sir William Macpherson', para. 6.34.

15. Counter-Terrorism and Security Act 2015.

16. Boswell, J. and Griffiths, S. (14 Feb. 2016). 'Police quiz teen over Palestine badge', *Sunday Times*.

17. Eddo-Lodge, R. (2018). *Why I'm No Longer Talking to White People About Race*, Bloomsbury, p. 64.

18. Gani, A. (16 Mar. 2016). 'Zac Goldsmith criticised over leaflet aimed at British Indians', *Guardian*.

19. Mason, R., Stewart, H. and Asthana, A. (20 Apr. 2016). 'MPs shout "racist" at Cameron after comments on Sadiq Khan during PMQs', *Guardian*; Stewart, H. (11 May 2016). 'David Cameron apologises after saying ex-imam "supported Islamic State"', *Guardian*.

20. Goldsmith, Z. (1 May 2016). 'On Thursday, are we really going to hand the world's greatest city to a Labour party that thinks terrorists is its friends? A passionate plea from ZAC GOLDSMITH four days before Mayoral election', *Mail on Sunday*.

21. Johnson, B. (5 Aug. 2018). 'Denmark has got it wrong. Yes, the burka is oppressive and ridiculous – but that's still no reason to ban it', *Telegraph*.

22. *BBC News* (21 Dec. 2018). 'Boris Johnson cleared of breaking Tory rules over burka comments'.

23. Toynbee, P. (14 Aug. 2018). 'Boris Johnson or the burqa? It's a false choice – both dehumanise Muslim women', *Guardian*.

24. Batty, D. (20 Jan. 2011). 'Lady Warsi claims Islamophobia is now socially acceptable in Britain', *Guardian*.

25. Griggs, I. (9 May 2016). 'London chooses "hope over fear" as Goldsmith's negative campaign criticised', *PRWeek*.

26. Murphy, J. (13 Apr. 2016). 'Zac Goldsmith accuses Sadiq Khan of "giving platform and oxygen to extremists"', *Evening Standard*.

27. Singh, H. (20 Jan. 2020). 'It's time to have an honest conversation about "Asian" grooming gangs', *Spectator*.

28. Norfolk, A. (28 Aug. 2017). 'Christian child forced into Muslim foster care', *The Times*.

29. Cathcart, B. and French, P. (Jun. 2019). 'Unmasked: Andrew Norfolk, The Times and anti-Muslim reporting – a case to answer', Media Reform Coalition.

30. Versi, M. (27 Apr. 2018). 'Islamophobia not an issue in the British press? You've got to be kidding', *Guardian*.

31. Wells, A. (10 Sep. 2011). '9/11: Ten years on', YouGov.

32. Show Racism the Red Card (19 May 2015). 'Study into attitudes of young people reveals widespread misconceptions about immigration'.

33. Embury-Dennis, T. (25 Apr. 2018). 'Daily Express helped create "Islamophobic sentiment", admits newspaper's editor', *Independent*.

34. Morrison, M. (20 May 1975). 'A humanist view', Portland State University's

Oregon Public Speakers Collection: 'Black Studies Center public dialogue. Pt. 2'.

35. Dodd, V. and Rawlinson, K. (1 Feb. 2018). 'Finsbury Park attack: Man "brainwashed by anti-Muslim propaganda" convicted', *Guardian*.

36. History drawn from Armstrong, K. (2001). *Islam: A Short History*, Phoenix, chapters 3 and 5; Armstrong, K. (2014). *Fields of Blood: Religion and the History of Violence*, Bodley Head, chapters 7 and 8.

37. Tolan, J. V. (2002). *Saracens – Islam in the Medieval European Imagination*, Columbia University Press, p. 87.

38. Armstrong, K., *Fields of Blood*, pp. 189–90.

39. Robert the Monk, cited in Armstrong, K., *Fields of Blood*, p. 194. See also, Asbridge, T. (2012). *The Crusades: The War for the Holy Land*, Simon & Schuster.

40. Grosfoguel, R. (2012). 'The multiple faces of Islamophobia', *Islamophobia Studies Journal*, *1*(1), pp. 9–33.

41. This erasure would prove unsuccessful. Muslim slaves led many of the slave riots, including the very first on the island of Hispaniola in 1521. See, Diouf, S. A. (1998). *Servants of Allah: African Muslims Enslaved in the Americas*, New York University Press; Mugabo, D. (2016). 'On rocks and hard places: A reflection on antiblackness in organizing against Islamophobia', *Critical Ethnic Studies*, *2*(2), pp. 159–83.

42. Djait, H. (1985). *Europe and Islam: Cultures and Modernity*, University of California Press, pp. 18–19.

43. Bohnstedt, J. W. (1968). 'The infidel scourge of God: The Turkish menace as seen by German pamphleteers of the Reformation era', *Transactions of the American Philosophical Society*, *58*(9), pp. 1–58.

44. Almond, I. (2012). *History of Islam in German Thought: From Leibniz to Nietzsche*, Routledge, p. 33.

45. Van der Lugt, M. (2017). 'The body of Mahomet: Pierre Bayle on war, sex, and Islam', *Journal of the History of Ideas*, *78*(1), pp. 27–50.

46. Prideaux, H. (1723). *The True Nature of Imposture Fully Display'd in the Life of Mahomet: With a Discourse Annex'd for the Vindication of Christianity from this Charge: Offered to the Consideration of the Deists of the Present Age*, E. Curll, 8th edition, pp. iii–viii; Gottschalk, P. and Greenberg, G. (2012). 'Common heritage, uncommon fear: Islamophobia in the United States and British India, 1687–1947', *Islamophobia Studies Journal*, *1*(1) p. 85.

47. Cited in Djait, pp. 24–5.

48. Samman, K. (2012). 'Islamophobia and the time and space of the Muslim other', *Islamophobia Studies Journal*, *1*(1) 107–30, p. 126.

49. Ernst, C. W. (2003). *Following Mohammad: Rethinking Islam in the Contemporary World*, The University of North Carolina Press, pp. 11–28.

50. *New York Daily Tribune* (15 Apr. 1854). 'The outbreak of the Crimean War – Moslems, Christians and Jews in the Ottoman Empire', quoted in Avineri, S. (1968). *Karl Marx on Colonialism and Modernization*, Doubleday, p. 146.

51. Samman, op. cit.

52. Grosfoguel, op. cit., p. 15; Grosfoguel, R. and Mielants, E. (2006). 'The long-durée entanglement between Islamophobia and racism in the modern/colonial capitalist/patriarchal world-system: An introduction', *Human Architecture: Journal of the Sociology of Self-knowledge*, 5(1), article 2; Meer, N. and Modood, T. (2012). 'For "Jewish" read "Muslim"? Islamophobia as a form of racialisation of ethno-religious groups in Britain today', *Islamophobia Studies Journal*, 1(1), pp. 34–53.

53. Lewis, B. (Sep. 1990). 'The roots of Muslim rage', *Atlantic*.

54. Huntington, S. P. (1993). 'The clash of civilization?', *Foreign Affairs*, 72(3), pp. 22–49.

55. Said, E. (1997). *Covering Islam: How the Media and the Experts Determine How We See the Rest of the World*, Vintage; Bazian, H. (2018). 'Islamophobia, "clash of civilizations", and forging a post-Cold War order!', *Religions*, 9(9), p. 282.

1. 'Muslims Don't Integrate'

1. Wiseman, E. (16 Dec. 2018). 'Nadiya Hussain: "This is more than a job – it's important to be out there"', *Guardian*.

2. Linning, S. (29 Oct. 2017). 'Bake Off's Nadiya Hussain reveals her husband does ALL the chores at Christmas as she shares her tips for a stress-free day – including three ways to entertain children of any age', *Mail Online*.

3. Powell, E. (31 Oct. 2017). 'GBBO star Nadiya Hussain hits back at racist Twitter trolls telling her to leave the UK', *Evening Standard*.

4. BBC One (19 May 2019). 'Nadiya: Anxiety and me'.

5. Dearden, L. (17 Feb. 2017). 'Danish opposition party demands immigrants celebrate Christmas "if they want to be Danish"', *Independent*.

6. Al-Azhar University (2009). 'The response', available at fixyourdeen.com.

7. Ministry of Housing, Communities and Local Government (Feb. 2019). 'Integrated Communities Strategy Green Paper: Summary of consultation responses and Government response'.

8. The People of Australia (16 Feb. 2011). 'Australia's multicultural policy'; German Federal Cabinet, 'National integration plan: Driver of integration policy' (2007) and 'National action plan on integration' (2012).

9. *Politics* (8 Dec. 2006). 'Blair warns of "duty" to integrate'.

10. *BBC News* (17 Oct. 2010). 'Merkel says German multicultural society has failed'.

11. Ngo, M. (3 Jul. 2018). 'Germany used to be a champion of open borders in Europe. Not anymore', *Vox*.

12. PM's speech at Munich Security Conference, Cabinet Office, Prime Minister's Office, 10 Downing Street (5 Feb. 2011); Hollinger, P. (10 Feb. 2011). 'Sarkozy joins multiculturalism attack', *Financial Times*.

13. Osborne, S. (22 Feb. 2017). 'Geert Wilders: Far-right Dutch PM frontrunner says "Islam and freedom are not compatible"', *Independent*.

14. Henley, J. (23 Jan. 2017). 'Netherlands PM says those who don't respect customs should leave', *Guardian*.

15. Kumar, D. (2012). *Islamophobia and the Politics of Empire*, Haymarket Books, pp. 55–9.

16. Kundnani, A. (2015). *The Muslims are Coming! Islamophobia, Extremism, and the Domestic War on Terror*, Verso, p. 251.

17. Malik, N. (4 Feb. 2019). 'High-profile Muslims have a right not to expect an inquisition', *Guardian*.

18. Rogers de Waal, J. (3 Feb. 2019). 'Western/MENA attitudes to religion portray a lack of faith in common values', YouGov.

19. Lowles, N., ed. (Feb. 2019). 'State of Hate 2019: People vs. the elite?', Hope Not Hate, pp. 17 and 22.

20. El-Menouar, Y. (Aug. 2017). 'Muslims in Europe: Integrated but not accepted?' Bertelsmann Stiftung.

21. Miera, F. (2008). 'Country report on migration: Germany', Edumigrom; Fernandez-Kelly, P. (2012). 'The unequal structure of the German education system: Structural reasons for educational failures of Turkish youth in Germany', *Spaces Flows*, 2(2), pp. 93–112.

22. Beauchemin, C., Hamel, C. and Simon, P., eds. (2018). *Trajectories and Origins: Survey on the Diversity of the French Population*, Springer.

23. Valfort, M. A. (Oct. 2015). 'Religious discrimination in access to employment: a reality', Institut Montaigne.

24. Full Fact (11 Aug. 2016). 'Are Muslim women more likely to be unemployed?'

25. Khattab, N. and Modood, T. (2018). 'Accounting for British Muslims' educational attainment: gender differences and the impact of expectations', *British Journal of Sociology of Education*, 39(2), pp. 242–59.

26. Cases C-157/15 Achbita, Centrum voor Gelijkheid van kansen en voor racismebestrijding v. G4S Secure Solutions and C-188/15 Bougnaoui and Association de défense des droits de l'homme (ADDH) v. Micropole Univers.

27. Barry, E. and Selsoe Sorensen, M. (1 Jul. 2018). 'In Denmark, harsh new laws for immigrant "ghettos"', *New York Times*.

28. Murray, D. (Feb. 2006). 'What are we to do about Islam? A speech to the Pim Fortuyn Memorial Conference on Europe and Islam'.

29. Casey, L. (5 Dec. 2016). 'The Casey Review: A review into opportunity and integration', Ministry of Housing, Communities & Local Government. Casey's hostility towards Muslims was further laid clear in an article for *The Sun* (13 Mar. 2018): 'We are sleepwalking into an increasingly segregated country – it's time to ignore "racism" fears and act to stop Britain falling apart.'

30. Press Association (18 May 2014). 'Immigrants need to learn English says new culture secretary Sajid Javid', *Guardian*; Refugee Action (Oct. 2017). 'Safe but alone'. The accompanying Refugee Action briefing detailed the impact of government cuts on integration: 'Government funding in England fell from £203m in 2010 to £90m in 2016 – a real terms cut of 60%.'

31. Runnymede Trust (Nov. 2018). 'Runnymede submission to UN Special Rapporteur'.

32. Stevenson, J., et al (Sep. 2017). 'The social mobility challenges faced by young Muslims', Social Mobility Commission.

33. Hourani, A. (1980). *Europe and the Middle East*, University of California Press, pp. 13 and 57.
34. Baldwin, R. (2016). *The Great Convergence*, Harvard University Press, p. 38.
35. Hourani, op. cit., p. 61.
36. Anievas, A. and Nişancioğlu, K. (2015). *How the West Came to Rule: The Geopolitical Origins of Capitalism*, Pluto Press; Nimako, N. and Willemsen, G. (2011). *The Dutch Atlantic: Slavery, Abolition and Emancipation*, Pluto Press.
37. Sen, A. K. (1999). 'Democracy as a universal value', *Journal of Democracy*, 10(3), pp. 3–17. See also, Sen, A. (2001). *Development as Freedom*, OUP.
38. Pew Research Center (10 Jul. 2012). 'Most Muslims want democracy, personal freedoms, and Islam in political life'.
39. Horovitz, D. (25 Feb. 2011). 'A mass expression of outrage against injustice', *Jerusalem Post*.
40. Kumar, op. cit., pp. 41–61.
41. Ibid.
42. Mishra, P. (20 Sep. 2019). 'The west's self-proclaimed custodians of democracy failed to notice it rotting away', *Guardian*.
43. More details on the Islamicity Indices can be found at http://islamicity-index.org/wp/ (accessed 3 Apr. 2020). See also, Askari, H. and Mirakhor, A. (2019). *Conceptions of Justice from Islam to the Present*, Palgrave Macmillan.
44. Black, N. (26 Sep. 2019). 'An interview with Farid Esack by Noah Black on liberation theology and Esack's scholarship', *Maydan*.
45. Said, E. (2003). *Orientalism*, Penguin; Hay, D. (1968). *Europe: The Emergence of an Idea*, Edinburgh University Press; Kaplan, R. D. (4 May 2016). 'How Islam created Europe', *Atlantic*.
46. Major, J. (22 Apr. 1993). Speech to Conservative Group for Europe.
47. Pankaj Mishra has written excellently on the myths surrounding British identity. For example, Mishra, P. (7 Dec. 2009). 'England's last roar: Pankaj Mishra on nationalism and the election', *Guardian*.
48. Wolfreys, J. (2018). *Republic of Islamophobia: The Rise of Respectable Racism in France*, Hurst, pp. 14–15.
49. Mill, J. S. 'Considerations on representative government', in Robson, J. M., ed. (1977). *The Collected Works of John Stuart Mill, Vol XVIII, Essays on Politics and Society*, Toronto, chapter xvi.
50. This was an open letter that Mesut Özil posted to Twitter on 22 Jul. 2018. A copy can be found here: Bryant, T. (23 Jul. 2018). 'Mesut Özil walks away from Germany team citing "racism and disrespect"', *Guardian*.
51. Scruton, R. (Sep. 2006). 'Should he have spoken?', *New Criterion*.
52. Addley, E. (11 Aug. 2012). 'Mo Farah also proved that we can cheer without stopping for 14 minutes', *Guardian*.
53. See ICM Unlimited (11 Apr. 2016). 'What Muslims really think: ICM Muslims survey for Channel 4'. This eventually led to a bigger survey conducted for the right-wing think tank, Policy Exchange: ICM Unlimited (Dec. 2016). '"What Muslims want" A survey of British Muslims by ICM on behalf of Policy Exchange'.

54. Pollack, D. et al, (Jun. 2016). 'Integration and religion as seen by people of Turkish origin in Germany', Cluster of Excellence of Religion and Politics, Münster University.

55. Harris, S. (8 Feb. 2006). 'The reality of Islam', *Truthdig*. The article is also available on his website.

56. Twomey, L. (18 Sep. 2018). 'Germany trio Toni Kroos, Thomas Muller and Manuel Neuer either "naive or scheming" against Mesut Özil, says agent', *Independent*.

57. Campbell, P. I. (17 Jan. 2020). 'Stormzy and Gary Neville: How privilege works in 21st-century Britain', *The Conversation*.

58. Orange, R. (10 Jun. 2018). 'Denmark swings right on immigration – and Muslims feel besieged', *Guardian*; Genevard, A. (7 Jun. 2016). 'Arabe enseigné dès le CP: Voulons-nous vraiment lutter contre le communautarisme?' *Le Figaro*.

59. Shackle, S. (1 Sep. 2017). 'Trojan horse: The real story behind the fake "Islamic plot" to take over schools', *Guardian*.

60. Coughlan, S. (6 Oct. 2016). 'Should there be more Muslim state schools?' *BBC News*.

61. Meer, N. 'Negotiating faith and politics: The emergence of British Muslim consciousness in Britain', in Ahmad, W. I. U. and Sardar, Z., eds. (2012), *Muslims in Britain: Making Social and Political Space*, Routledge.

62. All results can be found online on the Islamia School website: https://www.islamiaschools.com/the-school/results/ (accessed 3 Apr. 2020).

63. Meer, N. (2009). 'Identity articulations, mobilization and autonomy in the movement for Muslim schools in Britain', *Race Ethnicity and Education*, *12*(3), pp. 379–99.

64. *France 24* (29 Mar. 2013). 'France's first private Muslim school tops the ranks'.

65. Candles, N. and Vasiljeva, K. (20 Sep. 2016). 'Children from Muslim free-lance schools – how do they work?' Kraka.

66. Murphy, J. (15 Jan. 2018). 'Theresa May warned be "slow and careful" over faith school admissions changes', *Evening Standard*.

67. Parveen, N. (31 Jan. 2019). 'School defends LGBT lessons after religious parents complain', *Guardian*.

68. *Independent* (5 Sep. 2019). 'The government is hijacking LGBT+ sex education to bolster its counterterrorism strategy – it must stop now'.

69. Murray, D. (2018). *The Strange Death of Europe: Immigration, Identity, Islam*, Bloomsbury, p. 112.

70. Plenel, E. (2016). *For the Muslims: Islamophobia in France*, Verso, pp. 71–2. See also, Delphy, C. (2015). *Separate and Dominate: Feminism and Racism after the War on Terror*, Verso, pp. 47–8.

71. Défenseur des Droits (Jan. 2017). 'Enquête sur l'accès aux droits. Relations police/population: le cas des contrôles d'identité'.

72. Daillère, A. (2016). 'L'ordre et la force: enquête sur l'usage de la force par les représentants de la loi en France', ACAT France.

73. Carroll, R. (7 Aug. 2019). 'Meaning, without the white gaze', *Atlantic*.

74. Eisenberg, C. (22 Jan. 2005). 'Black Muslims seek acceptance from fellow Americans, adherents', *Seattle Times*.

2. 'Islam Is Violent'

1. Mortimer, C. (24 Aug. 2016). 'British Muslims marched off Easyjet flight after WhatsApp messages mistaken for "ISIS material"', *Independent*; Hassan, C. (19 Apr. 2016). 'Arabic-speaking student kicked off Southwest flight', *CNN News*.
2. Kundnani, A. (2015). *The Muslims are Coming! Islamophobia, Extremism, and the Domestic War on Terror*, Verso, pp. 153–6.
3. Boswell, J. and Griffiths, S. (14 Feb. 2016). 'Police quiz teen over Palestine badge', *Sunday Times*.
4. Pew Research Center (21 Jul. 2011). 'Muslim–Western tensions persist: Common concerns about Islamic extremism'; Pew Research Center (9 Aug. 2017). 'Muslims and Islam: Key findings in the U.S. and around the world'.
5. Bush, G. W. (20 Sep. 2001). 'Address to a joint session of Congress and the American people'; Waldman, P. and Pope, H. (21 Sep. 2001). '"Crusade" reference reinforces fears war on terrorism is against Muslims', *Wall Street Journal*.
6. Musharraf, P. (2006). *In the Line of Fire*, Simon & Schuster; also documented in Nelson, D. (6 Sep. 2011). 'Analysis: How the US and Pakistan are the best of frenemies', *Telegraph*.
7. Home Office (2004). 'Stop & Search Action Team, interim guidance', p. 12.
8. Dodd, V. and Travis, A. (2 Mar. 2005). 'Muslims face increased stop and search', *Guardian*.
9. Lai Quinlan, T. and Derfoufi, Z., 'Counter-terrorism policing', in Delsol, R., et al, eds. (2015). *Stop and Search: The Anatomy of a Police Power*, Springer, pp. 123–45. According to government figures, over 2017–2018, an Asian person was four times more likely to be stopped and searched than a white person; a Black person more than nine and a half times more likely. This has been a long-standing pattern for many years. More details can be found here: https://www.ethnicity-facts-figures.service.gov.uk/crime-justice-and-the-law/policing/stop-and-search/latest#by-ethnicity (accessed 5 Apr. 2019).
10. Kundnani, op. cit., pp. 188–95.
11. Ibid.
12. HM Government (Jun. 2011). 'Prevent strategy', presented to Parliament by the Secretary of State for the Home Department by Command of Her Majesty.
13. HM Government (19 Dec. 2019). 'Channel duty guidance: Protecting vulnerable people from being drawn into terrorism', statutory guidance for Channel panel members and partners of local panels.
14. Patel, F. and Kaushik, M. (2017). 'Countering violent extremism', Brennan Center for Justice.

15. New York Police Department (Aug. 2007). 'Radicalization in the West: The homegrown threat'.

16. Nessa (16 Jul. 2018). 'In surveillance's digital age, black Muslims are hit the hardest', The Establishment. For further reading: Crawford, M. (2015). *Black Muslims and the Law: Civil Liberties from Elijah Muhammad to Muhammad Ali*, Lexington Books; Evanzz, K. (1999). *The Messenger: The Rise and Fall of Elijah Muhammad*, Pantheon Books.

17. Taylor, V. (8 Jun. 2020). '"Why Minneapolis?": How deep surveillance of black Muslims paved the way for George Floyd's murder', The Progressive.

18. Eisenberg, C. (22 Jan. 2005). 'Black Muslims seek acceptance from fellow Americans, adherents', *Seattle Times*. See also, Auston, D. (Apr. 2017). 'Prayer, protest, and police brutality: Black Muslim spiritual resistance in the Ferguson era', *Transforming Anthropology, Special Issue: Baltimore and Beyond*, *25*(1) pp. 11–22.

19. Massoumi, N., Mills, T. and Miller, D., eds. (2017). *What is Islamophobia?: Racism, Social Movements and the State*, Pluto Press, pp. 10–11.

20. Ibid.

21. Quinn, B. (11 Mar. 2016). 'Nursery "raised fears of radicalisation over boy's cucumber drawing"', *Guardian*.

22. Boswell, J. and Griffiths, S. (14 Feb. 2016). 'Police quiz teen over Palestine badge', *Sunday Times*.

23. Grierson, J. (21 Feb. 2020). 'Revealed: how teachers could unwittingly trigger counter-terror inquiries', *Guardian*.

24. Grierson, J. (6 Oct. 2019). 'Counter-terror police running secret Prevent database', *Guardian*.

25. John, T. and Cotovio, V. (16 Aug. 2019). '"Woke" news platform aimed at young Muslims is actually a secret UK counter-terror program', *CNN News*; Iqbal, N. (15 Sep. 2019). '"We acknowledge we went wrong": Lifestyle website for Muslim teens admits it should have been clearer about Home Office funding', *Guardian*.

26. *BBC News* (1 Feb. 2017). 'Finsbury Park Mosque wins libel payout from Reuters'.

27. Cook, S. (22 Nov. 2017). 'Commission has a "disproportionate focus on Muslim charities", says Baroness Warsi', *Third Sector*.

28. Kerbaj, R. (20 Apr. 2014). '"Deadliest threat" to charities is extremism', *Sunday Times*.

29. Ramesh, R. (16 Nov. 2014). 'Quarter of Charity Commission inquiries target Muslim groups', *Guardian*.

30. *BBC News* (1 Feb. 2017). 'Finsbury Park Mosque wins libel payout from Reuters'.

31. Walker, P. (18 Feb. 2018). 'UKIP's Gerard Batten reiterates his belief that Islam is a "death cult"', *Guardian*.

32. Elkouche, M. 'Ahl al-kitab (people of the book) as Islam's religious and cultural others', in Morrow, J. A., ed. (2017). *Islam and the People of the Book, Volumes 1–3: Critical Studies on the Covenants of The Prophet*, Cambridge Scholars Publishing, p. 437. See also, Munir, H. (12 May 2018). 'Did Islam

spread by the sword?', Yaqeen Institute; Kennedy, H. (Feb. 2008). 'Was Islam spread by the sword?', paper given at the Yale Conference on Religion and Violence.

33. Cleveland, W. L. and Bunton, M. (2016). *A History of the Modern Middle East*, Westview Press, chapter 1; Bulliet, R. W. (1979). *Conversion to Islam in the Medieval Period: An Essay in Quantitative History*, Harvard University Press; 'Conversion to Islam and the emergence of a Muslim society in Iran', in Levtzion, N., ed. (1979). *Conversion to Islam: A Comparative Study of Islamization*, Holmes and Meier, pp. 30–51.

34. Hill, M. (Jan. 2009). 'The spread of Islam in West Africa: Containment, mixing and reform from the eighth to the twentieth century', SPICE Digest, Stanford University; Levtzion, N. and Pouwels, R. L., eds. (2000). *The History of Islam in Africa*, Ohio University Press; Islam, A. 'The spread of Islam in India and Southeast Asia' in Quayum, M. A. et al, eds. (2017). *Religion, Culture, Society: Readings in Humanities and Revealed Knowledge*, Silverfish Books, pp. 56–76.

35. Mishra, P. (11 Feb. 2019). 'See the Iranian Revolution as Iranians do', *Bloomberg*.

36. A 'war economy' has been defined as 'a system of producing, mobilizing and allocating resources to sustain the violence', Le Billon, P. (2005). *Geopolitics of Resource Wars: Resource Dependence, Governance and Violence*, Frank Cass, p. 288. See also, Ahmed, N. (20 Mar. 2014). 'Iraq invasion was about oil', *Guardian*; Emmons, A. (10 Sep. 2019). 'John Bolton tried his best to draw the U.S. into a war. Luckily, he failed', *Intercept*.

37. Kamali Dehghan, S. (11 Feb. 2014). 'Rouhani critics step up opposition to Iranian nuclear deal', *Guardian*; *Al-Monitor* (7 Aug. 2019). 'Rouhani takes fire from hard-liners for defending nuclear deal'.

38. Sergeant, J. (14 May 2019). 'Madonna, on Eurovision, says she won't bow "to suit someone's political agenda"', Reuters.

39. Modood, T. (Apr. 1990). 'British Asian Muslims and the Rushdie Affair', *Political Quarterly*, 61(2), pp. 143–60; Doward, J. (27 Apr. 2019). 'Industrial collapse of Thatcher years led to crime rise, study finds', *Guardian*.

40. Parekh, B. 'The Rushdie Affair and the British press', in Cohn-Sherbrook, D., ed. (1990). *The Salman Rushdie Controversy in Interreligious Perspective*, E. Mellen Press, pp. 72–96.

41. Burgess, A. (16 Feb. 1989). 'Islam's gangster tactics', *Independent*.

42. Parekh, op. cit.

43. Modood, op. cit., p. 160.

44. Azhar, M. (14 Feb. 2019). '"Salman Rushdie radicalised my generation"', *BBC News*.

45. Gartenstein-Ross, D. and Grossman, L. (Apr. 2009). 'Homegrown terrorists in the US and UK', FDD's Centre for Terrorism Research.

46. Kundnani, op. cit., pp. 123–6.

47. Knapton, S. and Gardham, D. (21 Aug. 2008). 'MI5: Terrorists not frustrated religious loners', *Telegraph*.

48. Roy, O. (2017). *Jihad and Death: The Global Appeal of Islamic State*, Hurst.

49. Knapton and Gardham, op. cit.

50. American Civil Liberties Union (Sep. 2011). 'A call to courage: Reclaiming our liberties ten years after 9/11'.

51. Sedgwick, M. (2010). 'The concept of radicalization as a source of confusion', *Terrorism and Political Violence*, *22*(4), pp. 479–94.

52. Taji-Farouki, S. (1996). *A Fundamental Quest: Hizb al-Tahrir and the Search for the Islamic Caliphate*, Grey Seal; Glynn, S. 'Liberalising Islam: Creating Brits of the Islamic persuasion', in Phillips, R., ed. (2009). *Muslim Spaces of Hope: Geographies of Possibility in Britain and the West*, Zed Books, pp. 179–97.

53. Kundnani, op. cit., pp. 141–50.

54. Lawrence, B., ed. (2005). *Messages to the World: The Statements of Osama Bin Laden*, Verso.

55. Gayle, D. (21 Apr. 2016). 'Prevent strategy "could end up promoting extremism"', *Guardian*; Human Rights Council (8 Jun. 2017). 'Report of the Special Rapporteur on the rights to freedom of peaceful assembly and of association on his follow-up mission to the United Kingdom of Great Britain and Northern Ireland', A/HRC/35/28/Add.1.

56. The Stationery Office (2011). *Report to the Home Secretary of Independent Oversight of Prevent Review and Strategy*, p. 11.

57. Commission for Countering Extremism (Oct. 2019). 'Challenging hateful extremism', p. 14.

58. Aslan, R. (2011). *No God But God: The Origins, Evolution and Future of Islam*, Arrow Books, pp. 86–7.

59. The full response can be found at: http://www.lettertobaghdadi.com/ (accessed 11 Jul. 2020).

60. Sardar, Z. (2016). *Islam Beyond the Violent Jihadis: An Optimistic Muslim Speaks*, Biteback Publishing.

61. Johnson, J. (20 May 2017). '"I think Islam hates us": a timeline of Trump's comments about Islam and Muslims', *Washington Post*.

62. Carroll, L. and Jacobsen, L. (9 Dec. 2015). 'Trump cites shaky survey in call to ban Muslims from entering US', *Politifact*.

63. Pew Research Center (30 Aug. 2011). 'Muslim Americans: No signs of growth in alienation or support for extremism'.

64. Dahlgreen, W. (3 Jun. 2015). 'Memories of Iraq: Did we ever support the war?' YouGov; Newport, F. (24 Mar. 2003). 'Seventy-two percent of Americans support war against Iraq', Gallup.

65. Cole, J. (9 Oct. 2018). 'Trump's unwavering adversary: Islam', *Nation*. In Feb. 2020, the ban was extended once more to include other countries with significant Muslim populations, such as Eritrea, Kyrgyzstan, Myanmar, Nigeria, Sudan and Tanzania.

66. Benjamin, M. and Davies, N. J. S. (19 Mar. 2018). 'The staggering death toll in Iraq', *Salon*.

67. Binns, D. (11 Mar. 2019). '"Too risky" to rescue jihadi baby, says Jeremy Hunt', *Metro*.

68. Mayhew, F. (18 Mar. 2019). 'Daily Mirror changes splash headline describing mosque killer as "angelic boy"', *Press Gazette*.

69. Hill, B. (17 Mar. 2019). 'From a bullied school boy to NZ's worst mass murderer: Christchurch mosque shooter was "badly picked on as a child because he was chubby"', *Daily Mail*.

70. *BBC News* (3 Apr. 2019). 'Fraser Anning: Australian MP censured for "appalling" Christchurch remarks'.

71. Soufan Center (Sep. 2019). 'White supremacy extremism: The transnational rise of the violent white supremacist movement'.

72. Dodd, V. and Grierson, J. (19 Sep. 2019). 'Fastest-growing UK terrorist threat is from far right, say police', *Guardian*; Dearden, L. (5 Dec. 2019). '"Far-right extremist" charged with 12 terror offences including encouraging attacks', *Independent*.

73. Neiwert, D. (22 Jun. 2017). 'Far-right extremists have hatched far more terror plots than anyone else in recent years', The Investigative Fund.

74. Chalabi, M. (20 Jul. 2018). 'Terror attacks by Muslims receive 357% more press attention, study finds', *Guardian*.

75. Al Gamah'ah al-Islamiya (2015), translated by Jackson, S. A. *Initiative to Stop the Violence: Sadat's Assassins and the Renunciation of Political Violence*, Yale University Press.

76. Curtis, A. (2015). *Bitter Lake*, BBC.

77. Shank, M. (27 Apr. 2011). 'Islam's nonviolent tradition', *Nation*.

3. 'Muslim Men Are Threatening'

1. Pulham, S. (8 Nov. 2005). 'Inflammatory language', *Guardian*.

2. Shaheen, J. G. (2015). *Reel Bad Arabs: How Hollywood Vilifies a People*, Interlink Books; Alsultany, E. (2012). *Arabs and Muslims in the Media: Race and Representation After 9/11*, NYU Press.

3. Auston, D. (Apr. 2017). 'Prayer, protest, and police brutality: Black Muslim spiritual resistance in the Ferguson era', *Transforming Anthropology, Special Issue: Baltimore and Beyond*, 25(1) pp. 11–22.

4. Kumar, D. (2012). *Islamophobia and the Politics of Empire*, Haymarket Books, chapter 3.

5. Patel, F. and Kaushik, M. (2017). 'Countering violent extremism', Brennan Center for Justice, p. 10; Patel, F. (2011). 'Rethinking radicalization', Brennan Center for Justice, pp. 14–18.

6. Mowat, L. (4 Jun. 2019). 'Cologne central station on lockdown after men in black vests storm train station', *Daily Express*; *DW* (5 Jun. 2019). 'Muslim Council demands apology for Cologne police "racial profiling"'.

7. Amnesty International (5 Mar. 1996). 'United Kingdom: Alleged ill-treatment of Amer Rafiq', EUR 45/005/1996.

8. François-Cerrah, M. (17 Sep. 2012). 'The truth about Muhammad and Aisha', *Guardian*; Malik, F. (4 Oct. 2018). 'The Age of Aisha (ra): Rejecting historical revisionism and modernist presumptions', Yaqeen Institute.

9. Lalami, L. (10 Mar. 2016). 'Who is to blame for the Cologne sex attacks?', *Nation*; Sokoll, L. (3 Jan. 2017). '"New Year's Eve in Cologne": The scapegoating of Muslims and refugees deepens', WSWJ.

10. *The Times* (5 Jan. 2011). 'Revealed: Conspiracy of silence on UK sex gangs'; Norfolk, A. (11 Aug. 2017). 'A disturbing pattern is repeated again, and more cases to come', *The Times*.

11. Champion, S. (18 Aug. 2017). 'British Pakistani men ARE raping and exploiting white girls… and it's time we faced up to it', *The Sun*.

12. *Telegraph* (8 May 2012). 'Rochdale grooming: BNP leader's tweet almost caused trial to collapse amid fears far-right had a mole in the jury'.

13. Patton, G. (10 May 2012). 'Asian sex gang "were acting within cultural norms"', *Telegraph*.

14. Walker, P. (3 Dec. 2018). 'Sajid Javid defends noting the ethnicity of child grooming gang', *Guardian*.

15. Culliford, G. (24 Jan. 2020). 'I've seen UK paedos preying on Gambian children and it's Britain's fault, says UN official', *The Sun*.

16. Chakelian, A. (19 Mar. 2018). '"Grooming rings are the biggest recruiter for the far right": Rochdale and Telford prosecutor', *New Statesman*.

17. Williams, M. (13 Sep. 2014). 'EDL supporters attack police during Rotherham sex abuse protest', *Guardian*.

18. Jay, A. (Apr. 2018). 'Interim report of the independent inquiry into child sexual abuse', HC 954-I; Casey, L. (5 Dec. 2016). 'The Casey Review: A review into opportunity and integration', Ministry of Housing, Communities & Local Government.

19. *BBC News* (29 Feb. 2016). 'Mushin Ahmed death: Two men jailed over racist Rotherham killing'.

20. JUST Yorkshire (2018). 'A temperature check report: Understanding and assessing the impact of Rotherham MP, Sarah Champion's comments in the Sun newspaper on 10 August 2017'.

21. Britton, J. (2019). 'Muslim men, racialised masculinities and personal life', *Sociology*, 53(1), pp. 36–51.

22. Memmi, A. (2016). *The Colonizer and the Colonized*, Souvenir Press.

23. Butt, R. (23 Jul. 2007). 'All the rage – victim of US bloggers' cartoon hits back', *Guardian*.

24. *Independent* (27 Feb. 2018). '"Senior member" of English Defence League jailed for sexually abusing 10-year-old girl'.

25. Williams, J. (14 Mar. 2019). 'Brexit was a working-class revolt', *Spiked*.

26. Anderson, C. (2017). *White Rage: The Unspoken Truth of Our Racial Divide*, Bloomsbury.

27. Office for National Statistics (11 Jul. 2019). 'Ethnicity pay gaps in Great Britain: 2018'.

28. Chouhoud, Y. (2 Oct. 2018). 'What's the hidden story behind American Muslim poverty?', Institute for Social Policy and Understanding (ISPU).

29. According to the Lammy Review, despite being less than 5 per cent of the population, Muslims accounted for almost 15 per cent of the prisoners in Britain, double what it was ten years ago. See, Lammy, D. (2017). 'The Lammy Review: An independent review into the treatment of, and outcomes for, Black, Asian and Minority Ethnic individuals in the criminal justice system'. See also, World Economic Forum (Jan. 2020). 'The Global

Social Mobility Report 2020: Equality, Opportunity and a New Economic Imperative'.

30. Hussain, M. (11 Feb. 2019). 'Liberté for whom? French Muslims grapple with a republic that codified their marginalization', *Intercept*.

31. Ramm, B. (26 Jul. 2016). 'We need to rethink the relationship between mental health and political violence', openDemocracy. It isn't clear where Ramm has taken this statistic from, but it may be drawn from the fact that 98 per cent of mass killers in the US were found to be male. See, Kluger, J. (25 May 2014). 'Why mass killers are always male', *Time*; Kimmel, M. (2018). *Healing from Hate: How Young Men Get Into – and Out of – Violent Extremism*, University of California Press.

32. Ibid.

33. Ibid.

34. Ibid.

35. Armstrong, K. (2014). *Fields of Blood: Religion and the History of Violence*, Bodley Head, p. 186.

36. Schuessler, J. (5 May 2019). 'Medieval scholars joust with white nationalists. And one another', *New York Times*; Walden, M. (18 Mar. 2019). 'New Zealand mosque attacks: Who is Brenton Tarrant?' Al Jazeera.

37. Hughes, D. (14 Nov. 2018). 'Poppy Appeal 2019: Why poppies symbolise Remembrance Day, when to stop wearing them and if there's a "right" side', *inews*.

38. Liew, J. (30 Oct. 2017). 'Tedious annual poppy circus reminds us that, for some, remembrance isn't about remembering, it's being seen to remember', *Independent*.

39. Keay, L. (15 Oct. 2018). '"Do you want to remember Nazis?": Piers Morgan blasts white poppy-sporting peace campaigner on GMB as St John Ambulance allows its volunteers to wear the pacifist symbol for the first time', *Daily Mail*.

40. Daly, H. (27 Oct. 2017). 'Colonel Richard Kemp SLAMS "insulting" white poppy activist on GMB over ISIS comments', *Daily Express*.

41. *BBC News* (22 Aug. 2018). 'Sweden rape: Most convicted attackers foreign-born, says TV'.

42. *The Local* (29 May 2019). 'New crime study: Rise in Sweden's rape stats can't be tied to refugee influx'.

43. Ibid. The actual statistics can be found here: https://www.bra.se/bra-in-english/home/crime-and-statistics/rape-and-sex-offences.html (accessed 7 Apr. 2020).

44. Rafiq, H. and Adil, M. (Dec. 2017). 'Group based child sexual exploitation – dissecting grooming gangs', Quilliam Foundation. This has been criticised by: Spooner, J. and Stubbs, J. (25 Jan. 2018). 'Grooming gangs and the myth of the 84%', Regressive Left Media and Malik, K. (11 Nov. 2018). 'We're told 84% of grooming gangs are Asian. But where's the evidence?' *Guardian*. For more reliable reading on this topic, see, Cockbain, E. and Tufail, W. (2020). 'Failing victims, fuelling hate: challenging the harms of the "Muslim grooming gangs" narrative', *Race & Class*, *61*(3), pp. 3–32 and Cockbain, E.

(20 Mar. 2019). 'When bad evidence is worse than no evidence: Quilliam's "grooming gangs" report and its legacy', *Policing Insight*.

45. Full Fact (6 Sep. 2017). 'What do we know about the ethnicity of people involved in sexual offences against children?'

46. Dearden, L. (5 Sep. 2017). 'Newcastle grooming gang "did not target white girls because of their race", judge rules', *Independent*.

47. European Union Agency for Fundamental Rights (3 Mar. 2014). 'Violence against women: An EU-wide survey'.

48. Foundation for European Progressive Studies (19 Nov. 2018). 'Women facing sexual violence and street harassment: Survey in Europe and in the United States'.

49. Fischer, T. (12 Jan. 2016). 'Fischer im recht: Unser sexmob', *Die Zeit*. Available to read in English at: https://www.europeanpressprize.com/article/our-sex-mob/ (accessed 11 Jul. 2020).

50. Prescott-Smith, S. (21 Jun. 2018). 'Two in five young female festival goers have been subjected to unwanted sexual behaviour', YouGov.

51. Apna Haq (2016). 'The Casey Review: Our response'; Sisters for Change (Nov. 2017). 'Unequal regard, unequal protection'.

52. Khaleeli, H. (19 Jan. 2015). 'Shaista Gohir: "I wish the words shame and honour could be deleted"', *Guardian*.

53. Islam Question & Answer (9 Dec. 2006). 'He likes to imitate women.'

54. Human Rights Watch (30 Mar. 2008). 'Kuwait: Halt dress-code crackdown'.

55. hooks, b. (2004). *The Will to Change: Men, Masculinity, and Love*, Washington Square Press, p. 66.

56. See, Gerami, S. (2003). 'Mullahs, martyrs and men – conceptualising masculinity in the Islamic Republic of Iran', *Men and Masculinities*, 5(3), pp. 257–74.

57. Siddiqui, M. (2016). *Hospitality and Islam: Welcoming in God's Name*, Yale University Press, p. 173.

58. Brustman, M. (14 Jun. 2017). 'Queer sexuality and identity in the Qur'an and Hadith'. Available at: https://people.well.com/user/aquarius/Qurannotes.htm (accessed 11 Jul. 2020).

59. Sunan an-Nasa'i 5113, Book 48, Hadith 74. Many biographies of Prophet Muhammad also set out his appearance. A more modern example of this is Athar Husain, S. (1983). *The Message of Muhammad*, Islamic Book Foundation: 'The hair of his head was long and thick with some waves in them. His forehead was large and prominent, his eyelashes were long and thick, his nose was sloping, his mouth was somewhat large and his teeth were well set… He kept his feelings under firm control – when annoyed, he would turn aside or keep silent, when pleased he would lower his eyes (Shamail Tirmizi).'

60. Lutfi, H. (1985). 'The feminine element in Ibn Arabi's mystical philosophy', *Journal of Comparative Poetics*, 5(1), pp. 7–19.

61. Stolworthy, J. (4 Mar. 2017). 'Riz Ahmed warns Parliament that a lack of diversity in TV is leading people to ISIS', *Independent*.

62. Ilott, S. (31 Jan. 2018). 'Man Like Mobeen: BBC comedy defies Muslim stereotypes', *The Conversation*.

63. Baumeister, R. F. (2007). 'Is there anything good about men?', paper presented at the 115th Annual Convention of the American Psychological Association.

4. 'Islam Hates Women'

1. Hughes, L. (17 Jan. 2016). 'David Cameron: More Muslim women should "learn English" to help tackle extremism', *Telegraph*; Bennett, A. and Dodds, L. (18 Jan. 2016). 'Are David Cameron's English lessons for Muslim women simply reversing his own cuts?', *Telegraph*.
2. *BBC News* (25 Jan. 2016). '"Traditionally submissive Muslim women" say who us?'
3. Samari, G., et al (Mar. 2018). 'Islamophobia, health, and public health: A systematic literature review', *American Journal of Public Health*, *108*(6), e1–e9.
4. Spivak, G. C. 'Can the subaltern speak?', in Williams, P. and Chrisman, L., eds. (1994). *Colonial Discourse and Post-Colonial Theory: A Reader*, Harvester Wheatsheaf, p. 93.
5. Ahmed, L. (1993). *Women and Gender in Islam: Historical Roots of a Modern Debate*, Yale University Press, p. 127.
6. Ahmed, L., ibid, pp. 127–38. See also, Rasool, H. (2017). 'The impact of colonial rule on women's rights: A case study specific to Egypt under the rule of British Consul-General Lord Evelyn Cromer', *Relics, Remnants, and Religion: An Undergraduate Journal in Religious Studies*, *2*(2), article 1.
7. Fanon, F. (1994). *A Dying Colonialism*, Grove Weidenfeld, pp. 37–8. See also, Woodhull, W. (1993). *Transfigurations of the Maghreb: Feminism, Decolonization, and Literatures*, University of Minnesota Press: 'The cultural record makes clear that women embody Algeria not only for Algerians in the days since independence, but also for the French colonizers… In the colonialist fantasy, to possess Algeria's women is to possess Algeria' (p. 16).
8. Hussein, S. (2016). *From Victims to Suspects: Muslim women since 9/11*, New South Publishing; Revolutionary Association of the Women of Afghanistan (RAWA) (Feb. 2001). 'US Supporters welcome RAWA at V-day in New York City & Washington, DC'.
9. White House Archives (17 Nov. 2001). 'Radio address by Mrs. Bush'.
10. 'CIA Red Cell: A Red Cell special memorandum/confidential/no foreign nationals', released by WikiLeaks on 26 Mar. 2010.
11. Janmohamed, S. (1 Mar. 2019). 'Long before Shamima Begum, Muslim women were targets', *Guardian*.
12. Janmohamed, S. (24 Sep. 2018). 'Bodyguard's worst offence? Its desperate stereotypes about Muslim women', *Telegraph*.
13. Dearden, L. (24 Sep. 2018). 'Bodyguard's Nadia shows the danger of underestimating female jihadis', *Independent*.
14. Tell MAMA (Nov. 2018). 'Gendered anti-Muslim hatred and Islamophobia: Interim report 2018'.
15. *ITV News* (21 Mar. 2019). 'Nearly two-thirds of Muslim women witness hate crime in Scotland – survey'.

16. Worley, W. (24 May 2017). '"Shabby racist" jailed after kicking pregnant Muslim woman in stomach "causing her to lose baby"', *Independent*.

17. *TRT World* (4 Jul. 2018). 'Muslim woman assaulted in Belgium, her hijab and shirt pulled off'.

18. Loyd, A. (14 Feb. 2019). 'How I found Shamima Begum', *The Times*.

19. Rawlinson, K. and Dodd, V. (19 Feb. 2019). 'Shamima Begum: ISIS Briton faces move to revoke citizenship', *Guardian*.

20. Jones, C. (27 Feb. 2019). 'Shooting range criticised for Shamima Begum target', *BBC News*.

21. Allen, C. (Nov. 2013). 'Maybe we are hated', University of Birmingham, pp. 19–24.

22. Mernissi, F. (1992). *The Veil and the Male Elite: A Feminist Interpretation of Women's Rights in Islam*, Basic Books, p. viii.

23. Ibid.

24. Ahmed, L., op. cit., from p. 66.

25. Mernissi, *The Veil and the Male Elite*, from p. 180.

26. Mark, J. J. (18 Mar. 2019). 'Women in the Middle Ages', Ancient History Encyclopaedia; Bovey, A. (30 Apr. 2015). 'Women in medieval society', British Library.

27. Goldziher, I. (1971). *Muslim Studies*, George Allen & Unwin Ltd, pp. 2:366–8. After Goldziher, several historians have discussed, to varying levels, the participation of women in Hadith transmission. These include: Ahmed, L. (1993). *Women and Gender in Islam: Historical Roots of a Modern Debate*, Yale University Press, pp. 46–7, 72–4, 113–15; Berkey, J. (1992). *Transmission of Knowledge in Medieval Cairo*, Princeton University Press, pp. 161–81; Lutfi, H. (1981). 'Al-Sakhawi's Kitab al-Nisa as a source for the social and economic history of Muslim women during the fifteenth century a.d.', *Muslim World*, *71*(2), pp. 104–24; Sayeed, A. (2002). 'Women and Ḥadīth transmission: two case studies from Mamluk Damascus', *Studia Islamica*, *95*, pp. 71–94 (which provides portraits of two female Hadith scholars).

28. Akram Nadwi, M. (2007). *Al-Muhaddithat: The Women Scholars in Islam*, Interface Publications.

29. Power, C. (25 Feb. 2007). 'A secret history', *New York Times*.

30. Sonbol, A. (2003). 'Women in Shari'ah courts: A historical and methodological discussion', *Fordham International Law Journal*, *27*, p. 225; Mansel, P. (1995). *Constantinople: City of the World's Desire 1453–1924*, St. Martin's Press, p. 171.

31. Mernissi, *The Veil and the Male Elite*, p. 180.

32. Spellberg, D. A. (Aug. 1996). 'Writing the unwritten life of the Islamic Eve: Menstruation and the demonization of motherhood', *International Journal of Middle Eastern Studies*, *28*(3), pp. 305–24; Lerner, A. (2019). 'Rib or side, right or left and the traits of women: Midrashic dilemmas about the creation of Eve in medieval Islamic tradition and literature', *Studia Islamica*, *114*(1), pp. 27–46.

33. Khan, A. (1 Apr. 2019). 'How Hind Makki is changing the conversation around women's inclusion in mosques', *Religion News*; Aly, R. (19 Feb. 2018). 'UK mosques must make space for women – not turn us away', *Guardian*.

34. Mernissi, F. (2011). *Beyond the Veil: Male-female Dynamics in a Muslim Society*, Saqi, pp. 27–30. Mernissi points to figures like Salama Musa who simultaneously believed that women's liberation was essential to the goal of overthrowing British occupation of Egypt, and yet, in his book, *Woman Is Not the Plaything of Man*, dismissed the Western example. Another intellectual, Qasim Amin, wrote that Islam had far greater capacity to liberate women than anything offered by the West: 'Muslim law, before any other legal system, legalized women's equality with men and asserted their freedom and liberty at times when women were still in the most debased condition in all the nations of the world. Islam granted them all human rights and recognized their legal capacity...' See Amin, Q. (1928). *The Liberation of Women and the New Woman: Two Documents in the History of Egyptian Feminism*, American University in Cairo Press, p. 18.

35. Ahmed, L., op. cit., p. 164.

36. Wax, E. (19 May 2002). 'The fabric of their faith', *Washington Post*.

37. London, B. (1 Feb. 2020). 'Four Muslim women reveal why they choose to wear – or not wear – the hijab in today's society', *Glamour*.

38. Ahmed, I. (2011). *The Politics of Religion in South and Southeast Asia*, Routledge, p. 108; Khan Burki, S. (2016). 'The politics of misogyny: General Zia-ul-Haq's Islamization of Pakistan's legal system', *Contemporary Justice Review*, *19*(1), pp. 103–19.

39. Lamrabet, A. (Jul. 2019). 'How does the Qur'an address the issue of Muslim woman's veil or "hijab"?'.

40. Zahedi, A. (2007). 'Contested meaning of the veil and political ideologies of Iranian regimes', *Journal of Middle East Women's Studies*, *3*(3), pp. 75–98.

41. Mernissi, *The Veil and the Male Elite*, from p. 49.

42. Some of these scholars include Ibrahim al-Nazzam (d. 221AH/836CE), Abu Jafar al-Iskafi (d. 241/855), Mahmud Abu Rayya (d. 1970); Mernissi, *The Veil and the Male Elite*, from p. 62; Abou El Fadl, K. (2001). *Speaking in God's Name: Islamic Law, Authority and Women*, Oneworld, pp. 215–17 and 224–31.

43. Barlas, A. (2013). 'Uncrossed bridges: Islam, feminism and secular democracy', *Philosophy and Social Criticism*, *39*(4–5), pp. 417–25.

44. Musawah (2015). *Men in Charge? Rethinking Authority in Muslim Legal Tradition*, Oneworld.

45. Esposito, J. L. et al (2002). *Muslim Women in Family Law*, Syracuse University Press, p. 14; Johnson, H. (2005). 'There are worse things than being alone: Polygamy in Islam, past, present, and future', *William & Mary Journal of Race, Gender, and Social Justice*, *11*(1), p. 563.

46. Blair, O. (14 Feb. 2015). 'Topless Femen protesters "kicked during scuffles" at Muslim conference about women', *Independent*.

47. Adams, R. (19 Nov. 2017). 'Inspectors to question primary school girls who wear hijab', *Guardian*.

48. Wolfreys, J. (2018). *Republic of Islamophobia: The Rise of Respectable Racism in France*, Hurst, p. 33.

49. *inews* (9 Aug. 2018). 'How many Muslim women actually wear the burka?'

50. Sanyal, M. (3 Mar. 2020). 'The Hanau terror attack shows the need for honesty about racism in Germany', *Guardian*.

51. Kroet, C. (17 Aug. 2016). 'Manuel Valls: Burkini "not compatible" with French values', *Politico*.

52. Poirier, A. (17 Aug. 2016). 'Burkini beach row puts French values to test', *BBC News*.

53. Stothard, M. (19 Aug. 2016). 'Burkini ban splits opinion in France', *Financial Times*.

54. Wolfreys, op. cit., p. 36.

55. Institut français d'opinion publique (Oct. 2019). 'Etat des lieux des discriminations et des agressions envers les Musulmans de France', reported in English at: *Daily Sabah* (6 Nov. 2019). '42% of Muslims in France harassed at least once in their lives, poll shows'.

56. Jaschok, M. and Jingjun, S. (2000). *The History of Women's Mosques in Chinese Islam: A Mosque of Their Own*, Curzon Press.

57. Barr, S. (28 Jun. 2019). 'Dalai Lama doubles down on belief female successor would have to be "attractive"', *Independent*.

58. Office for National Statistics (Nov. 2018). 'Domestic abuse in England and Wales: Year ending March 2018'.

59. Centers for Disease Control and Prevention (26 Feb. 2019). 'Preventing intimate partner violence'. See, https://www.cdc.gov/violenceprevention/intimatepartnerviolence/fastfact.html (accessed 7 Apr. 2020).

60. Thomson Reuters Foundation (2019). 'The world's 10 most dangerous countries for women', see, https://poll2018.trust.org/ (accessed 7 Apr. 2020).

61. World Health Organization (19 Nov. 2017). 'Violence against women'.

62. Schnall, M. (15 Dec. 2015). '2018 will be the year of women', *CNN*.

63. IPU Parline. 'Percentage of women in national parliaments (as of 1 March 2020)', Global Data on National Parliaments.

64. Ettachfini, L. (10 Feb. 2020). 'The argument for abortion as a religious right', *Vox*.

65. Malkin, N. (26 May 2019). 'Alabama, Iran, or Saudi Arabia? We checked where abortion laws are better for women', *Haaretz*.

66. Mahmood, S. 'Feminism, democracy and empire: Islam and the war on terror', in Wallach Scott, J., ed. (2008). *Women's Studies on the Edge*, Duke University Press, pp. 81–114, p. 97.

67. Shams, A. (30 Jun. 2012). 'Misreading feminism and women's rights in Tehran: Beyond chadors, ninjabis, and secular fantasies', Ajam Media Collective.

68. Taylor, L. (5 Sep. 2018). 'Islam shows its female face with rise of women mosques', Reuters.

69. wadud, a. (1999). *Qur'an and Woman: Rereading the Sacred Text from a Woman's Perspective*, Oxford University Press, pp. 25–6; wadud, a. (2006). *Inside the Gender Jihad: Women's Reform in Islam*, Oneworld, from p. 24.

70. Eltahawy, M. (2015). *Headscarves and Hymens: Why the Middle East Needs a Sexual Revolution*, Weidenfeld & Nicolson.

5. 'Islam Is Homophobic'

1. Hari, J. (24 Feb. 2011). 'Can we finally talk about Muslim homophobia in Britain?', *Huffington Post*.
2. Green, J. (9 Mar. 2011). 'Residents plan East End Gay Pride to combat hate', *PinkNews*.
3. *BBC News* (17 Mar. 2011). 'East End Gay Pride cancelled over EDL claims'.
4. Hill, D. (26 Sep. 2011). 'Courage and constructiveness distinguish East London Pride march', *Guardian*.
5. Taylor, V. (21 Mar. 2019). 'Queer Black Muslim women are still kept out of the LGBT+ community', *Wear Your Voice*.
6. Manzoor, S. (21 Mar. 2015). 'My boyfriend killed himself because his family couldn't accept that he was gay', *Guardian*.
7. Wildman, S. (5 May 2017). 'Marine Le Pen wants to protect France's LGBTQ community – but opposes same-sex marriage', *Vox*; Bayoumi, M. (7 Aug. 2017). 'How the "homophobic Muslim" became a populist bogeyman', *Guardian*.
8. Duffy, N. (1 Mar. 2017). '1 in 5 French gays are voting for anti-gay marriage Marine Le Pen', *PinkNews*.
9. *New York Times* (8 Nov. 2016). 'Election 2016: Exit poll'.
10. Murdock, D. (5 May 2017). 'Marine Le Pen: A surprising number of gay Frenchmen are with her', *National Review*.
11. Duffy, N. (26 Sep. 2015). 'Gay UKIP MEP claims refugees might stone him to death', *PinkNews*.
12. Weigel, D. (26 Jul. 2017). 'Trump's "LGBT rights" promises were tied to war on "radical Islam"', *Washington Post*; Matthews, D. (13 Jun. 2016). 'Donald Trump's pro-gay Islamophobia is straight out of the European right-wing playbook', *Vox*.
13. Signorile, M. (20 Aug. 2019). 'Trump has a devastating record on LGBTQ rights. Don't deny the truth', *Washington Post*.
14. Puar, J. K. (2017). *Terrorist Assemblages: Homonationalism in Queer Times*, Duke University Press.
15. Faye, F. (15 Feb. 2017). 'We're here, we're queer, we're racists', *Zed*; Wilkinson, S. (12 Mar. 2018). 'Is it okay to be gay (and in the far-right)?', *Vice*.
16. Naib, F. (29 Jul. 2015). 'Sweden far-right plans gay parade in mainly Muslim area', Al Jazeera.
17. Greenwald, G. and Hussain, M. (5 Mar. 2018). 'As the trial of Omar Mateen's wife begins, new evidence undermines beliefs about the Pulse massacre, including motive', *Intercept*.
18. Pilkington, E. and Elgot, J. (14 Jun. 2016). 'Orlando gunman Omar Mateen "was a regular at Pulse nightclub"', *Guardian*.
19. *PinkNews* (18 Apr. 2017). 'Far-right group exploiting Chechnya abuse and Pulse anniversary with fake LGBT march'.
20. Hendricks, M. (2010). 'Islamic texts: A source for acceptance of queer individuals into mainstream Muslim society', *Equal Rights Review*, 5.
21. Siraj al-Haqq Kugle, S. (2010). *Homosexuality in Islam: Critical Reflection on*

Gay, Lesbian, and Transgender Muslims, Oneworld, pp. 241–2. See also, Ali, K. (2008). *Sexual Ethics and Islam*, Oneworld.

22. Andrews, W. G. and Kalpakli, M. (2005). *The Age of Beloveds: Love and the Beloved in Early-Modern Ottoman and European Culture and Society*, Duke University Press.

23. Kseroof, O. (20 Dec. 2016). 'Abu Nuwas: The controversial poet and his most beautiful verses', *Step Feed*.

24. El-Rouayheb, K. (2005). *Before Homosexuality in the Arab-Islamic World, 1500–1800*, University of Chicago Press, p. 146.

25. Ibid, p. 116. See also, Bauer, T. (2013). *Die Kultur der Ambiguität: Eine andere Geschichte des Islam*, Verlag der Weltreligionen.

26. Ali, op. cit., p. 85; Ayubi, Z. (2019). *Gendered Morality*, Columbia University Press, pp. 196–200.

27. El-Rouayheb, op. cit., p. 150.

28. Irfan, L. (4 Aug. 2008). 'Stories of khwajasaras should be an important part of the study of Mughal history', *Wire*.

29. Murray, S. O. and Roscow, W., eds. (1998). *Boy-Wives and Female-Husbands: Studies in African Homosexualities*, Palgrave Macmillan; Independent Lens (11 Aug. 2015). 'A map of gender-diverse cultures'.

30. Fisher, M. (27 Jun. 2013). 'From colonialism to "kill the gays": The surprisingly recent roots of homophobia in Africa', *Washington Post*.

31. *The Economist* (6 Jun. 2018). 'How homosexuality became a crime in the Middle East'.

32. Stern, M. J. (3 Jul. 2014). 'Don't blame yesterday's colonialism for today's homophobia', *Slate*.

33. *BBC News* (2 Nov. 2011). 'Ghana refuses to grant gays' rights despite aid threat'.

34. *BBC News* (4 Jul. 2011). 'Pakistan: Religious groups condemn US embassy gay event'.

35. Reuters (10 Oct. 2007). 'President misquoted over gays in Iran: Aide'.

36. Kugle, op. cit., pp. 34–8.

37. Birt, J. 'Wahhabism in the United Kingdom: Manifestations and reactions', in Al-Rasheed, M., ed. (2005). *Transnational Connections and the Arab Gulf*, Routledge; Hamid, S. (2008). 'The development of British Salafism', *ISIM Review*, *21*(1), pp. 10–11; Abou El Fadl, K. (20 Jul. 2011). 'The emergence of supremacist puritanism in modern Islam', *ABC Religion and Ethics*; Trigg, C. (2018). 'Islam, puritanism, and secular time', *American Literature*, *90*(4), pp. 815–39; Baskara, B. (2010). 'Islamic puritanism movements in Indonesia as transnational movements', *DINIKA: Academic Journal of Islamic Studies*, *2*(1), pp. 1–22.

38. Armstrong, K. (2001). *Islam: A Short History*, Phoenix, p. 156.

39. Bukhari, M. (27 Jun. 2016). 'Pakistani clerics declare transgender marriages legal under Islamic law'.

40. Crown Prosecution Service (2018). 'Hate crime annual report – 2017–2018'.

41. Bachman, C. L. and Gooch, B. (2017). 'LGBT in Britain: Hate crime and discrimination', Stonewall.

42. Marsh, S., et al (14 Jun. 2019). 'Homophobic and transphobic hate crimes surge in England and Wales', *Guardian*.

43. Cadwalladr, C. (21 Jul. 2018). 'Shahmir Sanni: "Nobody was called to account. But I lost almost everything"', *Guardian*.

44. Goshal, N. (28 Aug. 2018). 'Success to savor but more challenges for LGBT rights in Lebanon', Human Rights Watch.

45. Mohydin, R. (22 Jan. 2019). 'With transgender rights, Pakistan has an opportunity to be a pathbreaker', Amnesty International.

46. Hari, op. cit.

47. Tevanian, P. (24 Oct. 2012). 'Pour 100% des musulmans, les sondages sont plutôt une menace', *Les mots sont importants*.

48. Ipsos MORI (Feb. 2018). 'A review of survey research on Muslims in Britain'.

49. BBC Three (screened on 8 Apr. 2014). *Free Speech*, episode 2: 'Can you be gay and Muslim?'

50. Sardar, Z. (2011). *Reading the Qur'an*, Hurst, pp. 327–8.

Conclusion: The Muslim Problem

1. Gilroy, P. (2002). *There Ain't No Black in the Union Jack: The Cultural Politics of Race and Nation*, Routledge Classics; Patterson, S. (1969). *Immigration and Race Relations 1960–1967*, Oxford University Press.

2. Ansari, H. (2007). 'Muslims in Britain', Minority Rights Group International.

3. Nye C. and Bright, S. (4 May 2016). 'Altab Ali: The racist murder that mobilised the East End', *BBC News*.

4. Blakeley, R., et al (3 Sep. 2019). 'Leaving the war on terror. A progressive alternative to counter-terrorism policy', Transnational Institute.

5. Lyons, K. (23 Dec. 2019). 'Stormzy hits back at media for "intentionally spinning my words" over racism comment', *Guardian*.

6. Pearson, A. (22 Dec. 2019). 'And I just retweeted a survey which showed the UK was one of the two least racist countries in Europe. This, the UK is 100% racist stuff is inflammatory, negative and such a distorted picture', Twitter post, 11.17pm.

7. Shoard, C. (2 Feb. 2020). 'Joaquin Phoenix's attack on Baftas for "systemic racism" hailed by film industry', *Guardian*.

8. Westbrook, C. (20 Jan. 2020). 'What has Laurence Fox said? From Question Time to wokies – a rundown of all the drama', *Metro*.

9. Jordan, M. (2005). *The Great Abolition Sham: The True Story of the End of the British Slave Trade*, The History Press.

10. Freedland, J. (12 Jun. 2020). 'Boris Johnson's polarising statue tweets are pure Trump', *Guardian*.

11. Sato, S. (2017). '"Operation Legacy": Britain's destruction and concealment of colonial records worldwide', *The Journal of Imperial and Commonwealth History*, 45(4), pp. 697–719.

12. Walker, P. (15 Jun. 2015). 'Boris Johnson criticised over "victimization" comment as he sets up racism inquiry', *Guardian*.

13. *BBC News* (14 Jun. 2020). 'Little Britain: Matt Lucas and David Walliams "very sorry" for blackface'.

14. All-Party Parliamentary Group on British Muslims (27 Nov. 2018). 'Islamophobia Defined: The inquiry into a working definition of Islamophobia'.

15. Dearden, L. (15 May 2019). 'Proposed Islamophobia definition "would undermine counterterror operations and threaten free speech," police tell prime minister', *Independent.*

16. Lowles, N., ed. (Feb. 2019). 'State of Hate 2019: People vs. the elite?', Hope Not Hate, p. 23.

17. *ITV News* (5 Mar. 2019). 'Baroness Warsi hits out at "institutional" Islamophobia in the Tory party'.

18. Murphy, S. (18 Dec. 2019). 'Tory Islamophobia inquiry chair in row over Kashmir views', *Guardian.*

19. Rawlinson, K. (17 Dec. 2019). 'Tories accused of ignoring Islamophobia after dropping inquiry', *Guardian.*

20. Grierson, J. (9 Jun. 2020). 'Labour attacks "complacency" over delayed Prevent review', *Guardian.*

21. Malik, N. (27 Mar. 2020). 'Mehdi Hasan: "Most people ask the question and move on. I don't"', *Guardian.*

22. Schulman, S. (10 Jun. 2020). '"Speak to me": A Yale School of Art forum organized with Claudia Rankine, Marta Kuzma, and Leah Mirakhor'.

23. Stewart, S. (2020). 'Building pathways: What works on developing young people's resilience to violent extremism', British Council: Community of Practice on Preventing Violent Extremism.

24. Grierson, J. (20 May 2020). 'UK government's new counter-terrorism bill: The key measures', *Guardian.*

25. Aizenman, N. (9 Feb. 2019). 'How to demand a medical breakthrough: Lessons from the AIDS fight', NPR.

26. Home Office (24 Feb. 1999). 'The Stephen Lawrence Inquiry: Report of an inquiry by Sir William Macpherson'.

27. Ellison, M. (6 Mar. 2014). 'The Stephen Lawrence Independent Review: Possible corruption and the role of undercover policing in the Stephen Lawrence case', HC 1094. Note that this particular review was commissioned by then Home Secretary Theresa May after discussions with Doreen Lawrence. See also, Bennetto, J. (2009). 'Police and racism: What has been achieved 10 years after the Stephen Lawrence Inquiry report?', Equality and Human Rights Commission.

28. Morrison, T. (1993). Interview with Charlie Rose, Public Broadcasting Service.

29. Dorling, D. (Jul. 2015). 'Income inequality in the UK: Comparisons with five large Western European countries and the USA', *Applied Geography*, *61*(1), pp. 24–34.

30. Examples of further reading on this topic include: Luce, E. (2017). *The Retreat of Western Liberalism*, Little Brown; Mahbubani, K. (2019). *Has the West Lost It?: A Provocation*, Penguin; Hawkins, K. A., et al (2019). 'Global

populism database', Harvard Dataverse; Global Burden of Disease (Institute of Health Metrics Evaluation) (2017). 'Global, regional, and national incidence, prevalence, and years lived with disability for 354 diseases and injuries for 195 countries and territories, 1990–2017: A systematic analysis for the Global Burden of Disease Study 2017'.

31. Auston, D. (Apr. 2017). 'Prayer, protest, and police brutality: Black Muslim spiritual resistance in the Ferguson era', *Transforming Anthropology, Special Issue: Baltimore and Beyond*, *25*(1) pp. 11–22; Esack, F. (1996). *Qur'an Liberation and Pluralism: An Islamic Perspective of Interreligious Solidarity Against Oppression*, Oneworld.

32. More information available at: https://mcb.org.uk/project/women-in-mosques-development-programme/ (accessed 2 Apr. 2020).

33. Walker, A. (23 May 2020). 'Eid celebrations to go virtual as UK Muslims urged to stay at home', *Guardian*.

Acknowledgements

Writing and publishing this book has been a long, at times gruelling, process. But it has also been the most fantastic blessing. I feel indebted to every person who made this happen – I can't quite believe it *has* happened – and want to share the depth of my gratitude.

Imogen Pelham, thank you for taking a small seed of an idea and turning it into a viable publishing prospect, one that resisted tokenization, one that stayed true to its political core. It sounds trite, but I want to say that I owe you, this book belongs to you too, and I hope that the world rewards you for what you did for me.

Matthew Turner, thank you for believing in this project as much as I do, for being as emotionally invested in its success, for fighting for its publication as you did. Thank you for the insight and ideas that you brought to the manuscript and for holding my hand throughout this process. We make a pretty awesome team.

Everybody at Atlantic Books, thank you for taking a leap of faith with both the book and me. It means so much. Mike Harpley and James Pulford, thank you for being such brilliant editors and champions of this book, I've so adored working with you.

Tom White, to you I give most of the credit: for encouraging me to write this book, for believing that I could, for being a sounding board for all my thoughts and ideas, for reading the terrible drafts and the slightly better ones, for holding me to account. Thanks for everything.

To all at New Writing North, particularly Will Mackie, thank you. How you support new writers, particularly those with no knowledge of the publishing industry and no concept of gaining access, is *everything*.

To all my elders, whose teachings I carry in life and into this book; I am forever your student. Thank you to my first teachers, my mum, dad and brother, Haseeb, from whom I have learned so much about Islam, about living a life committed to justice and kindness, about moving through the world with love and generosity. Thank you for always supporting my dreams and ambitions, for pushing me to be kind to myself, for lighting up with pride as I've shared bits of this journey with you. Thank you to my grandparents, who might be gone from this world, but whose lessons and prayers remain with me.

Thank you to M. C. Gorman, my high-school English teacher, for always looking out for me.

Thank you to Houyam, Leyla, Sahil, and Shanon for being safe places where I could ask questions and share thoughts. Thank you for listening to my fears and insecurities and responding with patience and bountiful knowledge. Thank you for challenging me when I've needed to be challenged. I look up to you all so much.

Thank you to Black feminist thought, which has done so much for my political consciousness and my ability to understand and articulate the language of justice; to the imams, scholars and leaders of my activist past, who sat with me, nurtured me and shared their wisdom; to the writers of books about Islam, who by refusing to reproduce stereotypes, helped me to rebuild my self-image and my relationship with faith; and to the scholars, thinkers, activists, archivists and statisticians who are fighting the good fight, and whose work I rely on in this book.

Thank you to my wonderful contributors for their generosity: Urooj Arshad, Reza Aslan, Ella Cockbain, Myriam François, Ruqaiya Haris, Leyla Jagiella, Hussein Kesvani, Magid Magid,

Suhaiymah Manzoor-Hussain, Saadat Munir, Samia Rahman, Omid Safi and amina wadud.

Thank you to Naeem for always uplifting me. Amna, you're the best big sister ever. Thank you to Karen, Laura and Sophie for your friendship and support as we travel on this crazy, frustrating, frightening, amazing journey together. Thank you Nemo, Shahid, Shoab and Tony. Thank you Jessica. Thank you Helen and Mariana. Shout out to my loved ones in Manchester, London and Norwich.

Most of all, thank you, God.

Index